1989

EDUCATIONAL FUTURES: SOURCEBOOK I

Selections from the First Conference of the Education Section
World Future Society

Edited by Fred Kierstead, Jim Bowman, and Christopher Dede

WORLD FUTURE SOCIETY

4916 St. Elmo Avenue
Washington, D.C. 20014 • U.S.A.

Published by
WORLD FUTURE SOCIETY
4916 St. Elmo Avenue
Washington, D.C. 20014 • U.S.A.

Copyright © 1979 by
World Future Society

International Standard Book Number 0-930242-08-4

Price: $5.95
          $5.25 to members of the World Future Society
Please inquire for reduced multiple copy price for classroom use.

In Memory of John McHale

CONTENTS

PREFACE

The Education Section is the largest of the specialized divisions within the World Future Society. Chartered in 1975, its purpose is to provide a forum for the exchange of ideas and to provide possible strategies for change. As part of fulfilling this goal, the Section held its First Conference at the University of Houston at Clear Lake City in October, 1978. The Conference had three main purposes: to share the results of state-of-the-art research in the future of education; to facilitate networking among those interested in similar issues in educational futures; and to provide frameworks for individuals to participate in the future directions of the Education Section, World Future Society.

SOURCEBOOK I is a selection from the one-hundred-forty Conference presentations submitted to the editors for possible inclusion. Its purpose is to provide a frame of reference for those interested in alternatives, models, and strategies for survival in a period of educational transition. Many similar volumes will follow from subsequent Education Section Conferences, to add to the knowledge base presented herein and to continuously reappraise educational goals, directions, and priorities.

If a person were to describe the general attitudes of the Education Section Conferees, one would sense both excitement and urgency: excitement about shared concern and vision; urgency to seek answers to a myriad of transformative problem areas. In education, this urgency seems more widespread than in other social institutions because of the tremendous number of critics and suggested improvements that have proliferated in the media, bookstores and classrooms. Futures research, however, indicates that most societal institutions continue to prepare their youth for a world that not only does not exist, but also will not exist; education continues to be the "whipping boy" for our frustrations.

The research presented by the authors took courage. Research in educational futures more often than not has been misinterpreted, misconstrued, and misused. Futures research is inherently risky, due to the high probability of error and elusivity of the "subject" being considered. Added to these liabilities is the wide range of alternative solutions to consider.

Perhaps that is why there are a large number of critics who analyze problems, but a small number of researchers who are willing to present possible solutions.

The editors believe that education has reached a turning point, just as society has reached a breakpoint in its development. Numerous futurists believe that America is transcending the industrial-era, but different perspectives abound on what will emerge. A few of many terms which depict this new era in human development are the post-industrial era, communications era, cybernetic era, and global era. Perceptions of the new era are diverse, as futurists debate future issues such as population size, allocation of world energy resources, food distribution, ecological controls, and quality of life in general.

There does seem to be considerable agreement, however, supporting the proposition that our lifeways are in a period of transformation. The transformation is perceived by some people as a time of crises, as highly industrialized people re-examine their past achievements (as well as their goals for the future). It is also seen as a challenging period in which to participate in the renewal that accompanies innovative decision-making.

How do we educate for a rapidly changing society? What are the alternatives? Educators are confronted with such questions as they examine probables, possibles and desirables in educational and societal future perspectives. Most teachers know that tomorrow is part of today. They realize that the foundation of a student's success or failure in adulthood is often formulated during the precollege years.

It would seem that in previous generations, industrial-era educators were successful in preparing youth for participation in society. There was reason for confidence in unchanging teaching competencies because of stability in projected societal needs (occupations, consumption patterns, etc.). During our present transitory period, however, educators are necessarily divided in their projections about what competencies will be needed. There are important efforts being made to establish accountability in the classroom (encompassing movements such as "back to basics," "open-education," "free school," and "tracked learning"). Like the matter of school integration, efforts at accountability establish that there are needs for changing education, but there is no consensus on the means or the ends for determining what education should be at this time.

Confusion and uncertainty are normal during periods of societal transition, but this does not necessarily make the decisions easier and can be especially frustrating for educators. One of the major characteristics of this transition that perplexes educators is "over-choice." As a way of coping with this problem, the articles in this book examine and contrast some of these choices. These contributions are compelling reading and confront futures issues for schools, industries, media, communities and families—our educational agencies.

Because SOURCEBOOK I is the first of many subsequent volumes, its central purpose is broadly construed: to ask what problems, methodologies, considerations and alternatives in the future of education are perceived to be most crucial and feasible, and why. The diversity of the alternatives and opinions presented is evidence that "education" implies more than attending school, preparing for a job, learning good citizenship skills, and marshaling degrees of specialization. The authors, as futurists, understand that the words "future" and "education" are operatives which require dynamic interpretation in light of anticipated (and unanticipated) consequences.

The contributors examine educational futures at two levels: some have designed theories about the possible directions of education (planned or unplanned), others are concerned with how to teach about the future. Section I of the book is devoted to theory; Section II provides educational models and methodologies; and Section III includes special topics related to future educational decisionmaking (i.e. work, multi-national corporations, special education). The selections collectively provide individual societal and global perspectives on these problem areas. Four of the authors originate from countries other than the United States, thereby giving added impetus to such an examination of education.

We, the editors, believe the resulting volume provides an exciting summary of current thought about dimensions and imperatives of educational futures. Of course, the sections presented do not offer absolute solutions to our problems, but do suggest ideas and directions which warrant consideration, analysis, and review for possible adoption. The papers suggest that present mindsets and methodologies in education will not be enough for survival; rather, courage and creativity, plurality and diversity are needed. Multicultural and transnational resolutions of educational goals and problems will require communications networks never before realized. The analyses presented offer only one "source" for this resolution, but this book and the Conference initiate a series of steps in the right direction.

University of Houston at Clear Lake City Fred Kierstead
Houston, Texas Jim Bowman
June, 1979 Chris Dede
  Editors

ACKNOWLEDGEMENTS

This work would not have come about without the inspiration and encouragement of Edward and Sally Cornish. We are also indebted to Chancellor Alfred Neumann, Vice Chancellor Louis Rodriguez, and Dean Rosemary Pledger of the University of Houston at Clear Lake City. Their support of the First Conference of the Education Section, WFS, is greatly appreciated.

Dean Calvin Cannon of UHCLC deserves special recognition for his overall support of the University's futures program as well as the Conference. George and Cynthia Mitchell provided additional support, for which we are sincerely grateful.

Special thanks is given to Mackie Ealick, whose dedication and efficiency are reflected in this publication. Finally, we would like to thank the authors for their cooperation in preparing the volume and for their dedication to the research which resulted in these articles.

F.D.K.
J.R.B.
C.J.D.

ABOUT THE AUTHORS

WILLIAM L. ASHLEY is a Research Specialist and acting project director of the Transferable Skills project at the National Center for Research in Vocational Education. He is the author of numerous papers, workshops, and presentations on transferable skills, occupational adaptability, and occupational and task analysis. Currently, he is the president of the Ohio Chapter of the National Society for Performance and Instruction, and was chosen for the Society's Outstanding Service award for 1978. Address responses to: Dr. William L. Ashley, Ohio State University, 1960 Kenny Road, Columbus, Ohio 43210.

JAMES W. BOTKIN is co-author and director of the Learning Report to The Club of Rome entitled *The Human Gap* (scheduled for publication in June, 1979). For the duration of The Club of Rome project, he was an Associate in Education at the Harvard Graduate School of Education. Previously he was the Academic Director of the Salzburg Seminar in Salzburg, Austria. His professional interests include the management of education, international relations, and computer-based systems, in which he holds a doctoral degree from the Harvard Business School. Address responses to: Dr. James W. Botkin, 26 Grozier Road, Cambridge, Massachusetts 02138.

JANEY CHEU is Associate Director of the Institute for Science, Technology, and Social Science Education at Rutgers—The State University of New Jersey. Most recently she has co-authored a series of fourteen interdisciplinary modules for secondary school students that focus on contemporary issues interfacing science and society. Her interests include futuristics in education, moral/ethical reasoning and environmental decision making. Currently, she is researching the development of formal operational thought as defined by Piaget. Address responses to: Ms. Janey Cheu, Institute for Science, Technology and Social Science Education, Rutgers—The State University of New Jersey, Doolittle Hall, New Brunswick, New Jersey 08903.

CONSTANCE R. FADDIS is a Program Assistant for the Transferable Skills project at the National Center for Research in Vocational Education. She was previously the technical editor for the Publication Series of the Learning Research and Development Center, University of Pittsburgh. Her major interests are in futurism, coping skills, and change. She also writes science fiction (*New Voyages*, Bantam Books; *Isaac Asimov's Science Fiction Magazine*), and has been a professional illustrator and cartoonist. Address responses to: Ms. Constance R. Faddis, Ohio State University, 1960 Kenny Road, Columbus, Ohio 43210.

JAMES P. GELATT is Director of Planning and Special Projects for the John F. Kennedy Institute, at Johns Hopkins University. He coordinated the first White House Conference on Handicapped Individuals, and is a consultant with the Washington Education Policy Institute, Washington, D.C. He is the author/editor of several publications regarding the education of handicapped children. Address responses to: Dr. James P. Gelatt, Director, Special Projects and Development, The John F. Kennedy Institute, 707 North Broadway, Baltimore, Maryland 21205.

HANS J. HARLOFF is professor of social and environmental psychology at Technische Universitat, Berlin, Federal Republic of Germany. He chaired the parallel conference on "Conditions of Life in the Future and Consequences for Education," Berlin 11/23.-26., 1978 and edited its proceedings *Konferenzdokumentation Bedingungen des Lebens in der Zukunft und die Folgen fur die Erziehung*. TUB-DOKUMENTATION aktuell 6/1978. He is mainly interested in social impact assessments from a psychological point of view and in economical, sociological, and psychological problems of the future. Address responses to: Dr. Hans J. Harloff, Technische Universitat Berlin, Fachbereich 2, 1 Berlin 10, den, Dovestrabe 1-5, Berlin, West Germany.

RICHARD B. HEYDINGER is an Assistant to the Vice President for Academic Affairs at the University of Minnesota. His current responsibilities include the development of information systems and staff work relating to institutional planning. Currently he is completing a chapter for a book on institutional planning and editing a volume on the same topic. Prior to this position, he was a co-founder and partner of Formative Evaluation Research Associates, an evaluation firm specializing in the assessment of innovative programs in post-secondary education. Mr. Heydinger has published articles on computing and non-traditional learning; he holds degrees from Carleton College, Indiana University and a Ph.D. from the University of Michigan. Address responses to: Dr. Richard

B. Heydinger, University of Minnesota, 213 Morrill Hall, 100 Church Street SE, Minneapolis, Minnesota 55455.

LOUIS A. IOZZI is Assistant Professor of Science and Environmental Education at Cook College, and Director of the Division of Science and Society at the Center for Coastal and Environmental Studies, at Rutgers—The State University of New Jersey. He has served on the faculty at Kean College of New Jersey and the Graduate School of Education, Rutgers University, and was the Director of Environmental Education in New Jersey. He is the author of numerous research papers in the area of environmental values and has developed several environmental and earth science programs for major publishers. Among his varied interests are futuristic decision making; the development of holistic problem solving; the application of Piagetian learning theory and environmental perceptions, attitudes and values. Address responses to: Dr. Louis A. Iozzi, Institute for Science, Technology and Social Science Education, Rutgers—The State University of New Jersey, Doolittle Hall, New Brunswick, New Jersey 08903.

GERALD L. KINCAID is Communications Education Specialist, Minnesota State Department of Education. He will retire in June, 1979, after serving 20 years as consultant, program coordinator, and specialist in Communications Education. He has taught in high school (Pekin, Ill.), at Michigan State University, Hillsdale College (Michigan), and Moorhead State College (Minnesota). His publications include *Language and Communication, A Resource Book*, K-12 (published by Minnesota State Department of Education) and articles that have appeared in professional journals. He is currently working on a booklength version of the enclosed paper, with the subtitle: "A Road to Peace with Dignity for All." Address responses to: Mr. Gerald L. Kincaid, Specialist, Minnesota State Department of Education, Capitol Square, 550 Cedar Street, St. Paul, Minnesota 55101.

ERVIN LASZLO has been a professor of philosophy as well as of futures studies, and is currently a Special Fellow at the United Nations Institute for Training and Research, in charge of international projects on the future of the world community. He has developed and applied general system theory in relation to international affairs and world order studies. He is the author of *Introduction to Systems Philosophy, The Systems View of the World*, and *Goals for Mankind, A Report to the Club of Rome*, among others. His most recent book is *The Inner Limits of Mankind: Heretical Reflections on Today's Values,*

Culture and Politics. Address responses to: Dr. Ervin Laszlo, 801 United Nations Plaza, New York, New York 10000.

W. BASIL MCDERMOTT has been teaching a course on "The Study of the Future" at Simon Fraser University, British Columbia, Canada, since 1968. His *stated* lament is that he does not know how to think "properly" about the seriousness of the future. He does believe, however, that the ideas of G.I. Gurdjieff as mediated by P.D. Ouspensky, *In Search of the Miraculous,* and Maurice Nicoll, *Psychological Commentaries,* have more than modest relevance for the future of mankind. As a member of the faculty of Interdisciplinary Studies, Professor McDermott has done extensive research in futures theory, and provides insight into the problem of "teaching" the future. Address responses to: Dr. W. Basil McDermott, Simon Fraser University, Burnaby, British Columbia, Canada V5A 156.

JAMES NOLFI is dean of the resident undergraduate program at Goddard College. He is the co-director of the Center for Studies in Food Self-Sufficiency, in Burlington, Vermont, and was resident director at Goddard's Institute for Social Ecology. Dr. Nolfi has published widely on computer mapping, decentralized planning, fisheries development, and comparative physiology. His current research includes work on minor breeds of livestock, crayfish, agriculture, and small scale energy systems. He and his wife operate a small hill farm in Central Vermont, and he is presently working on a book of poetry entitled *Manure.* Address responses to: Dr. James R. Nolfi, Dean, Resident Undergraduate Program, Goddard College, Plainfield, Vermont 05667.

JOHN D. PULLIAM is professor of Historical, Philosophical and Social Foundations of Education at the University of Oklahoma. He has been instrumental in the development of graduate seminars for the theoretical study of problems in educational futures. He is the author of numerous articles and chapters in anthologies and is contributing editor to *Education Tomorrow.* His books include *History of Education in America, Educational Futurism: In Pursuance of Survival* and *the Far Side of the Future: Social Problems and Educational Reconstruction.* Address responses to: Dr. John D. Pulliam, College of Education, University of Oklahoma, 820 Van Vleet Oval, Norman, Oklahoma 73019.

ELLIOTT SEIF is professor of education at Temple University, where he teaches courses in social studies education, humanistic education, and education for future living. He has been active in designing, coordinating, and teaching in several alternative programs for pre-service and in-service teachers and advanced graduate students. He has conducted sessions and workshops at national conventions and for local school districts. His research interests focus primarily on in-depth case studies of schools and classrooms. His writings include innovative curricula materials and several books, *Success With Open Education* and *Teaching Significant Social Studies in the Elementary School.* Currently he is writing a book and developing projects in the area of education for future living. Address responses to: Dr. Elliott Seif, Professor of Education, Temple University, Philadelphia, Pennsylvania 19122.

ROBERT B. TEXTOR has held postdoctoral appointments at Yale and Harvard Universities, and is currently Professor of Education and Anthropology at Stanford University, where he is a member of a multidisciplinary program focusing upon the instrumental use of education to promote "development," however this might be defined in a particular culture. This involvement has led to his current efforts to introduce an explicit futures dimension into anthropology/ethnography, and vice versa. Professor Textor is past president of the Council on Anthropology and Education. His works include *A Cross-Polity Survey* (co-author), *A Cross-Cultural Summary,* and *Cultural Frontiers of the Peace Corps* (editor-contributor). Address responses to: Dr. Robert B. Textor, Department of Anthropology, Stanford University, Stanford, California 94305.

ROBERT THEOBALD is President of Participation Publishers which deals with national transformation potentials and of Future Frontiers, a local, nonprofit educational organization trying to help people to see how to cope with issues of rapid growth. His publications include *An Alternative Future for America's Third Century, Futures Conditional, Teg's 1994, Beyond Despair,* and *Economizing Abundance.* He believes that one of the primary potentials for the future is the structuring of information and knowledge in new ways using the potentials of the new microelectronic technologies. Address responses to: Mr. Robert Theobald, Participation Publishers, Box 2240, 153 Jefferson Street, Wickenburg, Arizona 85358.

CHARLES WEINGARTNER is a professor of education at the University of South Florida, Tampa. He has long been interested in alternatives to conventional schooling, and is still active in exploring such possibilities. He is coauthor, with Neil Postman of NYU, of several books, including: *Teaching As A Subversive Activity; Linguistics: A Revolution in Teaching; Language in America; The Soft Revolution;* and *The School Book.* He has published articles in various professional journals, and has held editorial positions with three of them. In recent years he has become increasingly involved in "future studies," especially as they relate to schools. He is currently on a sabbatical leave visiting futurists and future studies centers around the U.S. Address responses to: Dr. Charles Weingartner, College of Education FA0283, University of South Florida, Tampa, Florida 33620.

ARTHUR G. WIRTH is professor of philosophy of education in the Graduate Institute of Education at Washington University, St. Louis, Missouri. He is the author of *John Dewey as Educator* and *Education in the Technological Society: The Vocational-Liberal Studies Controversy.* He is former editor of The John Dewey Lecture Series. Recently he has been publishing materials on education-work relations as, for example, in D. Vermilye, ed., *Relating Education and Work* and in the A.E.R.A. Reading Series, *Curriculum and Evaluation.* Address responses to: Dr. Arthur Wirth, Institute of Education, Washington University, St. Louis, Missouri 63130.

I
FUTURES THEORY IN EDUCATION

INTRODUCTION TO SECTION I
FUTURES THEORY IN
EDUCATION

This section is not recommended for readers who: (1) perceive education as something separate from society, (2) develop dichotomies between theory and practice, or (3) already know what will happen in the future.

In a rapidly changing world, continuous cooperation and communication between education and society are important; and the relationship between school (the present major component of general education) and society is of critical significance to everyone. As societies have learned throughout history, great ethical and economic costs are incurred in direct proportion to ignorance, obsolescence and intellectual deprivation. This is the essence of various "cultural lag" theories just as it is at the core of personal alienation. The editors suggest that these expenses—if they are deferred—become crimes against the future. This perspective is shared by the contributors to this section of the book. They all establish the imperative for education to relate closely to societal needs and for educators to serve society in a leadership capacity. Philosophers have argued since Plato's time about whether the school should reflect and adapt to the changes in society or whether the school should help direct the future of society. The authors are in consensus about this debate: educators should facilitate alternative societal directions.

The contributors of this section also agree that the integration of theory and practice is essential to an educational planning system. Practice (all life experiences), when separated from theory, results in conformity, internalized habit, and pretense—if it is conducted in a changing world. There is an equally obvious vacuum for theories which are far removed from practice. This is exemplified by theorists who do not test their ideas in the general society. This is a major criticism which has been thrust upon futurists. In this section, however, the futures theories presented are not removed from practice—the proposals are given within the general framework of alternative futures, and are founded in the present and the past. Thus, "the future" is replaced by the concept of "futures" which exist (in some form) at the present time, and may or may not continue.

The above assumptions necessitate alternative futures theories. The articles are, therefore, different in their approaches to probable, possible and desirable futures perspectives. Christopher Dede's paper provides an introduction to the fundamental definitions and assumptions underlying educational futures. He argues that the approach to technology that we choose is central in shaping our educational institutions. Dede's position is supported by James Botkin who discusses the world "problematique." The "world without borders" concept has become very meaningful in the context of work toward the world economic order. Scholars, however, have been slower to examine the world educational order. Botkin's analysis of this will make one wonder why there is not a "club of education" much like there is a Club of Rome.

Robert Theobald's paper presents what he terms as a "minority" futures theory. Theobald explains his conception of the transition from the industrial-era to the communications-era. The fundamental question, for him, is whether this transition can occur without a critical breakdown in social institutions. He maintains that change can occur through planning, but education about the alternatives must be a priority in contrast to theories set forth by other futurists such as Herman Kahn or Daniel Bell.

With less of a sense of the urgency than Theobald's proposal, Ervin Laszlo maintains that "a conscious and systematic plan must be evolved" to insure that intellectually prepared individuals participate in policy-making. He proposes that this will involve educational phases which bring educators into more contact with other decision-making institutions. Laszlo elaborates upon the practical applications of a more participatory educational system as well as the theory for this structure. James Nolfi's proposals also present a societal/educational view of reconstruction. Like Laszlo, he proposes a system for life-long learning. He believes that it should incorporate a social ecology which is "multi-disciplinary" and action-based. Nolfi proposes dramatic educational changes for "a whole variety of known quantum jumps of an evolutionary/revolutionary nature."

All of the articles in this section express the need for philosophic analysis in futures studies. John Pulliam examines major philosophic theories of education and expresses his conception of an educational philosophy of futurism. His article is in one way a summary and extension of the philosophic considerations of the previous papers. On another level, it stresses the demands for philosophic inquiry in emerging futures research. Pulliam suggests that "the future will not be understood by looking at a narrow slice of life or learning." The inquiry needed in futures research must be interdisciplinary and reflect normative approaches—something philosophers do as a matter of course.

THE "STATE OF THE UNION" IN EDUCATIONAL THEORY

Christopher J. Dede

This conference and its attendant Sourcebook are an essential step in the development of Educational Futures. In fact, they might qualify for what I have come to think of as a "Future Holiday." A friend of mine named Glenn Hawkes once said to me that all of our holidays were misdirected because they had to do with things in the past. We celebrate events such as Columbus Day, even though these happened hundreds of years ago and no longer have much meaning. He suggested that what we should celebrate would be, for example, World Disarmament Day. We could decide that, say, October 21st, 1998 would be World Disarmament Day; and on October 21st every year from now on, we would celebrate. We would enjoy our work toward the coming of world disarmament; and, when 1998 finally did come, disarmament would be complete and the holiday would terminate. Then we could set another future holiday, and in this way our holidays would always be meaningful and express our dreams and desires. For me, this conference has been a future holiday for about ten years, and so I am very glad to have helped to bring it about.

The overall issue I want to discuss in my State of the Union Address has to deal with how this conference is one essential component for creating a network that can deliberately shape the future. Such a network begins with the development of groups of future-oriented people all around the country, as has taken place in the last few years. I have been fortunate enough to help to begin several such groups: the degree granting Future Studies Programs at the University of Massachusetts and at the University of Houston-Clear Lake. In addition, by writing and speaking and traveling around the country, I have worked with many other action-oriented futures groups.

My sense, from all these groups, is that we have now come to the time at which a critical mass and a level of expertise have been reached that mandate linking all these futures groups together for support and evolution. A crucial question then becomes: what strategies can be used to create local, regional, national, international networks of people working in futures which will provide an opportunity for interaction, growth, and renewal? To evolve these strategies, we need to begin with a basic reformulation of educational theory.

BASIC DEFINITIONS AND GOALS

One way of initiating this reformation is to inquire: What does it mean to be a "futurist?" I know that is a question many of you are asked, usually by somebody with a half smile on his face. Most people have the notion that a futurist is someone who goes around saying, "The day after the day after tomorrow, is the third day of the rest of your life." Frankly, there are many quacks and trendy self-styled "experts" in the futures research to give such an impression.

In contrast, Jack McClellan's and Peter Wagschal's definition of a "futurist" is: a person who makes other people's futures more real for them. Most people live with an unconscious single image of what the future will be, and usually that image looks suspiciously like the present. If I interact with others, helping them to see that they have futures, in the plural, and that these alternatives are real choices for them, then I think of myself as a futurist.

This is consistent with the theory of futures research because the fundamental assumption of our field is that the future resembles a tree. The trunk is unitary, as is the present; the many branches are the different alternative futures. As we walk up the trunk towards the branches, through the present to the future, each decision we make cuts off a branch (eliminates an alternative future). By the time we get to the location of the branches (by the time the present becomes the future). By the time we get to the location of the branches (by the time the present becomes the future), only one branch is left (the new present) and again a host of alternative futures stretches out before us.

The theoretical futurists work primarily to explore what the different branches might be. The normative futurists work in the area of choosing which branch is the most desirable. Many of us in education work on helping people to act in the present, to make daily decisions which ultimately choose on which branch they wish to be. But the common factor, from the policy analyst in the think tank to the kindergarten teacher exploring the futures wheel in her classroom, is the concept of others seeing these alternative futures in a real sense.

Building the Education Section to an active professional organization carries this factor one step further. Unlike our work as individuals, in which we can simply hope to influence other people to see their options, as a group working together we can become a network which creates completely new branches on the tree, for ourselves and for others.

Such creation of futures ties into the question: What does it
mean to be an "educator?" Many people think of an educator
as the stereotypic teacher: lecturing endlessly to passive students; psychologically either forgetful or obsessive-compulsive
(depending on which end of the pathological spectrum the
teacher is being portrayed); and, of course, very dull. It is easy
to fall into the cultural trap of hearing the word "teacher"
and responding with those negative images.

In contrast, I think of an educator in a much broader sense:
in the sense of one who helps to realize human potential; in
the sense of one who shapes beliefs and values and most fundamental cultural ways that people look at the world. When
we visualize the profession of educators, we should include
news executives, newspaper reporters, media stars, cultural
idols, industrial trainees, community organizers, politicians,
and teachers. If we can link all these groups to discuss the
major goals and problems we have in common, we can make
a united, concerted, and complementary approach to shaping
a better future for education.

My own perspective is that the greatest challenge today for
educators is to take responsibility and power for what we can
and should accomplish. At present, society has many different
conflicting images of what education should be. We're supposed to socialize, we're supposed to train for jobs, we're supposed to screen for jobs, we're supposed to provide entertain-
ment, we're supposed to keep young people out of the job
market, we're supposed to screen for further education, we're
supposed to train for further education, we're supposed to
develop life skills and citizen's literacy, and if along the course
of those things we can turn out a healthy and happy human
being, so much the better!

I don't need to tell you that no one group of people in one
occupational role can do all that. But, looking at all the roles
and all the types of people that fall under the broad definition
of "educator," if all these people chose to work together and
to divide up the agendas for education according to each
group's particular abilities and resources, we could make a
major impact on building a better future and a giant step
toward satisfying what society wants from the educational
system.

As educators and futurists (using the two definitions just
given), where are we now in history? What will people fifty or
a hundred years from now write about education 1978: where
it was going and what it meant? One of the things that has
impressed me in may travels around the country has been
that the present shows many similarities to times in history
in which an entire civilization has rapidly changed its entire
cultural belief system. Today, our culture is pervaded by a
vacuum of leadership, many conflicting goals within the soci-

ety, and worsening economic distress. Some leading indicators which have consistently appeared historically when a civilization was about to shift are preoccupations with labyrinths and mazes, heavy use of hallucinogenic drugs, and a preoccupation with neurotic heroes—all of which we see in our society now. These indicators are external reflections of internal psychological conflicts which reflect a sense of fear and a loss of personal control over where the future is going.

Certainly, in education I talk to teachers everyday who are sick and tired of trendy innovations. Each year there's a new innovation: it's simplistic; there is no accountability; and, if one does implement it, the next year when an annual report is submitted, the school has already put all its money into the next trendy innovation and is no longer really interested in what has been done. I see teachers who are being forced out of the profession for economic reasons—students of mine who can make twice as much in other careers and who are tired of having two jobs to support a family on a teacher's salary. These dynamics are reflective of the larger trends in society just mentioned, and indicate educators' loss of control over the future of the learning process.

And yet, with all these problems, at the same time I've seen excitement, I've seen creativity, I've seen tremendous sacrifices from educators from across the country who have made an existential choice to stay in education. Such people are still committed because they find teaching personally rewarding and believe that we can build a better society through education. Of course, many of you are here today for just these reasons, and have come to share your ideas with others about improving our educational futures.

So, I think that the World Future Society slogan "Time of Crisis, Time of Opportunity" is very appropriate. In a sense, the stage for this conference was set by U Thant in 1969 when he was Secretary General of the United Nations, and said:

> "...the Members of the United Nations have perhaps ten years left in which to subordinate their ancient quarrels and launch a global partnership to curb the arms race, to improve the human environment, to defuse the population explosion, and to supply the required momentum to development efforts. If such a global partnership is not forged within the next decade, then I very much fear that the problems I have mentioned will have reached such staggering proportions that they will be beyond our capacity to control."

I don't need to tell you that in the last nine years of those ten, most of these problems have *worsened*. We can either view that as a failure and be doomsdayers, or we can view our situation as a call to action.

THE CONTEXT OF OUR PROBLEMS

Talking about civilization shifts is not productive unless one has a sense of why. I think I can explain part of what's happening to cause the dynamics discussed above. My own training is as a scientist, and although I teach "courses" at the senior or graduate level in biology, chemistry, geology, education, psychology, sociology, and studies of the future, the common thread that runs through these courses is a preoccupation with how science shapes society. When I look at the major schools of thought in futures research and ask how these schools see science affecting society, several distinct groups emerge. Despite the differences among these groups, one thing on which they all agree is the major trends in the last hundred years.

The last hundred years has been a unique time in human history. In the last hundred years, in the more developed countries, the speed of travel has increased by a factor of about a hundred. Our energy resources, despite the energy crisis, have increased by a factor of about a thousand. Data handling speed has increased by a factor of ten thousand, weaponry by a factor of one million, and communications speed by a factor of ten million.

What is especially impressive about these figures is that one hundred years is such a short period of time, given the scope of human history. We know that human beings have existed for the last five hundred thousand to two million years. If all of human history were to be compressed into a one hour period, the trends above all have occurred essentially within the last tenth of one second of that hour! No comparable time can be found in human history in which people have gained so much power over the environment so quickly.

One group of futurists, given these trends, has argued that unilateral and accelerating progress must therefore be the most likely alternative future, the major branch on the tree. Certainly all the first key works in futures research reflected this view point: Herman Kahn, Bucky Fuller, Daniel Bell, and so on. Year by year, however, this group of futurists has gained fewer supporters, relative to the total number of researchers in the field, as year by year the grounds for this optimism have been undermined.

The arguments for caution which have opposed this forecast of unilateral progress seem to center on the factory of social invention in society. We can discuss the future impact of technological inventions (such as the television and the computer), but perhaps more important in shaping the future are social inventions (such as marriage or the university), which consist of a set of myths and beliefs and rituals that structure individual and social behavior.

In prehistoric societies (before written language), the major mechanism of problem-solving was social invention. For example, prehistoric societies had an elegant mechanism for preventing war. Many prehistoric societies have very elaborate kinship networks, in which not only one's brothers and sisters are important, but one's second uncle's spouse by marriage. Similarly, there are very elaborate incest networks in prehistoric societies, networks which extend out to fifty, a hundred, one hundred and fifty of the closest relatives. Isolated, neither one of these social inventions makes much sense (at least to us), but combined in a tribal society they become an effective deterrent to war. Once a tribal member is married, that person becomes related to all their spouse's relatives. In a tribal society of two or three hundred people, within a very few generations marrying anyone within the tribe would be incest (since everyone is related), so tribal members must find marriage partners external to the tribe. But once someone from another tribe becomes one's spouse, then that entire tribe becomes related, and so are excluded as enemies with which to war.

In our society, we tend to rely on technological inventions rather than social inventions as our problem-solving mechanisms. We think of a new gadget, rather than a new set of behaviors, to solve whatever problems we have (e.g. the "balance of terror" to prevent war). As a result, in the last hundred years, while technological innovations have greatly increased in power, no comparable gains have occurred in education, in economics, in our political systems, in all of our social inventions. Therefore, many futurists argue that one of the grounds for caution about unilateral optimism is a current imbalance between technological power and social control stemming from an historical shift in emphasis between technological inventions and social inventions.

The "sorcerer's apprentice" problem prevents technological invention alone from being a satisfactory probelm-solving mechanism. Introducing a technology into the society intrinsically induces not only its benefits, but also its side effects (what technological assessors term secondary and tertiary effects). For example, one of the secondary effects of the automobile has been the development of vertical monopolies (controlling the coal mine, the lake steamer, the steel mill, the railroad, the automobile manufacturing plant, the rubber plant, the glass factory, the truck distribution system and the car dealership). A horizontal monopoly (owning all the gas stations) is illegal because of its erosion of the "free market," but a vertical monopoly just as effectively creates an oligopolistic economy and is completely legal. A different and unrelated side effect of the car has been a change in the sexual habits of Americans: the rate of premarital sex, the number of unwed mothers, and distinct changes in moral standards can be traced to having a portable bedroom readily available (that didn't eat the grass while one was busy trying to do other things).

Another illustration of the "sorcerer's apprentice" problem is detergents. Soap leaves a ring around the bathtub, so detergents were originally introduced because their salts with calcium and magnesium and some other metals were soluble and didn't leave a ring. A few years after detergents were introduced, people noticed that suddenly all the streams and ponds and glasses of drinking water were developing a head of foam, similar to a glass of beer; and so it was discovered that detergents weren't biodegradable and steadily built up in the water supply. Biodegradable detergents were quickly substituted, but a few years after that, people discovered that all of the lakes and streams were rapidly aging and filling up with algae because of phosphate additives in detergents, so another change had to be made. Now we are waiting to see what's going to happen from our biodegradable non-phosphate detergents that replaced the biodegradable phosphate detergents that replaced the non-biodegradable phosphate detergents that replaced soap. This is the kind of problem that one tends to encounter by using technology as a problem-solving mechanism.

Faced with these arguments, the unilateral optimists divided into two schools of thought, and a new approach to technology developed which might be called the "tiger by the tail" theory of technological invention. This group of futurists argues that, in the Middle Ages, perhaps we could have chosen a different relative balance between technological and social inventions, but such growth in population has taken place since then that if we don't create new technologies as fast as possible, we're doomed. These "tiger by the tail" futurists believe that without unlimited technologies there will be too many people, too many diseases, not enough food--back to the problems of the Middle Ages, without the resources readily available then, since now the easy-to-reach resources are exhausted. An anology that this school of futurists likes to use is Neanderthal Man freezing to death standing ten feet on top of a bed of coal. He doesn't know that the coal is there and wouldn't know how to get to it if he knew of its existence, but it is a resource that could keep him warm if he had the technological sophistication to use it.

Arthur C. Clarke, a "tiger by the tail" futurist, talks about the "cliff." In prehistoric societies, people lived in a "desert:" not much to eat and all of a person's time taken up with hunting and gathering activities just to keep up a minimum quality of life. With the development of agricultural technology, humanity "walked" from that desert into a "fertile valley": more things to eat, time available to be devoted to activities beyond subsistence--but population expands. Soon the "valley" gets crowded, people keep "walking," and another set of technologies developed in the industrial revolution creating a "greenhouse:" very intensive agriculture, again enough for everyone to eat--but population expands again.

Clarke says that our next "walk" is to the base of a "cliff," that the next set of technologies will be extremely difficult to create (e.g. fusion power, which may well take fifty years of intensive scientific research to develop). Clarke argues that we have to scramble up that "cliff" immediately, because if we stay at the bottom to let the rest of the world attain an equal standard of living, too few resources will be left to climb the cliff and we'll all starve to death in the wreckage of the "greenhouse." If we act now to climb the cliff alone with totally unrestricted technological advance, then at the top of the cliff we will find a "high" technology to create a "Garden of Eden" (a million pounds of copper in nationwide communications nets in the "greenhouse" can become one pound of copper in a communications satellite in the "Garden"). Once we're in the "Garden," we can pull the rest of the world up to our level. Thus, the "tiger-by-the-tail" futurists accept the difficulties of using technology as a sole problem-solver, but argue that it will work and that other choices are no longer possible.

However, a final group of futurists remains unconvinced by these arguments, and believes that social invention (coupled with appropriate technology) is an essential component of any desirable future. A few of their arguments can be summarized here; one has to do with social conformity. If we go back to Clarke's desert, valley, greenhouse, cliff, and Garden of Eden: In the desert (in the prehistoric society), there is very little need for social conformity. If half the people in the tribe dislike the decisions of the headman, they can split off to form their own tribe, use the same hunting territory and the same waterhole, and nothing is affected or disturbed.

However, once technology becomes a problem-solving mechanism, with the beginnings of agricultural society (the valley), a dramatic change occurs. No longer can even ten percent of the society deviate from social norms, because the irrigation canals must be maintained, the fortress of the cities must be secure (to keep the hill people from coming down and stealing the harvests), and no one can be allowed to throw salt on the fields. So, many social inventions are created simultaneous with agriculture's technological advance to increase social conformity: the god/king, organized religions, the military, private ownership, the walled city.

In the "greenhouse," this shift to increased social conformity becomes even more dramatic. A single person can throw a wrench into a modern manufacturing plant, causing million of dollars worth of damage and shutting down the plant for several months. A group of less than two hundred workers at the national Ford assembly plant can realistically menace the U.S. economy (as happened several years ago when such a group refused to ratify a national back-to-work order, thereby threatening the eventual shut-down of the other Ford plants as parts piled up, which in turn would close the steel plants, the glass factories, the rubber industry, the railroads, the coal mines, the lake steamers, and so on). A small group of terrorists can destroy power stations or transportation nets to disrupt the lives of hundreds of millions of people.

In the Garden of Eden, what extremes of social conformity will be required, with that level of high technology? Willis Harman, of the Stanford Research Institute, calls the probable outcome of climbing the cliff "Friendly Fascism," but friendly or unfriendly, the progression doesn't imply a desirable future.

A second argument against the "tiger-by-the-tail" theory is centered on the probability of "disaster" futures. The largest single branch on the tree may be made up of many many tiny little twigs, each a discrete, improbable but possible catastrophe. Maybe there is a one in ten thousand chance that we will dump enough oil into the ocean to kill the algae in the top one millimeter and destroy the major source of replenishing the oxygen in the atmosphere. Perhaps there is a one in a thousand chance that we will release enough fluorocarbons into the air to damage the ozone layer severely and cause a high rate of environmental cancer. A five in a hundred chance may exist that we will have a nuclear war; or a one in two hundred chance that we will emit enough carbon dioxide into the atmosphere to create a drastic climatic change. The interesting thing about all these tiny twigs is that if one looks at all of our new technologies and at all of the low probability, disastrous side effects respected scientists have predicted might happen from these technologies, the sum total of these tiny effects is massive and negative. About four hundred of these one-in-a-thousand chances can be cited; perhaps some are/one in a million, maybe some are one in two hundred, but four hundred one-in-a-thousand chances average out to forty percent of our possible futures! Therefore, with our current rate of technological innovation, we are risking a significant probability of a very undesirable future world.

One of the arguments of the "social invention" group that I have found most impressive has to do with the developmental cycles which take place in the different sciences. Each theoretical science has periods of relative productivity, followed by periods of relative consolidation. In the early 1900's, Einstein's work in the theory of space/time and relativity marks a period of productivity in the physical sciences. What we find is that, twenty or thirty years after such a revolution, a new set of technologies impacts on society, technologies which are byproducts of these new theoretical developments. (So, in the 1940s and the 1950s, the atomic bomb, the computer and the television were introduced, leading to huge changes in lifestyle and values).

People who are concerned about technology point to the fact that the biological sciences went into a period of theoretical productivity about 1955 with the initial work on the structure of DNA, a series of theoretical revolutions that has continued for the last twenty years. As a result, beginning now and extending for the next ten or twenty years, we can expect to see a set of biological technologies being introduced into the society: anti-aging strategies, intelligence boosting techniques, control of the fetus manipulations, and so on.

These biological technologies are perhaps more influential than the computer, the atomic bomb, and the television combined. All physical technologies, however powerful, are still somehow external; the television is a better set of eyes, the computer a better memory, the atomic bomb a better (or at least a bigger) fist. But, the biological technologies are *internal*, and affect what we call "human nature:" the fundamental set of jealousies, loves, dislikes, and attributes that we assume all human beings have in common. This shared heritage has been the basis of our religious and economic and educational and political institutions—all of our social inventions. Technologies that affect these human traits may be profoundly disturbing and disruptive to society; and yet, unplanned and unassessed, the biological technologies are surely coming.

On balance, I fall into the last group of futures researchers; I see the necessity for technology, my own training is in technology, I don't think a desirable future can be reached without some technological advance—but I have many concerns about the ways that we use technology now, and feel that many present problems can be solved only by social invention. No matter which group you believe, the insights I have discussed on the different schools of thought and their arguments explain much of the confusion and fear in society now—and also perhaps cast light on why this may be a civilization-shift period in human history. Further, each group's ideas have profound implications for the future of education.

IMPLICATIONS FOR EDUCATION

All three of these schools of thought, when pushed, end up stating that education is the most crucial, central force in shaping what the future will be. The unilateral optimists see education as the source of all the experts and the scientific elite and the bureaucrats who will run the post-industrial society for us. The "tiger-by-the-tail" futurists have similar goals for education, but also see the educational process as providing the necessary training in crisis intervention skills to help society cope with some of the short-term disasters we may hit as we try to scramble our way up the cliff. And, the futures researchers who are concerned with relying on social inventions see education as the key institution in society— both socially inventive itself in terms of new educational structures, and also producing the generalists and innovators and reconstructionists who will emerge and reshape our present directions. Thus, *we* are the crucial group for the future.

Now, what does all this imply for today, education 1979? I want to indicate what is right in education today, and not what's wrong. It's easy to be a pathologist, but it's very difficult to perform resurrections; everyone wants to criticize what's bad about education, but no one wants to propose solutions.

In a sense, I want to discuss the hope factor. If there's just one ghetto school in the United States that works without special resources, we can make any ghetto school work. If we learn to translate what this urban school is doing right into the similar schools across the rest of the country, we've solved the urban education problem. It seems to me that the hope factor is what we're discussing at this conference, because gathered here are more than two hundred people who are saying, "I've got something I'm doing that works for me and solves some of the problems I'm confronted with educationally." If we can pool that knowledge, we can move toward solving most of our problems in education.

I have my favorite success stories for education, but I'm not going to talk about them here; many of these ideas for change are contained in a book I co-authored with Jim Bowman, Fred Kierstead, and John Pulliam called *The Far Side of the Future*. Many other success stories will be in the Educational Futures Sourcebooks that will emerge out of this and future Education Section Conferences.

What can be summarized here are the major common themes in the two hundred forty plus success stories that this conference represents. One theme I've found is that "education" is more than schooling—that, in order to make sense of the future, we need to define education as including schools, media, industry, community action groups, and families, and then begin to allocate responsibility for all of the goals that society has for education to these different educational agents.

A second common theme in the papers at this conference is an emphasis on focusing education not on the disciplines as such, but on problems. Such a shift would make education *trans*disciplinary, in that real world problems would become the core content, and all the concepts and skills from all the different disciplines now taught would be used as needed to examine aspects of the problems. Such a curriculum would help teach students to apply the knowledge they receive, and would give them much more of a sense of control over their future.

A third common theme is the idea that education is for people of all ages, and should be oriented toward preparing students for both short range and long range challenges. No one claims that he can take someone now who is six years old, work with that student until he is eighteen, and then send him out totally prepared for the next fifty years—yet that is our present social model for manditory formal education. We can give students basic skills and a few projections of what may happen long-term, but continuous short range education for people of all age levels in our society is essential if we are to cope successfully with the oncoming futures in which there are so many branches on the tree, in which humanity will experience a discontinuous and a difficult series of crises.

Many of the papers here also discuss the need for a healthy diversity in education, for a move in education toward leading the society in terms of being non-racist, non-sexist, pluralist and egalitarian. The Education Section should take affirmative action so as to model what such diverse educational systems might resemble.

Finally, educational problems in the United States cannot be discussed in isolation. Many conference participants stress the need to be transnational, to recognize how interdependent we all are, to discuss the global problems that education faces and the global success stories that we can bring to bear on our national educational problems. Again, this is an area in which the Education Section should be leading the way to model such an approach to other educational agents.

Thus, if we take the notion of pooling ideas and support through interacting such as this conference and its Sourcebook, if we take the idea of assuming responsibility and power for what we want to do as educators, and if we conceive of both a broader definition of "futurist" and of "educator," then we can, as a group, make a major contribution to modeling how education might be an active society-shaping force, rather than its current status of passive, reactive past-oriented institution. Linking the isolated groups of futures educators working across the country and the world into a series of networks is a first step. As we do, I feel that we will be supported by many people who do not identify themselves as futurists, or perhaps even as educators, because I think that many people are tired of the "gurus" and the games that have marked a lot of what has happened recently both in futures research and in education. I think that people are ready to sit down and say, "we know some things that we can agree on; let's start to build with those rather than quarreling over which minor variation might be one percent more effective."

Two thoughts to close with: to change education, there is no sense in waiting for a big grant of a nationwide mandate or Santa Claus. Jim Bowman and Fred Kierstead and I made the decision to run this conference on the registration fees alone, and made a personal commitment of our time to see that that was done because we felt it was important, People in the World Future Society, people at the University of Houston—Clear Lake respected that commitment and took the risk with us. The results have been extremely impressive. So, one doesn't need a grant—even to run an international conference—one doesn't need money; one just needs the commitment.

Second thought: it's easy to be psychologically hypnotized by the relative stability of the present. As a result, part of human nature seems to be to wait and say, "Well, I'm not sure which of those futures on the tree is really going to happen, and I'm not sure in which of those schools of thought I really believe. Each of them has good arguments, so I'll be conservative and wait and see which future is coming for sure. I'll do a little bit in each area, so that I can present myself as being each type of futurist (depending on my audience) and then, when the future comes, I'll know which one to claim I was all along."

This is an easy human trait by which to be trapped, and through much of human history it hasn't been too damaging because we could wait until our crises were bad and still be able to solve them. What is characteristic of the crises that are coming is that, if we wait until they are fully apparent, it will be too late to reverse them. So, we need to get past our own individual willingness to not take risks and we must begin to make commitments now.

This university is a good illustration of what I am discussing. The campus is built on a flood plane, and the entire exterior of this building is glass. Sooner or later, a major hurricane is going to hit Houston; it may come next year, or twenty years from now. The building is on relatively high ground and is well built, so I'm not worried that the structure itself will blow away. But, at 90 miles an hour, every pane of glass on this building is going to go flying off into space, and someone is going to make a lot of money replacing them. Further, at wind speeds of 135 miles an hour, the roof of the Astrodome— like a giant frisbee—will sail across Houston and impale itself somewhere, probably in one of the oil company skyscrapers. This will happen, sooner or later, no matter how stable we feel!

I think San Francisco is probably the best example of being fooled by the stability of the present. If I wanted to make money betting on one prediction from my years of forecasting experience, I would wager that the largest single national disaster in American history will happen when the earthquake hits San Francisco, because there are elementary schools built on the fault, freeways and dams built within a few miles of the fault—there will be tremendous loss of life. And it *will* happen.

There is an old Chinese saying, "Too late to dig well, when house on fire." We need to dig wells for education here, now!

I would like to close with a blessing and a curse. My blessing is on all of you for making the personal sacrifices that I know you made to come here. The curse comes from ancient China: when you didn't like someone, you said to them, "May you live in exciting times." I'm afraid that we all do!

LINKING LEARNING TO GLOBAL ISSUES

James W. Botkin

Everyone is proposing a fresh look at global issues. The fact is that, since the complex of issues concerning energy, food, population, and the environment was first introduced in the early 1950s[1] and brought to international attention by The Club of Rome one decade ago,[2] the "problematique" (as this tangle of problems was termed) has grown worse. With the availability of Lester Brown's book *The Twenty-Ninth Day*,[3] the indicators of deterioration need not be detailed here.

To this "physical" problematique have been added a second and a third order set of world-class problems. The second order set would include the widening gap between rich and poor countries.[4] It would also include the renewed concern for the arms race, for difficulties in conflict resolution, and for the threat of international terrorism and war (in which the development of small mobile nuclear weapons adds a proliferation dimension to an already serious situation).

The third order set of problems, presently emerging, is associated less with physical concerns and more with mental, moral, or psychological questions. These comprise issues of cultural identity, the emancipation of women, the status of children (1979 has been designated by the U.N. as the "Year of the Child"), human rights, and the lack of consensus (or the lack of "global coherence") in human goals.[5] This lack of consensus seems to contradict to some extent the idea that some "globalizing process" is eroding cultural integrity and diversity.

METHODOLOGICAL CONCERNS

It becomes increasingly difficult or unrealistic to analyze these clusters of first, second, and third order issues with the computer modeling that served us well in the late 1960s. Perhaps second generation cybernetics will offer a new model in the 1980s, but for the time being these quantitative methodologies are seen by many as too mechanistic. The positivist idea—the notion that only what is observable and measurable

is valid—is under interrogation. Yet no alternative methodology has gained sufficient acceptance to take place alongside
systems theory. It is as if we were all in a room with our hands
raised, hoping to offer alternative ways to view the global
issues. In the latest project for The Club of Rome—the Learning Project[6]—we intend to offer *learning* as a focal point for a
fresh look at the critical issues facing humanity, both as methodology for analysis and, through education, as a vehicle for
possible, positive action.

In choosing a global methodology, it is no longer sufficient—
and these remarks apply equally to the methodologies of future studies—to rely upon methods of analysis appropriate
only to one culture. To the extent that the problems of the
future are increasingly global in scope, methodologies with
increasingly global acceptance will be required. No methodology is value free. There are currently at least three major
world-scale "modes of analysis" in use that reflect to some
extent the tripartite division of our world: cybernetics, ideology, and the development/basic needs approach. None of them
enjoys full support among the scholars and statesmen in all
world regions.

Is the lack of methodological consensus good or bad? If you
subscribe to a philosophy of decentralization such as proposed
by Johan Galtung,[7] you probably will see it as both good and
natural, since it would be an indicator that cultural diversity
is alive and well. If you advocate some measure of "global
coherence," as Mihajlo Mesarovic[8] might, then you would
likely see it as lamentable, since the global issues will persist
even when cultural diversity (or decentralization) is pushed to
its theoretical limits.

The requirement in choosing a methodology today may well
be that it has to include both universal and specific traits. Of
the many methodologies proposed, it seems that learning
meets this requirement as well as or better than most.

INDIVIDUAL AND SOCIETAL LEARNING: IS THERE A DIFFERENCE?

All people are involved in a continuous process of decision-
making (choices among alternatives *and* creating new alternatives) for their own lives (as individuals) and as participants
in society (social participation). They also affect and are affected by the choices of the community as a whole ("societal
learning"). From the myriad forms of learning, we will concentrate on that learning which improves our capacity to decide in new situations. Individual choice and societal choice
can then be distinguished. Although the elements (or forms)
of individual choice are different from the elements of societal
choice, the process is the same. That is, the elements of indi-

vidual learning might involve human brains (and their extensions); learning institutions (schools, media, some family functions, etc.); and specific sets of language, technological
understanding, and values. On the other hand, the elements
of societal learning might involve interactions among the subgroups of the society; "institutions" that would include research functions, laws, and proclamations (what Kenneth
Boulding[9] calls the "transcripts" of society); and a shared set
of language, technology, and values.

The processes, however, are the same. Societies decide and
make choices as individuals do. Political figures and diplomats
carry with them an implicit model of societal learning by
which they assess the learning capacity and knowledge resources of entire countries. Both individual and societal learning, like decision-making, contain the same basic ingredients—
preference (values and evaluation) and foresight (a continual
estimation of the likelihood of the occurrence of certain
courses of events). Given these similarities, the underdevel-
oped state of preference and foresight used in societal learning
is striking because many individual members of our own and
other societies possess humane preferences and extensive
foresight.

A widely accepted definition of societal learning still waits
to be articulated. The major problem has been that the boundaries of what is meant by "society" and what part of the
society can be said to have learned are seldom congruent.

HOW TO ASSESS A LEARNING SYSTEM? THE NOTION OF "PROBLEMATIQUE" APPLIED TO LEARNING

The Club of Rome Learning Project has tried to look at the
learning system for a society in order to assess its prepared-
ness to decide in new or unprecedented situations. Concep-
tually, it should be possible to "model" or simply to describe
a society's learning system by a careful examination of all its
elements, just as those who modeled the physical "problematique" could do so. Practically, however, this task in the area
of learning is difficult because: a) the number of elements is
large (learning and education is, by most counts, the largest
human activity in the world—even larger than the military or
health fields); b) the elements are only minimally quantifiable;
and c) even with key relationships, there is disagreement as
to whether they correlate negatively or positively (for example, do more schools detract from or enhance learning?). In
keeping with earlier Club of Rome language, such a description of a society's learning system has been termed a "learning
problematique."

To describe a society's learning problematique, an intermediate step has been used. Instead of focusing on the elements

themselves (such as schools, families, media, "transcripts," etc.), a series of characteristics are projected that cut across the elements. Instead of looking at teachers, textbooks, and television (as CBS Television recently did in America[10]), their degree of relevance/irrelevance, efficiency/waste, and so on is assessed. This makes the learning problematique more issue-oriented and less structually oriented. (It also tends to provoke a more normative assessment of a society's learning system.)

The characteristics which have been chosen to describe a society's learning problematique are: relevance/irrelevance, efficiency/waste, aids/impediments, and power (positive and negative). These can be said to be the "components" of the learning problematique. While the more detailed structural elements (such as schools or textbooks) may possess several or all of these charcteristics, certain of these elements can be used to illustrate the nature of the component parts.

Among many illustrations, one may note: a) groups excluded from learning as a waste of the human resource (for example, women especially in developing countries, and illiterates in both developed and less-developed societies); b) non-selective transfers of external learning models as contributing to irre-levance (importation of colonial or post-colonial schooling); c) the "imperialism" of schooling as an impediment to learning (the tendency to assume formative functions performed ear-lier by families, apprenticeship, or religion); and d) the slow rate of illiteracy eradication (a question of political will) and access to the mass media (a question of dispersed control out-side the reach of educators) as illustrations of different issues of power. These examples are, of course, not exhaustive.

The operation, behavior, or outcome of a learning proble-matique determines an individual's and a society's prepared-ness to make decisions in new situations such as those repre-sented by global issues. How well prepared are we as individuals and societies to make such decisions? The answer differs for each society (as of course for each individual). Some societies have a learning problematique that is blocked pri-marily for reasons of power: all of the efficiency in learning, relevant learning, and aids to learning are of no avail because the power structures will not change.

Most societies suffer from a severe case of irrelevance in their learning which may be defined as the lack of anticipa-tion. If one looks at what the children learn today compared to what they and their societies will need by the year 2000 (which coincidentally will be the graduating university class for American children born in 1978), then the irrelevance or "anticipation gap" looks forbidding. The past impact of this lack of anticipation is clear in fields such as energy, popula-tion, or any of the four bio-resources (croplands, grazing lands, fisheries, forests). Despite the efforts of so many individuals concerned with future studies in the United States, the American society as a learning system is still far behind in its capacity to anticipate, and runs the risks inherent to irrelevance: we are doomed to suffer in reality those situations we cannot anticipate and simulate mentally.[11]

IS LEARNING A GLOBAL ISSUE?

The learning problematique has been described as operating for all practical purposes at the national level, to the extent that learning and especially education take place within national contexts. (For federations like the United States, West Germany, or Switzerland, one should more accurately go to more decentralized levels.) This national or societal focus again distinguishes the learning problematique from the physical problematique, which was intrinsically global in nature. Increasingly, however, learning needs to be viewed in a global context.

A global view of learning can be visualized by piecing together all the world's learning problematiques. What is most striking about the mosaic is not so much its insularity and its divisions but its massive imbalances. Consider the following familiar facts:

—Three industrial countries (the USA, USSR, and Japan) account for over 50% of all organized higher educational activity (in terms of the number of teachers, number of students, and public expenditures on post-secondary education—see UNESCO *Statistical Yearbook* or Ruth L. Sivard, *World Military and Social Expenditures*.[12]

—Sixty percent of the world's population receives only six percent of world expenditures on public education (Sivard, 1977).

—Over 90% of world research and development (using R&D as an indicator of scientific capacity) is conducted in only 12 countries on the planet.[13]

—The USA exports television programs to every country in the world which has television broadcasting facilities, save five, but imports only 1% of its programming (primarily from Great Britain).[14]

Viewed from this perspective, we may say that learning itself is a global issue. Indeed, it may be seen as more than that. All of the processes and perceptions underlying the movements for a New International Economic Order or the Application of Science and Technology to Development are ultimately based on learning.[15] In a fundamental sense, learning can be seen as the issue of issues. A key question for learning as a global issue to be discussed in the forthcoming Learning Report to The Club of Rome is: How can we expect learning and education to help resolve issues that are globally distributed when learning itself is locally or regionally so mal-distributed?

NOTES

1. Harrison Brown, *Challenge of Man's Future*, Viking, New York, 1954.
2, D. Meadows, et al., *The Limits to Growth*, Potomac Associates, 1972. The Club of Rome, which initiated the study, was formed in 1968.
3. Lester Brown, *The Twenty-Ninth Day*, W.W. Norton and Co., 1978.
4. Jan Tinbergen, *Restructuring the International Order*, Dutton, New York, 1976.
5. Ervin Laszlo, *Goals for Mankind*, Dutton, New York, 1977.
6. M. Malitza, J. Botkin, M. Elmandjra, *Learning to Bridge the Human Gap*, in preparation for summer, 1979.
7. See Johan Galtung, series of papers presented to the World Future Studies Federation (Rome) conference on "Alternative Visions of Desirable Societies," Mexico City, April, 1978, sponsored by the Third World Center for Social and Economic Studies.
8. M. Mesarovic and E. Pestel, *Mankind at the Turning Point*, Signet Books, New York, 1974.
9. K. Boulding, *The Meaning of the Twentieth Century*, Harper and Row, New York, 1972. For another discussion of "societal learning," see Karl Deutsch, *The Nerves of Government*, The Free Press, New York, 1966.
10. CBS three-part series for television "Is Anyone Out There Learning?" shown in the USA in August, 1978.
11. There are other "orders" such as the "World Information Order" that deals specifically with communications, and of course the more comprehensive notion of "world order" as described by the Institute for World Order in New York (see S. Mendlovitz, *On the Creation of a Just World Order*, Free Press, New York, 1975). Also, UNESCO defines the "New International Economic Order" to contain educational and cultural aspects as well as economic ones.
12. Ruth L. Sivard, *World Military and Social Expenditures*, 1976, 1977, 1978. WMSE Publications, Box 1103, Leesburg, Virginia 22075. These excellent publications amplify and interpret the *UNESCO Statistical Yearbook* admirably.
13. These figures, from the *UNESCO Statistical Yearbook*, are widely disputed and to be viewed with some skepticism. Probably half the figure is military R&D.
14. S. Lane, "The Global Flow of Television," unpublished paper for the Learning Project, quoting from H. I. Schiller, *Mass Communications and American Empire*, Augustus M. Kelly, New York, 1970.
15. See P. G. Altbach, "Servitude of the Mind? Education, Dependency, and Neo-Colonialism" in *Teachers College Record*, December, 1977, Volume 79, Number 2.

THE NATURE OF EDUCATION: A FUNDAMENTAL RECONSIDERATION

Robert Theobald

Education should prepare each person to develop his or her unique strengths as fully as possible within the context of the world in which he or she will live.

It is suggested that this is essentially a tautological statement about the nature of education and that present educational systems operate in ways which fail to respect the implications of this tautology.

It should be stressed that as one begins to spell out the implications of the tautology, one discovers that there is much room for disagreement. Different people will perceive different potentials in themselves and others and there is obviously room for great controversy about the world that we are going to inherit as a result of our present patterns of action. In addition, this tautology calls for us to re-examine the theories of learning which presently underlie our educational patterns.

Those of us who believe that we are in the middle of a transformation from the industrial era to the communications era must move beyond challenging existing views which we believe to be incorrect and must be as clear as we can on the implications of the transformation model so that others can begin a careful, creative discussion of whether our approach is correct.

The viewpoint presented is not the majority one at the present time. Included in this paper are statements of the rationale for rejecting many other models which are today being put forward to guide our educational system and the overall direction of our socioeconomy.

The key assumption made in all of my work is that we are in the middle of a transformation from the industrial era into a period which has been given many names: here it is entitled the "communications era." This transformation implies that all the patterns and styles of the industrial era are obsolete and must be changed if we are to survive on this planet.

This viewpoint is often challenged on the grounds that societies do not pass through transformations. There have, in reality, been many transformations in past history. The correct question is not whether transformations *ever* take place but rather whether we are, in reality, moving through one at the present time. If we are, what are the similarities and differences between this transition and others?

Before going further, however, it is essential to stress that it is not being argued that a successful transformation will *necessarily* take place. Rather, it is argued that only a fundamental transformation will allow us to act upon the possibilities of the present time. Failure to achieve the necessary transformation will inevitably lead to a disastrous collapse that might even destroy the planet.

Why is this the case? In confronting present difficulties, the "obvious" feedback patterns which individuals and groups and communities and states and nations use to deal with existing problems are exactly those which will further destroy our present culture and society. Consider one individual example, one societal example and one example from the field of education. It is possible to multiply these examples as many times as one has the patience to explore.

First, let us look at individual behavior patterns. Those of us now living were taught that we should measure our success by the income levels and standards of living that we achieve. Most people are still trying to gain these symbols of success although it is now known that we shall have to limit the rate of growth if we are not to suffer from major economic, social and ecological breakdown. To make this problem worse, a great many people who still struggle to raise their living standards are also convinced of the necessity for society to develop a sparser life-style, and they therefore find two sets of personal convictions in conflict with each other.

Now let us examine socioeconomic concerns. During the 1930s, John Maynard Keynes carried through theoretical work which eventually convinced the world that the only way to order our economic system was to provide jobs for all who wanted them by continuously increasing effective demand. In the post World War II years, Keynes' disciples managed to convince Western politicians that this policy should be continued even though Keynes himself had pointed out that the time was coming when economic growth must be given a lower priority than social justice. A blind commitment to full employment has now developed and it is used to justify the ever-increasing intervention of government in the lives of individuals and institutions and has diminished the potential of effective personal initiatives. It is now even being suggested that we should decrease productivity in order to ensure that there are enough jobs to go around.

Finally, let us turn to the educational system and look at

the transformational issue here. Our educational system is designed to teach people specialized knowledge—to enable them to divide and dissect knowledge. Lying behind this pattern of teaching is a philosophical and epistemological view of the world which is quite simply false to the facts and realities that we now know. It appears that everything is indeed connected to everything else and that a great deal of the "reality" of any sentient being is defined by its relationships to others. Education needs to discover how to deal with complex relationships and wholes rather than only with analytical tools.

In effect, then, it is argued that the present educational system was designed to serve a world which no longer exists and is based on a philosophy and an epistemology which is known to be invalid. If this is true, only a total change based on new social goals and new understandings will make a difference to the present educational crisis.

Let me put this in anecdotal terms. I recently spoke to a group concerned with developmental disabilities: those people who have serious life-long disabilities. After listening to me, one perceptive person said; "Bob, all you are asking is for us to treat our clients with respect." I replied: "Yes, that is indeed the case, but I am also adding that it is impossible for you to treat clients with respect given present institutional structures because the rules are too constraining."

It is suggested that the same problem exists in education although others may want to argue that the problem is not impossible but merely needs "Superman" and "Superwoman." Let me stress that this is not challenging the commitment of most of those in the teaching professions, although the wave of strikes is certainly rapidly diminishing the credibility of educators. The thesis, however, is denying their ability to produce the results, which are necessary if the world is to survive, unless and until there is a fundamental change in beliefs and actions.

Recall the parable of the sabre-toothed tiger. Some young people in a stone-age village found a new and viscious animal which they called a sabre-toothed tiger. They then went to the elders of the village and argued the need to be taught to kill this new animal. The elders replied that they had always been taught to kill mastodons and what had been good enough for them was certainly good enough for their young people. The sabre-toothed tigers multiplied and eventually forced the tribe out of its village.

Many people are refusing to look at the new realities just as the stone-age elders did. Indeed, it is regrettable that there is less apparent evidence of a willingness to cope with the realities of change than there was in the sixties. However, this statement must immediately be modified, for although there is less apparent evidence of a willingness to cope with the realities of change, there is also a very large number of people in the educational world who are completely aware of the issues that have been raised. They do not know, however, how to act effectively at this time, and the job situation makes it difficult—if not impossible—for many people to take risks. Education is caught in the same problem as society in general—nobody feels able to stand up and announce that the emperor has no clothes on.

Unfortunately nothing much can happen until we admit the nakedness of the land, until we move Beyond Despair and admit that our present industrial-era system is non-functional. We must face up to the magnitude of the crisis we confront and reject the palliatives that are being offered us. For example, while it may well sense to get back to the basics, unfortunately the basics in the last quarter of the twentieth century are not those for which most people are calling.

Examine, therefore, the initial statement of what all parties should be doing in the field of education: *Education should prepare each person to develop his or her unique strengths as fully as possible within the context of the world in which he or she will live.* What does this imply about education in the future?

First, Americans must recognize the transformational nature of today and the rest of the century. All of us are going to be forced to deal with high levels of change, uncertainty and consequent stress. We need to teach coping and survival skills to enable people to adapt to the uncertain and the unexpected. The well-ordered and controlled world of the Victorians has vanished beyond recall.

As the medium is indeed the message, the style of educational establishments must be designed so that they call for coping skills from students rather than throwing all the responsibility for structure on the teaching and administrative staff. Children must learn as they grow up that they will always be structuring the world for themselves and that there is no "Big Daddy" with a slick, reliable set of answers.

It is not being argued that children can make *all* decisions for themselves. This is a different point which is necessarily difficult for us to grasp for it is a statement that is meaningless and/or threatening in industrial-era terms. The teacher and the administrator must take the responsibility for setting the context in which learners can explore and eventually, if they so desire, become teachers and administrators themselves. The task of those who accept the responsibility of creating contexts is to broaden the amount of freedom available to people on a continuing basis, without on the one hand moving so fast as to break the learner, or on the other, constraining the learner so closely that there is no sense of challenge.

One aspect of communications-era learning should therefore

already be clear. It is a process in which all those involved are continuously at risk. There are no pat formulas or decision paths. Each situation is new and all that one brings to it is a certain amount of experience which may help one to judge the right response. The moment one ceases to believe that there is necessarily uncertainty and risk in any real decision, at that moment one ceases to be an effective teacher. This statement is not new, of course. But schools and colleges have tried, with surprising success, to force formulas on all those concerned with education.

The primary task, then, is to teach people to deal with risk and uncertainty. Secondly, we must help people understand the realities of a finite universe. It is true that society can do anything it wants if it is important enough, but we cannot do everything we want. We need to learn that there is a state of "enoughness," a quantity which meets our real needs but does not encourage the continued accumulation of goods as we now do because we believe that more is always better than less.

Acceptance of the idea of limits necessarily forces on us the recognition that the communications era will be a time of pluralism and diversity. Quite clearly, the concept of enough will require very different quantities and types of goods for different people and different families. In addition, the same person and family will require different levels of resources at different times in their lives. Bureaucrats cannot determine a schedule of "enough" for various people: rather it would be necessary for people to decide responsibly what they need for themselves in the light of knowledge about what is available in total. Students must therefore be taught the meaning of responsible decision-making and ways to achieve it.

This then brings us to the third point. Responsible decision-making can only be achieved if accurate information is available. As a society we need to replace the control mechanisms which have grown up in the industrial era and have often distorted information flows. We need instead communication linkages which will provide accurate and up-to-date knowledge which can be used to make effective decisions. None of the consequent decisions will be right in any *absolute* sense, for the belief in clear-cut right and wrong will vanish along with all other dichotomies. It will be possible for people to develop responses which will be effective over a wide range of conditions thus coping as best one can with the inevitability of uncertainty.

Responsible and effective communication, however, requires knowledge of three communication styles:

—one involves the skill to structure "messes:" the confused patterns of reality which confront one as a new situation develops. By what processes does one sort the essential

from the trivial, the real relationships from the apparent?
Jeanne Scott and I named this communication skill
OUTER in our book *Teg's 1994*.
—the second involves the capacity for close reasoning in a
clearly defined situation: specific skills and information
will be required for each area. We called this communication skill INTER.
—the third involves the ability to understand the culture of
a group, community or society, the historical reasons for
the culture, its future dreams and the acceptable political
processes for creating change. We called this communication style SITUATIONAL.

But none of the changes so far discussed can possibly develop unless we recreate a fundamental moral tradition. Some
people believe that religion is for the weak who cannot make
their own decisions. System theorists and others have now
discovered that honesty, responsibility, humility and love are
the minimal requirements for the achievement of a functioning society. If we cannot, through our education, reintroduce
values, then we have no chance of individual fulfillment or
societal transformation. World social collapse then becomes
inevitable. What would happen to educational systems if these
changes, and of course many others on which I have not had
time to touch, were to be accepted?

First, we should break out of the extraordinary division
between education and the real world which has developed as
we have cut the student off from day-to-day life in order to
teach theory in the classroom. It is not denied that there is a
place for theory, but it is argued that it is useful only as it
meets the actual needs of a person as he/she grows up.

Second, education would cease to be seen as a period of
preparation for life which must be essentially completed by a
certain date—instead we should take seriously the arguments
which have been made by those pushing for life-time learning.
Indeed, the whole life-cycle would change: for example, a large
proportion of people in their late teens might go out and do
some of the heavy and less pleasant work of the society. This
would provide the physical and psychic challenge which many
teenagers seem to need, and certainly do not get in all too
many parts of Western society at the present time.

Third, there would be far less weight put on the process of
credentializing and far more attention given to enabling the
individual to be aware of his/her limitations and potentials. It
would be reasonable to ask a person whether or not he/she
expected to be able to do a task and to expect an honest and
realistic answer. Fundamental changes in the relationships
between work and income would be necessary if such honesty

is to be feasible but these are essential if *any* effective alternations in education are to be conceived.

This leads to a point which cannot be stressed too heavily. It is not possible to transform a part of society. Transformation necessarily means changes *throughout* the society. But if this is the case, is a successful transformation conceivable at this time? Is there any evidence that proves we can achieve the transformational process?

The answer to this question is "no." However, it *is* certain that we shall not achieve the necessary transformation if we do not try to do so. If, on the other hand, we do make the effort then there is a real possibility. What more can one reasonably ask from today's world?

Let me now turn to the second part of my subject. Some reasons for the transformation have been given, but it is necessary to explain the fallacies in various sets of views which are more generally held in our society today.

The most common view, of course, is that the present form of the society can continue to function with some limited adaptation to meet changing conditions. It is argued that we have been passing through a bad period in the last decade of fifteen years but that the system has proven remarkably resilient to the shocks that have fallen upon it and that a significant number of changes have already been made which should improve the functioning of the system. (It is also often stated that even if we are not in reality doing very well, any of the ways out are so risky that the dangers will be less if we continue the present system than if we move off into uncharted waters.)

Those who forecast the validity and/or desirability of this type of future are indulging in what the weather forecaster calls "persistence:" it is assumed that things will stay the same. For long periods, such a forecast about social trends is the best possible. Unfortunately, of course, forecasting on the basis of persistance causes one to miss all the turning points when dangers and opportunities are greatest. It *is* certainly true that social systems do not often undergo fundamental change: it is also true that they do change on occasion. The critical question therefore is *when*.

At this point the argument becomes somewhat complex. It is not assumed that transformation is inevitable. It is required. From my point of view, the most likely pattern is a continued inability to come to grips with the critical problems of our time: unemployment, inflation, balance of payments difficulties, global arms race, etc. These problems are symptoms of the central and critical breakdown of our time. We seem unable to make decisions about our problems and our possibilities.

These problems and these possibilities in themselves are not beyond our ability to control. We cannot, however, be effective in restructuring knowledge and the educational system which is supported by it so long as we persist with industrial-era styles. Only a holistic view of the world, which also encompasses the analytical one, can enable us to come to grips with the issues which presently exist. Unfortunately, this holistic view is incompatible with industrial-era bureaucratic systems. Thus, any solution to the central decision-making dilemma of our time cannot be achieved within the present industrial-era system and the culture which underlies it.

This viewpoint is not shared by a large number of futurists. They are generally in four non-compatible groups. Let me describe first the view of such writers as Herman Kahn and Daniel Bell. They agree that we are moving through an inflection point of an S-shaped growth curve and that rates of economic and population growth are beginning to slow down. They believe that the process of change will be gradual and will cause only limited stress. They argue that we have learned the critical lessons from our rather bad experiences of the past fifteen years and that both individuals and decisionmaking groups are beginning to act intelligently. I call this viewpoint "Utopian."

It would be enjoyable to share this Utopian vision, but there is no evidence to support it. My assessment of the state of the world is quite different and far more depressing. Individuals are increasingly "frustrated, baffled and angry" by a world which refuses to conform to the hopes they had of it. In a recent Arizona Magazine poll, two thirds of those who replied used these words to describe their reactions to the overall direction of socioeconomic change.

Individuals seem to be increasingly open to accepting panaceas wished upon them by social activists: California's Proposition 13 which reduced local taxes will have effects far different from those hoped for. (We usually think of activists on the "left," but they also exist on the "right.") The consequences of Proposition 13 and similar movements around the country *could* be good, but it strains my credulity to believe that they will be unless we can create an effective conservative political philosophy rather than the "know-nothing" styles which so far dominate the move to the right.

If the Utopian model is invalid, what then of the work of the disaster theorists, who show the many ways in which the present socioeconomic system can break down? Writers such as Commoner and Ehrlich help us to understand the patterns of breakdown, some of which are inevitable in coming years and decades. We cannot avoid major problems in the eighties. For me, the key question is whether they can be kept from spreading and engulfing the total society.

My problem with disaster theorists does not stem from the

pessimistic conclusions they reach about our *present* directions but from the conclusions they advance about appropriate
policy. It is my conviction that we continue to drift toward
disaster because of our faulty perceptions of the world and
therefore our only hope is to learn to understand the world
better so that we can avoid the risk of disaster. However, this
stress on new learning is not shared by either of the two
disaster schools of thought.

One of the groups argues that the necessary types and magnitude of change can only be achieved after society breaks
down completely: it is hoped and believed that the desirable
measures would then seem attractive. It is my conviction that
a collapse of the magnitude required to break through our
resistance to change would be so total that recreation of a
functional society might well be impossible and that the proposed level of risk is therefore intolerable. Indeed, one can go
further and ask fundamental questions about the validity of
this approach because there is both pragmatic and theoretical
evidence which shows that culture shock and future shock
decrease the willingness of people to consider significant
change rather than increase it and that under these circumstances people want to go back to the "good old days." The
drive to "return to the basics" seems to me to be part of this
phenomenon.

The other dominant school of disaster theorists suggests
that the only hope of dealing with the certainty of breakdown
is to separate the United States (and the rest of the rich world)
from the poor countries. There is no way in which such an
approach would not inevitably lead to total disaster. The belief
that rich countries as a whole, or the United States in particular, could subdue the people from the rest of the world in any
feasible way seems to be wildly unrealistic. Both numbers and
terrorist technology seem to argue against the validity of such
an approach.

The fourth significant futurist stream argues the case for
personal transformation which will then bring in its wake
societal change. This view is advanced by such thinkers as
George Leonard and by groups like Esalen, and more recently
EST. It should already be clear from this paper that this
writer is sympathetic to the viewpoint that one's personal
success criteria must change as one works on these issues (I
am personally only too conscious of how differently I see the
world today than in the past and am aware that my personal
process of change is continuing).

The hope, however, that personal change will necessarily
force societal change seems to me to be highly unrealistic at
two levels. First, there is a great deal of evidence that many
of the human potential movements are themselves deeply
caught up in the pathologies of the industrial era and that the

styles they teach may not effectively help people to put their well-established patterns behind them. Second, unless we face and deal with the myriad ways in which the industrial era makes humanistic, concerned behavior difficult or impossible, we are unlikely to be able to cope with the reality of its constraints.

We are probably all familiar with the experience of coming off the high of a humanistic conference and going back to the real world and finding that it operates in different ways which are not concerned with or responsive to the types of patterns which we would like to introduce.

Assumptions determine conclusions. Problems with the assumptions of several sets of perspectives, which are far more dominant at the present time than my own, have been stated. In concluding, therefore, I feel it is my obligation to suggest at least some of the steps which are feasible and necessary at this time.

First, there is one critical issue in the educational context which we can only ignore at our peril and on which all our hopes will flounder unless we can find imaginative ways to deal with it.

The "lack-of-numbers" crunch is now moving steadily up the educational ladder. For years now, primary school enrollments have been declining with few new teachers hired. This problem is presently hitting secondary schools significantly and is already having effects on colleges and universities. The movement of teachers between educational establishments has been greatly slowed and the resulting in-breeding of ideas is greatly worsened by the decrease in travel budgets.

Let us be realistic. If you're going to work with the same group of people for much of your life, the need to rub along with your colleagues is going to take a high priority. Rocking the boat will be even less attractive than in the past. In addition, the fact that colleges and universities are going to be engaged in a frantic search for any living body who can pay tuition or for whom the government may pay, is going to still further degrade the educational atmosphere.

What then can we do? You will have recognized from the whole tenor of my paper that there are no panaceas. It is time that we gave up the search for technological fixes for complex problems. But, there are some suggestions both in general terms and ideas about specific actions that you might take as individuals and as a communal body.

What should education be about? First, we need to teach people survival skills to cope with risk, uncertainty and stress which are going to be very difficult for us to manage as individuals and as a society in the remainder of this century.

Second, we need to teach people to cope with the realities of a finite universe and to learn the values implied by it.

Third, these first two requirements can only be accomplished if we break out of the division between education and the day-to-day world.

Fourth, we should also have to perceive education as life-long process.

Fifth, we should give less stress to the process of credentializing.

All of this would lead to a *fundamental* change in our understanding of teaching. Effective learning takes place when there is mutual respect between the teacher and the student. It is for this reason that studies are increasingly showing that many forms of teaching are compatible with success, but that authenticity is an *absolute* requirement, that the teacher must be comfortable with the approach he/she is using.

In addition, there must be a belief that students can really benefit from the knowledge that is being advanced. There will be no creative, imaginative, energy-creating teaching unless the teacher is convinced that some of those present will not only learn the factual material which is being communicated but also, and more importantly, the role model being presented by the teacher. In watching the Today Show one day during one of the fillers on the program, somebody asked about good teachers, and the various anchor people came alive. Each clearly felt that one or more teachers had been largely responsible for his/her attitude toward life.

It is proposed that we now know enough to develop a network among those interested in education. The organizers of the First Assembly of the Education Section share this hope and believe that you will hear more about this subject in the future. Let me stress, however, that a network is not the latest "inword" for justifying the traditional academic style of activities: papers, a journal, annual conferences, etc. Rather it implies a search for more effective inter-active techniques. Indeed, there is research which suggests that networks are a traditional form of organization which tends to emerge when there are great possibilities in a particular field at a particular time: the critical aspect is that patterns of relationships are far more intense and informal than in more settled disciplines.

Finally, there is an invitation for those of you who are interested in cross-linking between education and other areas to join a linkage system which has been developing over the last year. One of the primary purposes of this effort will be to create the communications-era encyclopedia using the potential of computers and teleconferencing. This linkage system now brings together about 150 people of *very* diverse interests and may appeal to those of you who see your "educational" role very widely, who do believe that everything is connected to everything else and that this should have immediate consequences for the ways we act and the styles in which we organize knowledge. To learn about this write me at Box 2240, Wichenburg, AZ 85358.

In looking back on the process of the educational discussion since I joined it in the early sixties, it seems to me that we have lost ground throughout the seventies. This does not mean that everything that developed during the sixties was good, but we were at least willing to admit that there were critical questions which needed consideration. It is my hope that as we look back at the beginning of the eighties, we shall be able to see the First Assembly of the Education Section of the World Future Society as one of the points from which we reopened the critical educational questions which so urgently confront us.

SOCIAL ECOLOGY: A RECONSTRUCTIVE APPROACH TO RENEWAL OF LIBERAL EDUCATION

James R. Nolfi

In 1926 the sharp-eyed and thin-skinned critic Julien Benda wrote a famous book, *La Trahison des Clercs*, in which he accused the *clercs*, writers and thinkers who by their vocation had the duty to defend the ideals of freedom, justice and dignity of the individual, of treason by embracing dogma of one sort or another, such as obscurantism, class hatred, or the creed of extreme nationalism. Twenty years later when he re-edited his book, his foresight was sadly vindicated; by that time his bad *clercs* had turned into overt traitors in Vichy, France. What I call the new treason of the *clercs* is nothing as crude and criminal; it is not treason by commission but by omission, by not giving us a vision, a faith for living.

Dennis Gabor
Inventing the Future

Each year a sizeable number of liberal arts colleges in the United States close. This occurrence is intimately linked to the intellectual and ideological assault on the conventional notions of liberal education which has gone on for nearly three decades. If liberal arts institutions, and liberal education, are to be viable, and, in fact, to become a vital force in higher education, root changes must take place in conceptualization and *praxis*.

But, how do we arrive at the new direction for liberal education? What is the process? One can plan the future by making extrapolations from known present conditions, i.e., logical rates of growth, change, trends, etc., and derive a vision of the future in this fashion. Unfortunately, this leads to the fallacious view that the future is a direct derivation of the present. Such a technique does not allow for unexpected technological breakthroughs, mutations, cataclysmic changes, cyclic phenomena of greater than human lifetimes, of a whole variety of known quantum jumps of an evolutionary/revolutionary nature. It also locks one into having to *react* to the future rather than feeling the power to *create* it.

A different planning technique is known as future-invention. The term was apparently coined in 1964 by Dennis Gabor, who states:

> ...Future cannot be predicted, but futures can be invented. ...
> The first step of the technological or social inventor is to visualize by an act of imagination a thing or state of things which does not yet exist. ... He can then start rationally arguing backward from the invention and forward from the means at his disposal until a way is found from one to the other.[1]

We, as faculty and administrators, need to "invent a future" for liberal education and, through that institution, for the whole society. What is the new direction for liberal education for the 1980s, '90s, for the year 2000? First, we must look to the root meaning of the *liberal arts*. The liberal arts are the things which free people, the things that free people do. What then are the liberating arts for the near future? What situations in which learning is likely to occur, as Tim Pitkin has said, can be constructed to help our students (and ourselves) become more free? Ziegler gives us reason to believe that the *process* of future invention itself, as well as the *product*, may be useful:

> Inventive planning is grounded in a belief in the intrinsic worth of human beings who, by their nature and irrespective of their official position in society, possess the potential—and often the actual—to act competently with a view to their own future.[2]

Ziegler emphasizes that the social *setting* for this process is important: it must take place within their homes, churches, workplaces, neighborhoods, communities. In this setting they can be encouraged to "bring their practical wisdom and critical imagination to play."[3]

This approach is critically important since we currently face a growing belief in personal impotency, lack of power, and lack of control over our own destiny. It is the necessity to act in the present, to use the power of the present, to shape a future which can free us from the grinding inertia and emptiness of mass culture.

> The percentage of people who feel "left out of things" going on around them has risen from 9% (in 1966) to 29% (in 1974) and the proportion of people indicating that what they think doesn't mean much anymore has risen from 37% to 61%.[4]

Centralization of planning and power has increased the sense of powerlessness. We need to break this trend through creation of *anticipatory democracy*. Alvin Toffler writes:

> A democracy that doesn't anticipate the future cannot survive.
> A society that is good at anticipating but allows the future to
> be captured by elites is no longer a democracy. As we move into
> the future, anticipatory democracies will be the only surviving
> kind.[5]

Science fiction and utopian literature, the great social experiments of the people's utopias in Spain, the Paris Commune, and the communal movement of the late '60s and early
'70s in this country as well as social experiments of the People's Republics of China, Cuba, and Tanzania give us visions
of the future. Murray Bookchin, in his seminal essay "Ecology
and Revolutionary Thought" applies principles of natural ecology to social ecological theory and develops the concept of
social ecology.

Ecology is a critical, integrative, and reconstructive science.
Ecology is concerned with inter-relationships, functional in-
terdependency of components in systems. Ecology is a study
of systems, hence part of general systems theory, holistic analysis, the paradigm of the emerging scientific revolution. Hol-
ism stands in stark contrast to reductionism, which has been
the predominant scientific paradigm. Bookchin states:

> Broadly conceived..., ecology deals with the balance of nature.
> In as much as nature includes man, the science basically deals
> with the harmonization of nature and man... in the final anal-
> ysis, it is impossible to achieve a harmonization of man and
> nature without creating a human community that lives in last-
> ing balance with its natural environment.[6]

Bookchin finds that the critical edge of ecology as a science
derives from an examination of the impact of human culture
on natural systems. Man, Bookchin states, produces imbalances in the natural world as a consequence of the imbalances
he has produced in the social world.

> The notion that man must dominate nature emerges directly
> from the domination of man by man.... Owing to its inherently
> competitive nature, bourgeois society not only pits humans
> against each other, it also pits the mass humanity against the
> natural world. Just as men are converted into commodities, so
> every aspect of nature is converted into a commodity, a resource
> to be manufactured and merchandized wantonly.[7]

The critical, yet integrative perspective of ecology unfolds
into a reconstructive vision. The same fundamental concepts
of ecology which allow us to critique the present relationship
of man to nature, provide us with guidance for developing a

reconstructive perspective, a vision of new social ecological relationships. The destructive aspects of our present society stem from the reductionist/industrial/managerial/commodity approach to problem solving. This paradigm calls for simplification, but the ecological consequence of this simplification is a reduction in natural diversity; hence a lack of stability. The reconstructive message of ecology is that we must conserve and promote variety in order to promote diversity.

The ecological society proposed by Bookchin is humanly-scaled, relations between persons on the face-to-face level. The society which develops is self-sufficient, individuals are self-reliant. ". . .far from producing provincialism, relative self-sufficiency would create a new matrix for individual and community development—a oneness with surroundings that would revitalize the community."[8] Work roles and leadership responsibility in the community would be flexible and floating, resulting in diversification of experiences such that the engineer would dip hands in the humus, the intellectual stretch muscles in physical labor, the husbandman would experience the industrial plant. Thus society would be able to achieve the vital goal of "the harmonization of nature by the technician and the naturalization of society by the biologist."[9]

Bookchin further states:

> We will witness a creative interplay between individual and group, community and environment, humanity and nature. . . . This sense of unity will reflect the harmonization of interests between individuals and between society and nature. Freed from an oppressive routine, from paralyzing repressions and insecurities, from the burdens of toil and false needs, from the trammels of authority and irrational compulsion, individuals will finally, for the first time in history, be in a position to realize their potentialities as members of the human community and the natural world.[10]

Lest we regard such a vision as utopian, that is, fantastical and unobtainable, Bookchin notes:

> . . .The anarchist concept of a balanced community, a face to face democracy, a humanistic technology and a decentralized society—these rich libertarian concepts—are not only desirable, they are necessary. They belong not only to the great vision of man's future, they now constitute the preconditions for human survival.[11]

These statements of Bookchin, written more than a decade ago, offer a vision of the future and, consequently, a role for liberal-liberating education in the realization of that vision. The form of the learning experience must follow these philosophical/ecological tenets. It must be individualized, part of a

face-to-face process. It must be analytical and integrative in
its approach. It must be inherently positive, reconstructive,
and action based. Social ecology should be the underlying philosophical base, the structure through which individual learn-
experiences are organized, not a discipline or a multi-disciplinary field. Social ecology becomes the perspective through
which knowledge and experience can be interpreted.

There is a need to create a liberating learning environment
characterized by a critical, active *ferment* of ideas and creative
energies. Just as John Milton responded to Roundhead book-
burning by calling for promiscuous reading as a primary necessity for free people, this writer calls for promiscuous fan-
tasizing, promiscuous exchange of ideas, and promiscuous exposure to conflicting views, not to achieve a liberal, balanced
view, but to threaten one's ideas, to move, to expand consciousness. This is what the liberating arts college ought to be like!

Experiences, however, or learning situations cannot be viable in a vacuum. Self-knowledge is important, but it is not
enough. Developing self-knowledge must not become invo-
luted, egocentric education; it must be relational; i.e., the life
of the individual must be placed in context of space and time.
Experiences can no longer be justified for their own sake without calling for a connectedness with other experiences, ideas,
phenomena. Faculty have a major responsibility to constantly
ask: What is this experience? How does this experience, piece
of information, relate? ...to what? We need to see and seek
the relationship ourselves, to challenge students to do the
same. These are not hollow, artificial exercises, but fundamental explorations in understanding the underlying inter-
relatedness. This approach unfolds as we orient our educational focus to a bioregional perspective.

Bioregions are natural areas in which geology, geography,
climate, and topography inter-relate to produce a characteristic landscape. Plant and animal associations—*biocoenoses*—
or biotic communities develop which are characteristic and
unique to each bioregion.

> The differing regions of the world have long had—each—their
> own precise subsistence pattern developed over millennia by
> people who settled in there and learned what particular kinds
> of plants the ground would "say" at that spot. ... Countless
> local ecosystem habitation styles emerged. People developed
> specific ways to *be* in each of those niches: plant knowledge,
> boats, dogs, traps, nets, fishing, the smaller animals, and
> smaller tools. From steep jungle slopes to Southwest China to
> coral atolls to barren arctic deserts—*a spirit of what it was to be
> there evolved*, that spoke of a direct sense of relation to the
> "land"—which really means the totality of the local bio-region
> system from cirrus clouds to leafmold.[12]

Mercantilism, colonialism, industrialization, and associated social, intellectual, and machine technologies have created "mass culture," a smoothing out of regional and continental differences causing great disparity between the forms of culture presently existing in a given locale and those most *appropriate* given the parameters of the bioregion. Gary Snyder develops the idea that this cultural imperialism stems from the conflict of *ecosystem-based cultures* and *biosphere cultures* who:

> . . .discovered—seven or eight thousand years ago in a few corners of the globe—that it was "profitable" to spill over into another drainage, another watershed, another people's territory, and steal away its resources, natural or human. . .all that wealth and power forming into a few centers had bizarre results. Philosophies and religions based on fascination with society, hierarchy, manipulation and "the absolute." A great edifice called "the state" and the symbols of central power—in China what they used to call "the true dragon," in the West as Mumford says, symbolized perhaps by that bronze age fort called the Pentagon. No wonder Levi-Strauss says that civilization has been in a long incline since the Neolithic.[13]

The bioregionally focused liberal education must center on that which is most closely around us. We can begin, again, to explore in detail the quality of life, biology, social organization, political forms, an aesthetics of the place where we are. We can muster our human resources to begin to attack the pressing needs of each particular "appalachia" where creative ideas and energy are more critical than expensive research establishments or massive budgets. These studies should be part of daily life, not special events; historical and anthropological ideas and current events on the national and international level then become material to be integrated into regional studies. How does an event in Italy relate to the price of milk for Vermont farmers? How does Shakespeare fit into our understanding of life in a small Midwest town? Integrated intimately into such studies are ways in which electronic recording, interpretive writing, theatre as a means for communication of ideas, etc., can be utilized. It is imperative to develop a sense of bioregional creative expression. Can there be forms of dance, sculpture, ceramics, theatre; are there materials, subject matter, concepts which are richly and appropriate bioregional? Can there be analogs in Vermont of the urban neighborhood murals? How do travel and the transfer of ideas in space and time relate to such studies? Can networks between bioregional educational centers in New England and the Midwest be developed?

This is not a call for the migration of students to permanent residence near the college, but for a curriculum *focusing* primarily on the daily life around us. It can create an approach, a concern with a "sense of place" *wherever* one resides, an awareness, a lively sense of vision, a grounding. This approach can create a multidisciplinary problem-defining, problem-solving attitude toward the world. Moreover, the detailed study of the particular and the development of a critical awareness open us, as students and teachers, to a more concrete and deeper exploration of the universal.

Social ecology and bioregionally-based education can lead clearly to moral and ethical questions. As Gary Snyder states:

> The ethics and mortality of this is far more subtle than merely being nice to squirrels. The biological-ecological sciences have been laying out (implicitly) a spiritual dimension. We must find our way to seeing the mineral cycles, the water cycles, air cycles, nutrient cycles as sacramental—and we must incorporate that insight into our own personal spiritual quest and integrate it with all the wisdom and teachings we have received from the near past. The expression of it is simple: gratitude to it all, taking responsibility for your own acts; keeping contact with the sources of the energy that flow into your own life (i.e. dirt, water, flesh).[14]

Rather than isolating the study of the ways of inhabitory people, actual inhabitants of "the land," to the cultural anthropology classroom or the "objective" field study, there is a need to humbly look at these cultures for their own sake and our own curiosity. We may find in the richness, diversity, and perception of these people ways for us to unfold our own ways, a new inhabitory education.

> The wisdom and skill of those who studied the universe firsthand, by both direct knowledge and experience, for millennia, both inside and outside themselves, is what we might call the old ways. Those who envision a possible future planet on which we might continue that study, and where we live by the Green and the Sun, have no choice but to bring whatever science, imagination, strength, and political finesse they have to the support of inhabitory people—natives and peasants of the world. Entering such paths, we begin to learn a little of the old ways, which are outside of history and forever new.[15]

Another rich and fertile area for exploration of ideas of social ecology is in the future presented in the great body of science fiction literature. The novels of John Brunner, such as *The Sheep Look Up* and *Stand on Zanzibar*, present logical extensions of present pollution and population pressures to very pessimistic conclusions. Ernest Callenbach's *Ecotopia* presents a vision of a "social-ecological society." Robert Heinlein's *Farnham's Freehold* presents the "fall-out shelter" rugged individualist vision of the future; survival of the fittest, not far removed from the mentality of a sizeable portion of the readership of *Mother Earth News*. Virtually all the novels of Ursula LeGuin are excellent culturally detailed studies which pose questions concerning a "new society." What would be the effect on gender questions—sexism—in a society in which all individuals are physiologically and psychologically androgynous? *The Left Hand of Darkness* explores that question. What is the nature of conflict between the individual and the community in a society built on libertarian principles? *The Dispossessed* focuses on this issue. These few examples are meant to indicate that, rather than being a curiosity or a manifestation of popular culture, science fiction and speculative fiction can be a very valuable resource for exploration of ideas of social ecology.

Growing directly from the bioregional aspect of social ecology, focused on self-sufficiency, is the vast potential for development of humanistic technologies. Daniel Bell, in *Post Industrial Society*, categorizes technologies into machine technologies, i.e., tools and machines through which man extends his physical capabilities; intellectual technologies, which formalize decision-making rules thus extending man's intellectual capability for dealing with organized complexity; and social technologies, institutions that use scientific knowledge to specify ways of doing things in a reproducible manner, thus extending man's social and economic capabilities. Jacques Ellul, in *The Technological Society*, expresses a fatalistic view of technology which basically sees present technology as dominating man through the development of addictive dependencies. Bookchin, rather than taking an anti-technological approach typical of the reaction to the "inhumane" technology, poses questions to be answered in the revitalized liberal arts institution. He asks how machine and other technologies can be used in a liberatory fashion: to promote the balance of nature, and the creation of humanistic communities.[16]

Richard Brautigan's poem, "All Watched over by Machines of loving grace," expresses this integration of human-centered technology in a harmonious relation to the natural world:

> "I like to think (and
> the sooner the better!)
> of a cybernetic meadow
> where mammals and computers
> live together in mutually
> programming harmony
> like pure water
> touching clear sky.

I like to think
    (right now please!)
of a cybernetic forest
filled with pines and electronics
where deer stroll peacefully
past computers
as if they were flowers
with spring blossoms.

I like to think
    (it has to be!)
of a cybernetic ecology
where we are free of our labors
and joined back to nature,
returned to our mammal
brothers and sisters,
and all watched over
by machines of loving grace." [17]

The development of *appropriate technologies*, tuned to the bioregion within which the liberal arts institution is situated, can become a rich educational opportunity when students and faculty are involved with members of the surrounding community in analytical problem-solving experiences with a real social context. Moreover, direct interaction of students with persons from the community in such projects may ameliorate the problem of race, culture, and class prejudices which the traditional university environment tends to reinforce and the separation between college and life. In addition, one need not construct self-conscious interdisciplinary learning experiences since the problem-solving demands mustering of all available tools, from whatever "discipline" toward the analytical statement of the problem and movement to its resolution.

Often in the past, small liberal arts colleges and community colleges have not engaged in active research programs. While lacking funding for such research and heavy demands on staff time for course teaching is certainly an impediment, these institutions have seen their societal role as "pure teaching." Additionally, they have suffered from the step-child complex that, even with the time, faculty of such institutions aren't "good enough" to be creative researchers and that undergraduate students are not capable of being involved in a productive manner in carrying out research activities. It must be made clear that research on appropriate technology is educationally justified, financially feasible, and may be capably carried out by staff and students in these institutions.

The development of bioregionally appropriate technologies in the context of community, as part of action-based learning programs in liberal arts institutions, can give participants the opportunity to see the potential for local responses of global problems:

> Some of the most important achievements in providing food, upgrading housing, improving human health, and tapping new energy sources will come not through highly centralized national and international efforts, but through people doing more to help themselves. When those most affected by a problem assume the primary responsibility for solving it they gain the understanding and skill to deal with the broader political and economic issues of their society. . . .

> When those in need participate in defining their problems, in deciding on a solution, in carrying out what needs to be done, in distributing the benefits of the solution, and in assessing their own work, the impact of self-help multiplies. Through cooperative self-help, individuals gain a sense of competence and self-respect as well as strengthen their ties to their community.[18]

The material presented in this paper is intended to serve as a stimulus for the consideration of the implications of social ecology, its concerns and its critical tools, "for the renewal and redefinition of liberal education. Those of us who have begun this process have seen in our students and in ourselves the shape of a vision of the future, the formulation of a faith for living. Perhaps the most important aspect of social ecology and its greatest significance for change in liberal education is its ability to convert the often nihilistic rejection of the *status quo* into an emphatic affirmation of life; indeed, into a reconstructive credo for a humanistic society."[19]

NOTES

1. Dennis Gabor, *Inventing the Future*, 1964.
2. Warren Ziegler, *Planning As Action*, 1972.
3. *Ibid.*
4. "The Future of Citizen Involvement," Lind, 1975.
5. Alvin Toffler, "What is Anticipatory Democracy," 1975.
6. Murray Bookchin, "Ecology and Revolutionary Thought," in *Post Scarcity Anarchism*, 1971, p. 58.
7. *Ibid.*, p. 62.
8. *Ibid.*, pp. 80–81.
9. *Ibid.*, p. 80.
10. *Ibid.*, pp. 81–82.
11. *Ibid.*, pp. 69–79.
12. Gary Snyder, "Reinhabitation," in *The Old Ways*, 1977.
13. *Ibid.*, pp. 60–61.
14. *Ibid.*, p. 63.
15. *Ibid.*, p. 66.
16. Murray Bookchin, "Toward a Liberatory Technology," in *Post Scarcity Anarchism*, 1971, p. 86.

17. Richard Brautigan, "All watched over by Machines of loving grace," in *The Pill Versus the Spring Hill Mine Disaster*, 1973.
18. Bruce Stokes, *Local Responses to Global Problems: A Key to Meeting Basic Human Needs*, Worldwatch Paper #17, Worldwatch Institute, Washington, D.C., 1978, pp. 5-6.
19. Murray Bookchin, "Ecology and Revolutionary Thought," in *Post Scarcity Anarchism*, 1971, p. 70.

THE EDUCATION OF EDUCATORS

Ervin Laszlo

The most crucial problem of contemporary education is that, while society is changing and in a generation will be very different from the present, education in matters of social concern is hardly changing and seems to be bent on remaining what it has been for the last generation or two. This will create an increasing gap between society and the educational establishment, making the latter irrelevant and the former dangerously adrift in the absence of widespread and reliable knowledge.

Education and society need to be brought together. This calls for educational reform to create a corps of more informed and involved educators. However, educating the educators cannot be done by the educators themselves, by administrators, or politicians; only by society as a whole. But for society to educate the educators, the latter must have access to its workings. A kind of "dialectical" relationship must be maintained between academia and government, to infuse government with relevant and reliable knowledge and at the same time to maintain an independent source of knowledge of high integrity.

The problem of bringing together knowledge of integrity and relevance with participation in policy decisions has not been properly solved in any contemporary political system. Western liberal systems create a wide gap between academics and politics, allowing the compartmentalization of knowledge and the specialization of social roles to erect a barrier between those who research or teach, and those who make practical decisions. The barrier can be crossed by a few: those academics whose speciality is in a policy-related field and who fit themselves into the ideological frame of the governing establishment with advice that is acceptable to policy-makers; and by those policy-makers who, upon retiring or temporarily leaving office, decide to don the academic robe to tell a small group of respectful students of the ideas and motivations that inspired their past political actions. The benefit derived from such oc-

casional cross-overs is small: except for a few outstanding
personalities, the information provided is routine and overwhelmed by concern with short-term politics. Communist societies mobilize their academics and bring them into decision-
making environments, but they do so by suspending the independence of scholarly inquiry and subjugating it to the of-
ficially adopted ideology.

Aware of the shortcomings of both kinds of systems, Western
socialists and Eurocommunists, as well as the Chinese Com-
munists, attempt to find further viable alternatives. The
Chinese have gone farthest in creating a dialectical balance
between theory and practice, academia and social participation. But their highly planified and disciplined model does not
appear to be applicable to a liberal society such as the United
States. The problem here is not to create a master plan for all
to follow, but rather to creat opportunities that those so inclined can seize, for their own fulfillment and the betterment
of society. Thus the proposal that follows is not to be taken as
a rigid 50-year plan for the programming of select educators,
but as a flexible framework offering appropriate niches of
social relevance for persons to fill of their own accord.

The proposal concerns the creation of adequate career
niches for persons inclined to, and capable of, becoming "practical theoreticians"—new educators educated enough to educate the next generation and advise this one in our rapidly
changing society. The principle is to create a series of successive career opportunities of occupational niches which would
have the cumulative effect of shaping the mind and personality of the new educator. These would constitute a sequence
of intellectual and practical environments conducive to evolving the kind of normative and yet relevant thinking so badly
needed in today's society. The environments would inspire in
turn theoretical thinking and practical activism. Individuals
following their sequence would tack back and forth between
academia and politics, drawing on the integrity and depth of
the former and the concreteness and practicality of the latter.
Each environment would constitute a phase through which
the new educator passes in his or her process of lifelong development.

The phases do not lock individuals into preconceived path-
ways, but permit a wide variety of theoretical and practical
activities. Moreover, they are open in the sense that in a democratic society each individual is free to leave the sequence at
any point he or she desires. Their *raison d'etre* is to assure the
fusion of normative societal theory and actual policy-making
practice in the life and personality of a few individuals who,
by virtue of this sequence of experiences, come to fulfill an
important social role.

THE FIRST THEORY PHASE

The lifelong development of the mind and personality of the new educator would begin with a well-balanced curriculum encompassing studies in the humanities, as well as the natural and social sciences. The future educator must acquire a broad perspective embracing the history of culture and civilization, as well as the history of science and technology. The perspective must rest on a thorough familiarity with the main concepts and tenets of the contemporary natural sciences, with special regard for those branches whose applications influence the lives of people and the development of societies. It must also include a knowledge of diverse schools of thought for the explanation of social phenomena, representing the principal social and ideological currents of our times.

The second portion, at the level of graduate studies, would concentrate on familiarizing the student with the major trends, problems and prospects of humanity, in the immediate as well as in the long-term future. The undergraduate studies in history would be deepened, with special attention to broad patterns which have significance for the future. Studies of human needs and problems in the global context would provide the new frame for reviewing the accomplishments of the natural and social sciences. A comparison of need with possibility, and of problem with opportunity in the world at present and in coming decades, would offer a setting for assessing human prospects on this planet.

Throughout these graduate studies, the globality and wholeness of vision is to be carefully maintained. In an interdependent world, the further one looks ahead the more the effects of diverse and distant actions interpenetrate, creating a common though differentiated future for all. Even in a medium time horizon of 20-25 years, global and holistic thinking are imperative. In looking ahead to the year 2000, the world cannot be conveniently divided into autonomous nation-states, each pursuing its own policies independently of the others, nor can problems and opportunities be neatly classified into single scientific fields of study for research and resolution by specialists.

THE FIRST PRAXIS PHASE

Prior to receiving the doctorate or another highest form of professional qualification, the new educator should spend a year in internship at a major policy planning or executing agency or organization. The host institution may be operating on the local, state or provincial, federal, regional, or international level. It may be concerned with a single sector (such as energy or communication) or with a broad range of issues such as development or foreign policy. Unless it is an international organization directly concerned with the broadest range of issues, it will offer a contrast to the new educator in virtue of the restriction of its scope compared with those of his or her previous studies. This contrast will create a valuable insight into sectoralism, specialization, and/or political constraints in the real world, and should trigger a healthy motivation to expand scope and concern and to place matters of immediate policy interest into a global and holistic context.

The new educator will receive much needed insight into the values and workings of public bodies, while he or she will be stimulated to outline and advocate ways and means for appropriate organization and functioning in such bodies in the light of insights won in previous studies. This combination of theoretical knowledge and practical experience can properly suggest the topic for a doctoral thesis, which should be shorter and more imaginative—even more controversial—than the lengthy scholarship required in most fields today.

THE SECOND THEORY PHASE

According to statistical studies of the time of life when great conceptual and scientific discoveries and innovations are performed, the period of greatest personal creativity is in the late twenties and early thirties. Hence, the new educators should be given the opportunity to work out their ideas and conceptions from their mid-twenties onwards by making good use of the best that the academic environment has to offer. This includes constructive dialogue with students, for this reason they should be entrusted with at least one research seminar each term on a subject related to their current interests (assumed to be likewise related to the topic of their doctoral thesis and experience during the internship).

This working out also includes dialogue with colleagues (perhaps in a setting of revolving open discussion groups on topics of interest to faculty members) as well as access to a good library. The academic environment offers time to reflect and write: during the summer, on nonteaching days, on weekends, and on leaves of absence requested for this purpose. Such leaves should normally be given favorable consideration, with special funds devoted to provide at least a minimal livelihood.

The second theory phase should culminate in the publication of some major studies—articles, research notes, or books—stating the normative, global and holistic approach adopted by the new educators in reference to some selected problems or issues of long-term social relevance. In their mid-thirties, the new educators should then be ready to embark on a practical testing of their theories and concepts, rejecting the role of a life-long specialist in theorizing and teaching in favor of that of an integrated personality and an active and responsible citizen, bringing the best he or she knows to bear on problems confronting society.

THE SECOND PRAXIS PHASE

Like Plato in Syracuse and Aristotle in tutoring Alexander, the new educators should enter the maelstrom of practical policy-making armed with vision and knowledge, but ready to learn and to adapt, to modify and make practical their aims and goals, without sacrificing their integrity and the expected benefits. In order to make the new educator's presence as attractive as possible to public institutions, he or she should be given a title such as Research or Adjunct Professor, on long-term leave from the home institution. The terms of leave should specify intermittent contact through periodic lectures and accounts to the university administrators, faculty and student body, some directed study of advanced students, and participation in a few pertinent committees. These activities take little time and require but sporadic presence on campus.

The new educators are to be given ample opportunity to immerse themselves in the practical workings of a policy making institution. They are an attractive presence in such organizations; not being career civil servants they are not a threat to the regular staff, while being professors they confer additional status on the section with which they are associated. Moreover, they bring to the organization fresh knowledge documented in relevant publications.

The activity of the new educators during their second praxis phase cannot be predicted in detail; it can, however, be characterized in general terms. The new educators must forget all specialty and professional status associated with academia, and behave not like benevolent professors advising lay colleagues from the depth of their wisdom, but as concerned and dedicated civil servants desirous of bringing about changes and realizing goals according to the best of their insight and conviction. The educators have a real ax to grind—their own normative conceptions deriving from a global and holistic vision—but past exposure to public policy bodies prevents them from falling into utopianism or dogmatism. They know what is politically feasible and what is not; they know the meaning of "green lights" and going through "channels" and how to size up the ambitions and rivalries of various personalities and offices.

THE THIRD THEORY PHASE

Now in their late forties, the new educators return to the academic world to further reflect on their experiences, to hand them down to the next generation, and to disseminate their knowledge through appropriate professional and public media. Given the title and privileges of a full professor (or equivalent), they may turn their attention to curriculum design, to academic structure and organization, to student affairs, to the revision of old and the creation of new textbooks, or to the conceptual foundations of their previously espoused theories and conceptions. In the two decades or so of active life in academia ahead of them, the new educators should endeavor to come in contact with the broadest range of academic and civic groups. They should not become traditional professors with an "interesting past" (now safely behind), but should continue to fuse theory and practice from an academic base. They are not to be forced by administrators to spend the greater part of their time in the classroom and serving on committees, but are to be allowed to consult, to lecture, to publish, and to engage in other relevant public activities. They should be allowed to offer seminars and courses on a flexible basis, more in one term, less in another, to balance in a multi-year period.

The changing societal landscape offers ever new opportunities for the intellectual and personal involvement of the new educators, and for the further testing, deepening and refining of their conceptions. Thus, they would not settle into the sterile routine of teaching the same courses year after year, with the only change limited to the names of students and the date. Their personal involvement would trigger continuous intellectual growth, or direct benefit to students, colleagues, community, and society.

A sixth phase will no doubt be added by new educators who reach official retirement age in good physical health. This phase could mean a return to the active life of policy-making bodies, now with the status of an elder academic and public personality; it could mean a search for seclusion to think through, or perhaps rethink entirely, the concepts and norms espoused and advocated in previous decades; or it could be devoted to a combination of the academic and the activist lifestyles, It could be exercised until ripe old age, for society's need for people with knowledge and experience and the ability to think deeply and in context on practical problems is and will not doubt remain great.

SUMMARY

There is a great and urgent need to bring innovative, global and holistic thinking to bear on problems confronting society today and in decades ahead. The infusion of intellectuals properly equipped to cope with the mushrooming problems of a rapidly changing society cannot be left to the serendipity of geniuses appearing at the right time and coming to be appreciated by the right people. A conscious and systematic plan must be evolved to encourage a constant and reliable flow of intellectually equipped people into the policy-making environment.

These people cannot be simply "borrowed" from academia, filling ancillary roles in the political context, but must become fused with the appropriate institutional bodies as members of their staff. At the same time they cannot be totally integrated into the political environment, for this would remove the vital element of academic freedom and integrity. Hence periodic alternations are called for between academic research, reflection and teaching, on the one hand, and policy-oriented activism in appropriate institutions on the other. The five-phase sequence outlined above responds to these requirements.

TOWARD A FUTURISTIC
THEORY OF EDUCATION
John D. Pulliam

It will not be easy for most of us to relinquish to the machine the arts and techniques which have taken us decades to master, and to concentrate on the even more demanding tasks of generalization, synthesis, and judgment which only man can carry out. Perhaps the greatest demands for ingenuity will fall upon the field of education, once it is decided to hand over to other means the mere memorization of information, the computing of sums, and such other routine intellectual tasks as may be found appropriate. It will be an excellent teacher indeed who shows us how to program our school and college experience so as to maximize the capacity to grasp general principles, detect relevance where none was seen before, and to create new conceptual schemes. When that day comes, all education will in a sense be general education, since the technical problems which now divide the specialties will in large part be handed over to the computers, and we will have taught ourselves a language we can all use in common.

—Robert S. Morison, "New Types of Excellence"

"To learn is to change. Education is a process that changes the learner"

—George B. Leonard, *Education and Ecstasy*

With the wide interest in the future of education for which conferences, workshops, courses and the proliferation of literature provide evidence, the question arises, "Does a need exist for a philosophy of educational futurism?" Since those concerned with shaping or inventing the future represent a wide variety of backgrounds, interests, abilities and values, it appears that some type of broad conceptual framework upon which a theory of educational futurology might rest is necessary and timely.

It should be obvious that existing systems of educational theory are manifestly inadequate for the task. Indeed, so far as speculative and normative philosophy are concerned, there has been very little recent work applicable to futurism. Available systems consist of the historical record of great thinkers of the past or are based on sets of assumptions not acceptable to most futurists. Many of those who currently practice philosophy of education are devoted to using philosophy as a means of clarifying issues and sharpening arguments or to the analyzing of educational concepts and language. Necessary and useful as these activities are, they do little to establish a set of norms or identify the major themes central to a futures approach to education. However risky the effort, it seems imperative to propose some basic principles and a priority of values which might serve to guide futuristic thinking about education. This paper is aimed at that task.

That educators are in a quandary about the direction they should take is not news to anyone familiar with the crisis-oriented literature in the field. Unstable social conditions and conflicting values have perpetuated educational issues since the time of Plato, but twentieth century conflicts are more intense because of the lack of commonly accepted core values and an easily identified cultural synthesis. Scholars look in vain for enduring structures in modern society while deep cultural arguments create tremendous strain on the moral texture of education.

Today, accelerating change, exponential growth of science and technology, and numerous unresolved problems contributing to human anxiety on a global scale have stretched the educational crisis to the breaking point. The transition from the industrial era into something else (post-industrial society, the age of automation, cybernated/computer culture, the information age, the era of mass communications) demands an educational response on a scale never before imagined. Education is charged not only with teaching skills and information necessary for survival, coping with change and controlling the human life space, it is also expected to socialize the young and it is used as an instrument for enforcing public policy. Consequently, old standards become increasingly suspect and there is a lack of new criteria by which to judge whether departures from accepted customs and plans of action represent a step forward or merely a weakening of established norms.

Even those longstanding beliefs such as that the school should cultivate intelligence as a tool for problem solving rather than as an end in itself must be evaluated pursuant to alternative life styles, increased leisure, the decline of the work ethic and new concern for the creative imagination of the individual. Yet the absurd notion persists that vitally important cultural issues and their concomitant educational problems may be solved by mere reorganization and the expenditure of enormous sums of money. Beyond question technological improvement is needed and information in the future may become man's most prized possession but information alone furnishes no answers. Whitehead called the merely well-informed man "the most useless bore on God's earth," or as T. S. Eliot put it:

"Where is the wisdom we have lost in knowledge?
Where is the knowledge we have lost in information?"

It is the nature of philosophy to encourage constant re-examination of existing ideas and institutions and to suggest their modification or, if necessary, their elimination. Effective philosophy must be part and parcel of human life and education. It must utilize critical and reflective thought in developing a *Weltanschauung* (or world view) from which consensus on the most vital issues may be reached. There must be constant experimentation, the testing of hypotheses against experience, re-examination of plans of action in the light of new data and the constant reconstruction of past experience. Such a philosophy is dynamic, evolutionary and never finished. If philosophy fails to achieve a common synthesis, negativeness, disillusionment, apathy, materialism, greed, resource exploitation and individualistic hedonism will prevail. Under such conditions, there is virtually no hope that education can be made the tool of human control over the future or the means of human survival with maximum realization of the human potential.

Assuming a need for an educational theory of futurism has been established, it is necessary to state what is intended by such a philosophy and to indicate how its basic framework might be erected. Futuristic educational theory is not system building. It is not something which can be derived from the assumptions of philosophical premises of idealism, realism, pragmatism or essentialism. It is neither a set of metaphysical assumptions nor a process of applying philosophical tools to previously identified problems of education. Certainly no argument (including the one here presented) which will not withstand the test of critical analysis is adequate, but linguistic analysis offers no new directions or guides for the future. It is too narrow because the most important educational issues are not clear and many are emerging rather than existing. It is therefore the thesis of this paper that the best approach to a futuristic educational theory is not speculative or analytic, but normative.

If the approach to futuristic educational philosophy is to be that of advocating certain ends, objectives, or values which are regarded as better than others, some common areas of agreement must be identified. There are no limits to futurism. Futures thinkers are found among educators, economists, sociologists, political scientists, biologists, communications theorists and representatives of all the known disciplines. Many, such as R. Buckminster Fuller, are interdisciplinary and no area of learning can be logically excluded from futurism. That future thinking is anything but monolithic can be illustrated by the gap between Herman Kahn and the "Limits to Growth" people. Futurists examine present trends in the culture and attempt to project what these trends might mean in the world of tomorrow. Some, like John McHale, see a new planetary culture the chief characteristics of which are accelerating industrial technology, automation, and a multiplicity of new communications channels to accommodate vastly expanding levels of information. Others, like Donald Michael, are concerned with the ability of man to control cybernation. Still others merely extrapolate from the present in an effort to predict future demographic figures or other statistical data. It seems likely that the interest in the future will continue as will the diversity of planning tools. In spite of differences, however, evidence suggests consensus on several areas critical to global human survival and to education. These areas of agreement are not assumptions to be accepted on faith. They are all grounded in evidence which has been tested or is at least potentially verifiable by empirical means. They may be modified or rejected if they fail the test of experience as new data comes to light but they serve as current guides to action. Inventing the future is dependent on human action (but failure to act also influences it) and it is no mere cliche to say that the future is now.

BASIC CONCEPTS

Human Survival with Maximum Realization of Potential

While there is no ultimate end in a fixed or cosmic sense for futuristic educational theory, the aim of human survival is central. This alone is inadequate unless it is linked with maximum realization of the human potential and the greatest possible opportunity to achieve the good life. The good life, in turn, is one that realizes the greatest value, which implies availability of alternatives, the ability to choose, and the removal of barriers or inhibitions to choice. Schools, in the past, have often attempted to set arbitrary limits to the definition of the good life. They have often stifled creativity and implied that only the models provided by history or the current social order were viable choices for students. Life-styles of the ancient Greek polis, the Indian tribe or the village on the Peruvian plateau and others not yet invented may offer better opportunities for future survival than those of the materialistic, consumer-oriented industrial states. It is also necessary to evaluate educational ideas in the light of the whole future of mankind and to avoid the narrow view dictated by proximate ends. As Alec Guinness so well illustrated as the British colonel in *The Bridge on the River Kwai*, it is very easy to internalize immediate or proximate purposes while losing sight of the overall or ultimate goals which can only be understood by keeping the whole situation in mind. Every educational plan for the future should be required to show that it enhances the chances for survival and the quality of life.

Accept Change for What It Is and Learn to Use It

Futurism is based on the continuation of an accelerating rate of technological change and the constant emergence of new problems in the adaptive nonmaterial culture. The tide cannot be turned and mankind must use technology to serve his needs but this does not require man to be a slave to his machines. "Back to nature" or a revival of the agrarian past may be useful for psychological reasons or for models of life styles which maximize freedom while easing the stress on non-renewable natural resources. "Appropriate technology" is necessary for the solution of most of the great problems and to abandon it would be an act as futile as that of the Luddites who tried to halt industrial growth by smashing machines in 1811. Rapid change and invention are very much a part of our future and education must make them instruments for the identification and resolution of major problems. This is not to say that change for the sake of change is good or that the rate of change is beyond human control. Technology is certainly not valueless and human beings can select the fields in which they wish to stimulate invention as well as those which might be allowed to slow down. Planned educational change is difficult but it can be accomplished. Following World War II, the Japanese realized that their future welfare depended on a decrease in their population growth rate. This required a change of cultural values which was successfully accomplished by using the mass media for informing adults and a deliberate alteration of the school curriculum to include family planning, sex education and personal economics.

Have Faith in the Human Ability to Control the Future

The assumption of Sumner and others that human beings are unable to understand and powerless to control their world must be abandoned. Athenians in the fourth century B.C. believed in an intelligible universe but the Greek nerve failed in Hellenistic times and for two thousand years men doubted their own ability to know and manage their environments. Immanuel Kant described the Enlightenment as the process of leaving man's self-imposed state of immaturity and proposed the slogan *Aude spere* ("Dare to know") as a guide for free people. Daniel Bell holds that there are no *inherent* secrets in the universe. Quite obviously there is a great deal to learn but there must be no failure of nerve and no abandonment of reason to fate or to imagined but unknown forces. All too often in the past people beset by obscure difficulties or problems that appeared insurmountable have adopted the "whatever will be, will be" attitude. Inventing the educational future requires faith in the capacity of human intelligence to comprehend the world and control its own destiny. It is also well to keep in mind that imagination and intuition are as much a part of the human mind as logic and reason. They should not be dichotomized.

Use the Past But Avoid Obsolete Values and Attitudes

Historians rightly claim that the past is a useful guide to the present and the future but it is important to guard against the uncritical acceptance of past values. The traditional mind-set and industrial era attitudes may prevent clarity of perceptions and inhibit the choice of alternatives. A preference for keeping things as they are, rejecting unfamiliar or unknown plans or casting aside all choices that require significant behavioral change is common in human society. The more deeply a value is cherished, the more difficult it is to see it as relative to our own culture, tastes and experience. Parents who are uncomfortable with the world in which their children live often want the schools to recreate the environment they knew when they were students. This rear view mirror approach to the educational future is dangerous and counterproductive. Just as the Puritan work ethic still casts its shadow over modern America, so the values of the future will be shaped by the industrial era unless we prevent it. Following the crowd to materialistic values and situational ethics as fostered by the mass media and advertising is a powerful force that is far from healthy. Extrapolism from the age of conspicuous consumption is a poor approach to the good life and future survival. Theobald has pointed out that except for food, clothing, shelter and a little love, the things we want are not determined by us but by the culture in which we live. Balance is needed to the weight of production, consumption and exploitation. Perhaps it is time to review the humanism of Erasmus, to value the psychology of Maslow and to give scholarly attention to Roszak's *Making of a Counter Culture*. It is especially difficult for people engaged in the process of teaching to realize that the values they hold dear are drawn from past experience and may not be relevant for tomorrow.

Future Educational Theory Must Not Be Confined to Schooling

Most of the theoretical literature in education deals with teaching and learning in institutions called schools. It is quite possible that schools will be significant in the future but alternative means of education will surely increase in importance too. Problem solving/resource distribution centers, life-long learning, community education centers, universities without walls, the mass media, learning webs, home based computer assisted instruction and prenatal training are already in use. The work of Illich and other critics who call for deschooling society must be seriously studied. Too many educational philosophers have taken a narrow and myopic view which is centered upon the American public school rather than on the whole of education. Some futurists suggest that all human beings will spend most of their lives in alternative teaching and learning activities by the year 2000.

In many parts of the world, basic adult education cannot be accomplished by schools because they do not exist and the means for their establishment is lacking. Some form of education utilizing mass media or a special system of electronic communications seems the most promising solution. Even in the highly technical culture of the United States, media—especially the medium of television—play a major educational role. Some of the most provocative philosophical questions to face this age and the future have been formulated by theorists interested in the impact of electronic media and computer technology on the culture. Marshall McLuhan suggests that the perceptions of children exposed to television are altered so that causal connections and subtle relationships are understood as never before. The question of whether a "canned" culture stored in memory banks and television tapes will have the same iconic value as permanent and unique objects in the "real" world is treated by John McHale in "The Plastic Parthenon." A philosophy for the future of education must be as broad as education itself and not confined to schools alone.

Means and Ends Must Be Kept in Perspective

There is a strong tendency for futures authors, especially science fiction writers and utopian novelists, to suggest desirable goals without saying how these goals might be achieved. John Dewey gave a great deal of thought to his argument that means and ends cannot be separated and that the ends do not justify the means. Goals, ends or aims in future education should be evaluated not only on the basis of desirability but also on the criterion of the possibilities for implementation. The social reconstructionism of Theodore Brameld postulates using the schools as an instrument of social change and calls for a new world social order. The weakness of the theory is that no means for its realization have yet been identified. It is not suggested that desired and needed ends be given up merely because the means have not been found but only that means and ends be given equal attention. Drastic action, major alteration of institutions and systems, innovative learning programs and alternate life styles may be required in the future. But nothing is ever done in a vacuum and what is involved in getting from here to there is just as important as the goal identified as "there."

Future Educational Philosophy Must Be Broadly Based

The future will not be understood by looking at a narrow slice of life or learning. However important specialization may remain, the task of understanding and analyzing the forces which shape man and his world must have the broadest possible base. Futurism is interdisciplinary. McLuhan has attacked the "fragmented unrelation" of industrial era school curricula and pointed out that any subject studied in depth immediately relates to other subjects. Leonard has called for an educational experience as wide as life itself and one that does not ignore creativity, aesthetics or ecstasy. Ecologists stress the symbiotic relationship of many plants and animals; Brown has demonstrated that virtually all the major human problems are global; Theobald may be justly called a socio-economist-educator; Fuller uses the term synergy to show that combined action is necessary in almost all aspects of life. If futurism is comprehensive, interrelated and synergetic, it follows that a theory of futuristic education must be the same. Theories about how human beings behave come from psychology, anthropology and the other social sciences. Theories about how they *ought* to behave come from axiology and are therefore philosophic. But axiology, ethics and aesthetics are too important to be left to philosophers alone. Marx, Myrdal, Boulding, Toffler, Platt, Coleman, Skinner, Lilly and Illich are names just as relevant to futuristic educational philosophy as are Dewey, Whitehead, Hutchins, Buber and Ryle. Unless futurism remains synergetic, open, interdisciplinary and oriented toward a cultural synthesis, it will become just another academic discipline to be studied in the ivory towers of universities.

II
MODELS AND
METHODOLOGIES IN
EDUCATIONAL
FUTURES

INTRODUCTION TO SECTION II
MODELS AND
METHODOLOGIES IN
EDUCATIONAL FUTURES

Educational modeling is not new, nor is it a specialty only of futurists. Models can help clarify existing systems, they can be useful tools for the resolution of alternatives, and they do provide a framework of action. They can solidify choices and open other avenues of approach. All models have purposes and sets of assumptions, no matter how loose or tight their design; and it is the responsibility of futurists in educational research to clarify, evaluate and redesign these priorities and assumptions on a continuous basis.

The models suggested by the authors of this section seem to have a central purpose: to replace present educational models with more flexible approaches to learning. Reasons for the suggested changes vary from the anticipated need for global learning approaches to projected demands for more responsive educational systems that meet the demand of information overload. Some of the authors anticipate the collapse of the public school system; others merely see a radical restructuring. Whatever the reader's personal convictions, all the models suggested deserve consideration.

Charles Weingartner is one who questions the use of "steamboat construction" (schools) to get to the moon (need for new ways of thinking). He cites accountability, "back to basics" movements, and the denial of the use of electronic media as symptoms of the steamboat psychology. The author describes a diploma as a "badge of endurance" which makes a difference only if you *do not* have one. He criticizes American schools for being credentialing agencies, rather than places for learning.

Professor Weingartner equates America's public schools with other "art forms" such as ballet or opera. Without extensive faith on the part of its patronage, it would die. Already the taxpayer is feeling the economic pressure of publicly supported programs, and the author believes the general public is losing respect for the educational "products" (students) of the present "efficiency model" (public school) in terms of its return for investment.

Weingartner believes that computers have the capability of replacing conventional schooling. Teachers could assume the role of "programmers." Many of the problems of finance, discipline, violence, busing, absenteeism, and scheduling facing schools today could be answered with this approach. Responsibility for learning would be placed ultimately on the shoulders of the learner (where the author thinks it should be). Many may view with horror the prospect of schools being closed, but Weingartner believes this may be a blessing in disguise.

Elliott Seif, unlike Weingartner, believes present schools can be salvaged, if the stress is shifted to "knowledge and skills for future living." He suggests citizenship knowledge, everyday living knowledge, personal growth knowledge, thinking skills, problem-solving skills, decision-making skills, research skills, relating and interacting skills, communication skills, and technical skills as the types of learning needed for future survival and self-determination.

Professor Seif adds that such knowledge and related skills are only the beginning. Attitudinal shifts are also required, if in fact societies will be capable of directing their future. He provides samples of his instructional model that parallel cross-impact matrices ("subjects" are interdependent and require holistic interpretation). His goal for educational institutions is to include the knowledge, skills, and attitudes necessary for future living in a model that would parallel future life-models.

Gerald Kincade examines the "ifs" and "whys" of education in America. He first criticizes those who equate "human behavior" with "human nature." Much of what is considered human nature (greed, violence, selfishness) might be due, according to the author, to the lack of belongingness, or a need to be needed (Maslow's heirarchy). Kincaid believes that education should stress development of potentials (such as creativity, curiosity, self-reflection, and learning capacity) rather than emphasizing competitive and alienating practices.

Kincade agrees with Robert Theobald—create a new set of myths that value wholeness over specialization, quality over quantity, people over things, and cooperation over competition. Education can promote these myths, but only if the society recognized them as valuable.

In his scenario of the "Global Village School," Kincaid provides insight for the conversion of old myths into new myths. Planning and implementing this model would require much more community participation, but the author expresses his faith in humankind's ability to care about posterity.

Louis Iozzi and Janey Cheu introduce a "social-scientific reasoning model," based on the research of Piaget and Kohlberg. Problem-solving skills are combined with moral/ethical reasoning as a precondition for higher levels of decision-making. They believe their curriculum promotes higher levels of reasoning because alternatives, clarification of ideas, others' viewpoints, and examinations of consequences are included in the learning process.

The authors' curriculum materials are organized in module form, primarily because as such they can easily be introduced into existing educational structures. Examples of the modules include topics such as food, energy, bioethics, technology and changing lifestyles. The authors have purposely left the topics broad enough to be included in several "subject areas," mainly because of the interdisciplinary nature of futures studies. Suggestions are provided for the reader's own implementation of transitional models.

Hans Harloff proposes that some futurist and utopian models for living have striking similarity. His model for living is not inevitable, but rather requires conscious efforts by groups who wish to fashion their own destiny. He uses the broadest meaning of utopia: "a fountain of hope, guideline for political action, ... a solution of social problems, the ideal toward which we must strive."

Although utopian *thinking* is important to the author, he also believes that advanced industrialized countries should reevaluate lifestyles and consider the adoption of several possible utopian-like models. Many readers might find his writing "radical," but the author contends that no matter what the style of life chosen, education must reflect equality, love, and individual purposes so necessary for self-determined living.

The last two papers in this section deal with new educational methodologies. Richard Heydinger suggests that computer conferencing could be used not only for public involvement in the learning process, but also in specific areas of study. Heydinger points out that computer conferencing offers the potential for location-free learning, and provides feedback for the evolution (rather than fixed structure) of knowledge and skills. Furthermore, the author dispels the myth that computers are best for narrow topics—to the contrary, they could encourage more integration of knowledge and more participation.

Potential pitfalls such as access, faculty and student reluctance, learning the language, high costs and the potential for lost time are addressed by Heydinger. He realizes that this pedogogical tool is not a panacea, but feels that it does offer an alternative to other learning environments.

Robert Textor has designed an ethnographic approach to futures research. His EFR (Ethnographic Futures Research) methodology is designed both to study extent cultures and to elicit from interviewees their perception of a possible future cultures. The author describes his method as interactive, cummulative, and evaluative in nature. Not only will the interviewer better comprehend the culture being studied, but at the same time, the interviewee can gain a perspective on his own implicit values.

Professor Textor uses interviews with Buddhist monks from Thailand as an example of how EFR works. He believes that Western social planners today assume "standards" in ways of thinking that are not only dangerous but counter-productive to world problem-solving; valuable insights can be gained from the Thais who do not have an advanced technological society, and therefore do not assume the same conditions. This methodology may well reshape techniques for the study of cross-cultural variabilities.

The authors of this section do not all agree about what could or should be accomplished in education, given the plethora of alternatives and possible effects. The utility of these models and methodologies, however, is that they do inspire action and decision-making behavior. The prospect of living through a societal transformation without weighing alternatives is very sobering. Discovery of "appropriate" or suitable models is, therefore, a critical element of directed futures.

NO MORE PENCILS, NO MORE BOOKS, NO MORE TEACHERS' DIRTY LOOKS

Charles Weingartner

TECHNOLOGICAL CHANGE

Have you ever wondered what candle-snuffer manufacturers said when the electric light was developed? I would guess that they talked about the "quality" of their product, and how they could produce an even better product and market it more efficiently in order to maintain their great tradition in the face of possible competition from the "new-fangled" gadget. That's what they probably said, if they said anything at all. It is possible that they did not even consider the electric light bulb to be "competition" since it was so "impractical," expensive, flimsy and fragile, etc.

If there is one point that the continuing story of technological innovation makes, especially in relation to media of communication, it is that no one seems to have the faintest idea as to what the new development will mean. One of the reasons for this is that the most common and primitive process used to form meanings is that of analogic thinking. That is, the new is assigned meaning in relation to the old, analogically. Most people say, "Oh, that's just a newer form of this." This tendency is what Marshall McLuhan is getting at with his reference to the "rear-view mirror" syndrome. We are apparently limited in the range of meanings that we can conceive by what we already know, and by our emotional investment in it; that is, by our preference for the familiar. We are a precedent-oriented society, and that turns out to be a tremendous liability in a rapidly changing environment. It is a liability in any case, even when change occurs so slowly as to be imperceptible. Conversely, when change is occurring exponentially, it produces anxiety, hysteria, and chaos, and a psychopathically intense search for simple, unchanging "truths."

The need to squeeze the new into old metaphors (or paradigms as Kuhn calls them in *The Structure of Scientific Revolutions*) is the largest single obstacle to planning—even to planning short-term strategies for dealing with the new and its consequences. We are racing into the future while looking relentlessly backward. Using precedent as a basis for assigning meaning is relatively feasible when today is pretty much like yesterday and when tomorrow will be pretty much like today. But, when today is unprecedented, when today has made a quantum-like leap from the past, using the past as reference (except in negative ways) insures catastrophic decisions and choices.

We are all familiar with examples of how wrong "experts" have been in making predictions because they based them only on precedent and simply extrapolated from familiar trends in order to infer future meanings. In *Profiles of the Future*, Arthur Clarke identifies this as the single, most common cause of faulty prognostication. Completely unforeseen (unforeseen because the preferred perspective is backwards) developments seem always to render expert predictions ludicrous or harmful, even within a relatively short time. The generalization most obvious to draw from this record is that predictions are usually grossly inaccurate on the short side. The degree to which they fall short seems to be a function of the rate at which change—technologically induced change—is occurring. It seems fair to say that technologically induced change is now occurring at an incomprehensible rate. Both the rate and the magnitude of change is so great that, paradoxically, most people in technological societies are inured to it—possibly as a result of some primitive "self-defense" mechanism in the psyche.

OUR SCHOOLS IN A CHANGE ERA

When we are "overloaded" by anything that impinges on our sensorium, we seem to "turn it off" even without a conscious decision to do so. The most obvious form that this tendency is taking currently in relation to schools is the "back to basics" movement. The emphasis here is on "refining" anachronistic techniques to make them more "efficient" for the purpose of achieving anachronistic purposes, All it takes to focus the resources and energy of the schools in this way is a denial of the complex changes that have occurred since World War II. The schools are a vast machine devoted exclusively to print/ book "literacy" in the most minimal sense. This exclusivity simultaneously and ludicrously denies and denigrates the presence of all electric and electronic media that comprise the essential environment of the school clientele. School conventions are based on assumptions that were marginally appropriate to the realities of 50 or 60 years ago. They have little to do with the realities of the last 25 years, and they have nothing to do with the realities of today and the probable realities of tomorrow and beyond.

The already observable effects of "accountability" are manifest in increasing emphasis on fungibility—on the relentless standardization of both student and teacher roles. "Accountability," measured solely by "achievement" measured by scores on standardized tests, intensifies the confinement of students and teachers to roles that have never made much sense, even in conventional school terms. The student is confined solely to the role of temporary memorizer of random bits and pieces of assorted and unrelated taxonomies comprised almost exclusively of nouns—that is, of names. The teacher is confined solely to the role of enforcer-imparter of these taxonomies. The "effectiveness" of the imparter and the memorizer is determined by the quantity of nouns the memorizer can recognize—or can feign recognizing—on a standardized, multiple-choice test. All of this despite the fact the we live and change in a world of verbs.

Operationally, accountability is equivalent to a mindless, and expensive, game in which the participants are essentially engaged in an attempt to remember a sufficient quantity of nonsense syllables to "pass" a test at a specified time. There is no expectation that anyone would remember a sufficient number of these "correct answers" beyond the point where they were tested (via "recognition") on them. Indeed, anyone who entertains such an expectation is regarded as unreasonable, at the very least. When a prescribed number of such taxonomical "tests" have been "passed," this is equivalent to "passing" whatever "course" the particular taxonomy comprised.

Note, too, that during this process neither the student nor the teachers are engaged in any intellectual activity except the most minimal—that of temporarily memorizing trivia. The "teachers," by virtue of their access to the teachers edition of the text which contains the "correct answers" in a special section in the back, are spared even this amount of "effort." (It is worth ruminating over the fact that the "competencies" that are "measured" by "competency tests" are *minimal* competencies.)

So, we have the school with all of its appurtenances—administrators, teachers, counselors, coaches, clerks, custodians, buses, bus drivers, managers, uniforms, instruments, etc., devoted solely to the task of somehow inducing "students" to temporarily memorize assorted lists of essentially useless names of people, places, events, and things, none of which can be "controversial," that is, having much to do with anything currently crucial or that might possibly be useful to any of the "students" in their real lives outside of school. What does accrue from a nominal participation in this process over a period of time—for the "students" at least—is a certificate called a "diploma" which symbolizes nothing so much as the "ability" of the student to acquiesce to a series of mindless "requirements" over a specified period of time. It is a certificate that represents the nominally quantifiable "credits" and time spent in "earning" them. It bears no relationship to quality, which is notoriously difficult to quantify. A diploma is a badge of endurance. It is also an appropriate index of the assymetrical nature of many bureaucratic values; it makes virtually no difference if you have one, but it can make a great deal of difference if you do not—depending upon how you decide to use up your life.

Virtually every close look at the results of the schooling process described above has produced negative conclusions about it. The range of negative conclusions runs from vigorous condemnation to wistful despair. Just about every attempt at "school reform" has resulted from such a close look at the process and its consequences. The most obvious and durable of the consequences have been on the negative side themselves, producing in turn the negative conclusions about schooling. It seems fair to say that those students who ultimately produce positive contributions to society—and themselves—do so in spite of the conventional schooling process rather than because of it. These people comprise a distressingly small percentage of the total number who endure schooling. The various "school reform" efforts had as their romantic purpose increasing the number of those who might benefit substantively—that is in more than a certificate earning sense—from school experience.

The history of school reform is itself a depressing chronicle. For all of the efforts made by one person or another, or one institution or another, in one place or another at one time or another, there is virtually nothing to show for it. The relentlessness of the inertia in the conventional school bureaucracy is truly impressive. It has been almost totally unaffected by dramatic changes in society resulting from technological developments, by knowledge of how human learning proceeds, and by the efforts of informed, and even subsidized, school reformers. Even church conventions and prison conventions are characterized by more innovation than are school conventions. By and large, schools, both public and private, at all "grade levels," have been impervious to change from within and without.

PUBLIC SCHOOLS, PATRONAGE, AND SHIFTING VALUES

Schools, then, can be compared to an anachronistic "art form," such as ballet or opera, which cannot survive without substantial subsidies from patrons of those "arts." That is, in a "free market"—without patrons willing to subsidize the costs of keeping them "alive"—schools would simply disappear. They have no way of generating sufficient funds to sustain themseleves; so small is their free-will patronage and so great is their cost. The "benefits" that are alleged to accrue from such anachronistic forms are largely a matter of "faith" rather than a series of consequences that can be verified by any empirical means. The patrons, for whatever reasons, believe it is desirable to keep such forms "alive," and so they contribute money—heavily—to do so. If the patrons should (for whatever reasons) "lose their faith," the subsidies would stop and the forms would disappear since there is no way for them to survive on their own.

This analogy between schools and anachronistic art forms seems feasible since what has produced the financial support for conventional schools to date is a "faith" in them that has endured despite massive evidence that such faith is unwarranted.

We may, however, be reaching (or even be at) a point where this "faith" is experiencing unprecedented challenges. Partly because the school population now includes virtually all cohorts in the "school age" range, and partly because of the technical means of "informing" the population at large—via "media"—there is unprecedented disenchantment with the results that schooling produces or fails to produce. It is almost irrelevant to note that *no* single institution or process could possibly fulfill all of the expectations that schools presently have imposed on them. It is one of the curiosities of our time that schooling—notoriously ineffective in producing the most minimal changes in attitude or behavior even in relation to trivial tasks—is assigned the role of solving any and all "problems." There is apparently a widely held belief that all that has to be done to "remedy" any conceivable problem is to "require a course" in relation to it in school. The absence of *any* evidence that any course in any school on any level ever "remedied" any problem (personal or social) has no apparent effect on this belief. The degree to which any schooling ever achieved any perceptible portion of the objectives it was established to achieve is primarily a function of the degree to which the school as an institution and its constituents enjoyed a system of shared values. That is, in order for a school (or any other institution) to be "successful" in its own terms (at least) it *must* have a set of values (and policies and procedures which both derive from and complement them) that is shared by the administration, the faculty, the students, and the parents.

To say that most schools (both public and private) do not enjoy such a circumstance today is a massive understatement.

The diversity of values characterizing contemporary society is largely a result of that form of technological development called "media." There is enormous power for proselytizing, propagandizing, and persuading in the media environment outside of school, and there is, operationally, a total absence of such power inside school. The values, expectations, and, indeed, the *demands* that are learned by the various "audiences" that comprise the society are a product of forces at work outside the school. The adolescent and young adult sub-culture of the 60s did not "learn" its value system from anything in any "formal" institution such as the family or the church or the school. It learned it—both in form and sub-stance—from trend-setters of the youth culture accessible via long-playing records. The messages of these heroes and heroines, sung to a guitar accompaniment in most cases, shaped both the appearance and behavior of millions of youth around the world in a relatively brief period of time, producing what was probably the first international sub-culture in human history. The evidence of the potency of this source of "values education" is visible today even in the most conservative portions of the population which initially castigated both the form and substance of the "youth movement." Young executives with conservative political orientations and single-minded cor-porate aspirations now sport long hair and use marijuana without any awareness of the origins of either. In the face of powerful electronic mind-shaping capability in the "real world" outside the school, the school is rendered not only an-achronistic in its traditional form, it is also ineffectual.

The inability of the conventional school to have any percep-tible effect on the values and behavior of such a constituency is a primary source of the "lack of faith" mentioned earlier. The current disaffection with schooling is not merely a result of disappointment at the schools' ineffectuality in coping with environmentally produced changes in the constituents it nom-inally exists to "serve," but is also a result of a less visible source of discontent. Deep anxiety and hostility in schools are characteristic of an increasing feeling that nothing is under control. The absence of anything that might be called "confi-dence" in just about any institution, agency, department, cor-poration, profession, or politician on the part of the public is one of the more obvious characteristics of our social-psychol-ogy. And, because schools are the "closest" to most of our disaffected citizenry, being subsidized by local property taxes, they are most vulnerable to criticism and reprisal.

So, what do we have so far? An anachronistic and ineffectual institution, the school, condemned by its assumptions and con-ventions to remain out of touch with its constituents, and vulnerable to attack from its increasingly disaffected patrons.

ECONOMICS AND DEMOGRAPHY: NEW CHANGE PARADIGMS

If we add to this social-psychological mix two other layers of "outside forces" affecting schools, we can develop at least one scenario. The two most obvious "forces" to consider (both actual rather than theoretical) are demographic shifts and economic trends.

Testimony given before the House Subcommittee on Education in hearings held in May, 1977 dwelt primarily on demographic shifts that affect schools. While it may be presumptous to attempt to "summarize" more than 700 pages of testimony in a line or two, there are a few generalizations that are more obvious that others. The most obvious generalization is that the conventional school age population is declining nationally. From 1970 to 1975, school populations declined in 38 states, and of those 12 that didn't, only two had appreciable increases in both number and percentage: Florida and Arizona. While I do not know about Arizona, in the three years since these figures were tabulated, a curious pattern has developed in Florida. Hillsborough County is a representative example of it. The pattern is one of an overall increase in population, including school age population, paralleled by a decline in the public school population. Where this decline is acknowledged, it is generally attributed to a disaffection with public schools because the population in nonpublic (primarily so-called "Christian") schools is increasing dramatically.

The portion of the public school population coming from white, middle-class, "nuclear" families is also diminishing. The non-white, lower socioeconomic, single parent "family" is the source of this increasing number of the public school population. While "hard" figures are not easy to come by in census taking, there is no question but that the non-white population is increasing at a rate that is several times greater than the white.

From 1970 to 1975, the number of single/parent families doubled, and the number of "out of wedlock" births trebled. When the fact that the number of married women in the work force doubled in that period is added, it is clear that the source of the school population is less and less liable to be characterized by values, attitudes, expectations, and beliefs that complement the conventional white school. One of the most obvious manifestations of this dissonance is the escalating rate of violence and vandalism in the schools. There is no way to overstate the magnitude of this problem. The cost in money is the easiest way to quantify this problem, but it is much more difficult to assess the cost in human terms for both teachers and students. For example, Los Angeles spent more than

seven million dollars directly as a result of vandalism in 1974-
1975 at a time when the school system was already facing a
$40 million deficit. According to Birch Bayh, formerly chair-
man of the Senate Subcommittee to Investigate Juvenile Delinquency, the Chicago school system suffered $3.5 million in
property loss in 1974, to which can be added $3.2 million for
school security programs and $3 million for guards necessi-
tated by the violence and vandalism! On a national level, the
National Association of School Security Directors estimates
that school vandalism diverts almost $600 million from annual
education budgets. This sum exceeds the total amount spent
on school textbooks in 1972.[1] The NEA completed a study in
1977 that showed the average age of public school teachers to
be declining. This, it turned out, was not attributable to an
increasing number of younger teachers entering the schools,
but rather to an increasing number of older, experienced
teachers resigning. Many teachers resigning were within a
few years of retirement, but said that "it wasn't worth it" to
stay in a school environment characterized by increasing pun-
ishments (of all sorts) and decreasing rewards. The demographic shifts seem to be a direct source of the increase in
school violence and vandalism with its consequent increase in
school costs.

What we have then is a nationally declining public school
population that is characterized by attitudes inimical to the
conventional school culture. And, this population produces
both directly and indirectly a dramatic increase in the cost of
schooling. Since 1970 the cost of public schooling has increased
at a rate considerably in excess of the rate of inflation.

It is difficult to describe briefly, and perhaps even at length,
what the current and probable future rate of inflation means
in relation to the daily life circumstances of the much ma-
ligned middle-class, working, taxpayer. To put it melodramat-
ically, perhaps, the American dream is turning into a night-
mare. As inflation continues, it becomes more and more
apparent that the values which the middle-class, working, taxpayer lived by have turned to dust. He and/or she "did everything right": stayed in school, followed the rules, went to work,
got married, had kids, mortgages, and debts for all the "ne-
cessities" and now finds that a single-income is insufficient to
pay all the bills. Prices and taxes are eating him and her alive,
and the hostility this middle-class, working, taxpayer feels
toward those drawing welfare checks and other subsidies
should surprise nobody. There is only a narrow band in our
economic spectrum of middle-class, working, taxpayers that is
carrying both ends of the society: (1) the younger end, characterized by "dependent children" and (usually) their single
mothers plus assorted other recipients of one form or another

of "welfare," and (2) the older end, drawing social security and other benefits of one sort or another.

This narrow band of the overtaxed is narrowing even further. What this means is that the portion of the population that is paying the taxes that make most "social services" possible is in a relentless squeeze economically and emotionally. It feels as if it has been lied to, tricked, gypped, and generally duped. It is less and less willing to pay for the increasing costs of public schooling at the same time that the school population is decreasing in numbers and (as nearly as anyone can tell) is also failing to master "basic skills."

COMPUTER-BASED INSTRUCTION: REDEFINING "SCHOOL"

That is the crux of it. At the point where the downward line on the graph representing the size of the school population and its "achievement" intersects with the line representing the sharply upward cost of schooling, we have a very large "X."

The meaning of this big "X" for public schools seems obvious; given these demographics and economics, schools are simply insupportable. A systems break has occurred, but it is just becoming apparent, and it will be denied and resisted by all of those who can only use precedent as a source of meaning. The anachronistic art form we call the public school is about to lose its patronage—unless there is a radical, not just dramatic, but *radical* shift in the source of funding for it. At the moment, the most "radical" of the shifts being proposed is that of moving to "casino gambling," which both predictably and paradoxically is being resisted by those most beset by the present pattern of funding.

What seems to this author to be as probable as anything else is that we will be "deschooled" for reasons that have nothing to do with Illich's perspective. The ultimate "reform" of public schooling will not come from any informed education philosophy within, but from uncontrollable socio-economic forces in the society at large.

The collapse of public schooling, already well underway as nearly as I can tell, need not be the "catastrophe" that most will consider it to be. It can be regarded as an opportunity— an opportunity to shift from an ineffectual set of assumptions and conventions to a completely different set that is already available.

There is nothing that the present public school is said to exist to do that cannot be done better by shifting to electronic information handling systems. The base of these systems, as has been elaborately and eloquently described by many, is the

computer. The computer is the ultimate medium of communication—it combines in a synergistic manner all other existing media. The shift to computer-based instruction has been
exotically slow because of the apparent "supportability" of
conventional schooling. In those instances where computer-
based instruction has been and is being used, its desirability
and effectiveness are unquestionable. From the early efforts
of O. K. Moore and his "learning environment" at Yale where
three- and four-year-olds learned all kinds of things (including
"the basics") while they thought they were just playing in an
interesting environment, up to the current range of computer
based instruction at all grade levels, the feasibility of such a
mode is unquestionable.

The current state of the art now makes it possible to say
that just about anyone can learn just about anything that the
conventional school "teaches" and this learning is much more
effective and efficient via computer than it is in conventional
schooling. The rapidity with which computer technology and
capability is developing is indescribable. With mini and micro-
computers now available in combination with multiple-simul-
taneous access to data systems, there is no imaginable limit
to what can be learned in an interesting and intellectually
engaging manner via computer-based instruction. As described in *Creative Computing* for example, the Learning Research Group of the Xerox Palo Alto Research Center (PARC)
has produced the "Dynabook." The "Dynabook" is a "knowledge manipulator" the size and shape of an ordinary notebook.
"...the software which will give life to the 'Dynabook' concept
must go through a long and arduous process of development
if it is to aid and not hinder the goals of a personal dynamic
medium." This "long and arduous development" suggests a
crucial future role for educators.

"The software system being developed for Dynabook is
known as Smalltalk and its capabilities are truly amazing.
With the graphic capabilities of an 8½ by 11" display composed
of over one million points, some really fantastic things are
possible, from the planned book quality printing in any desired
font up to animated cartoons, musical scores that can control
a synthesizer, all manner of simulations, the ability to 'paint'
on the display as if it were a canvas, and just about anything
else that an imaginative person can think of!"[2] Right now,
every household in the country can be equipped with a mini-
computer for less than half of what it costs to keep one student
in public school for a single year.

It will take the implosion of conventional public schooling as
a result of the intersection of the declining school population
and increasing school costs to produce a forum in which substantive (and to date unthinkable) alternatives can be explored. "Conventional Wisdom" will doubtless perceive the dis-

appearance of conventional schools as a catastrophe. But, it can also be viewed as an opportunity. The opportunity resides in developing feasible strategies for capitalizing on the synergistic educational potential of computer-based instruction.

The implosion of conventional schooling, while it will be regarded as something on the order of an "insurmountable problem," will curiously, perhaps, "solve" all of the current real problems characterizing conventional schooling. These include: the school finance problem; the discipline, violence, and vandalism problem; the busing problem; the "equality of opportunity" problem; the absenteeism problem; the lack of achievement problem; the burgeoning administrative bureaucracy problem; the accountability problem; the increasing cost of school fuel problem; the school cafeteria problem; the school library problem; the school year calendar problem; and the costly litigation problems that result from many of these. All of these problems exist because the anachronistic conventional school exists. When it is gone, all of its attendant problems which consume so much time, energy, and resources will also be gone. It is as if we have been engaged in a protracted and incalculably expensive debate as to how we should go about refurbishing a stern-wheel steamboat for a trip to the moon. We may finally have the opportunity to see that what we need is an entirely different kind of vehicle, and that it already exists.

At some point, the current era may be referred to as "the age of redefinition." Virtually all conventional institutions, values, roles, and relationships are undergoing dramatic redefinition. As economics, demographic changes, and social psychology redefine the form of schooling, the opportunity to redefine the purposes of education and the role of educators becomes available. Rather than investing more resources and energy in attempting to resist redefinition, educators can best use their time and imagination in developing new roles complementary to new information-handling media. One of the more obvious of these roles derives from what will be an insatiable need for suitable "software," for imaginative and effective "programs" to help learners make the most of this unprecedented learning resource. The process of redefinition will also require that the responsibility for learning be shifted to the only component in the learning process where there is any palpable result—the learner. It is not possible to teach anybody anything that they do not want to know. The knowledge and skills that computer instruction makes available finally makes operational the concept that you can't keep anybody from learning anything that they really want to know, and in their own time and on their own terms. Doubtless, there will be problems, requiring new questions in order to produce new answers, but they will be oriented toward the future rather than rooted in some romantically inaccurate vision of the past.

We are literally at a point where it is no longer necessary for anyone to "go to school" because "school" can now go to them, wherever they are, whenever they want it to. It is as if the "ultimate summer vacation from school" is in view, and all students, of all ages, and of all "grade levels" can sing, once and for all, that old end-of-the-school-year song, "No more pencils, no more books, no more teachers' dirty looks."

NOTES

1. Statistics taken from "School Violence and Vandalism: Problems and Solutions," *American Educator*, Summer, 1978, pp. 4-5.
2. John Lees, "The World in Your Notebook," *Creative Computing*, May, 1977, pp. 54-56.

PLANNING SCHOOLING FOR FUTURE LIVING

Elliott Seif

Predicting the future is, of course, fraught with difficulties. There are those who believe that the future holds the promise of rosy and glowing technological and social progress.[1] In this scenario, the world will overcome its pressing problems through technological innovation, and be able to adequately support increasing populations on earth. In the United States, life will go on as it does today for most middle and upper-middle class Americans, except that more people will be able to enjoy the fruits of technological progress. There will be increasing benefits from technological progress. People will increasingly be in white collar, service-oriented jobs.

Another scenario is extremely pessimistic.[2] In this view, the world's problems will not be solved and the peoples of the earth will increasingly turn to war and other negative means to solve conflicts. The earth's resources will continue to be depleted and become more limited. Energy will become a more serious problem, and other energy sources will not be found in time. Increasingly abundant lifestyles will gradually be reduced. People's lives will change dramatically, with the quality of life deteriorating.

Amidst these two scenarios are many others. Some advocate, for example, that people should move to a simpler lifestyle today, and our future will certainly be more positive.[3] Others see an increasingly interdependent earth.[4] One recent forecast suggests that we will find the means to reduce or eliminate the aging process, and thus become nearly immortal.[5]

These previews and forecasts are helpful in projecting ideas and scenarios for the future. But they are not the future. They are future *possibilities*. They will or will not occur, depending in part on what people do or do not do. The future will probably be guided by people's actions or lack of actions and their effects on what happens in the future. For example, many believe that a future war is inevitable, but it is in fact the actions of individuals and nations that will cause war to happen. As Cornish states, the future is often a series of gradual events accumulating over many years to produce or solve problems.[6] If, for example, the Soviet Union and United States agree on a nuclear arms treaty that greatly reduces arms spending and the arms race, then this would have a profound effect on the potential for war and on the economy of the world. If during the next ten years there are serious efforts in the United States to reduce oil and other energy consumption and begin instituting sunpower and other simpler forms of energy, then our energy problems could be very different in the future. Individual and collective decisions will influence and help determine how we will live in the future.

A major goal of education is to prepare students for future living. Schools, as the major educational force in the public sector, have both the obligation and the responsibility to provide students with the training necessary to allow them to lead fulfilling lives in the future. If people play a major role in what happens in the future, then it is imperative that schools train students with knowledge, skills and attitudes to help them build their own future world.

Schools have, in the past, focused on the concept of "literacy". Literacy has traditionally meant becoming competent in basic reading, comprehension and writing skills. Currently there is a major focus on these basic academic competencies, even though most students in the United States have achieved basic literacy skills in schools today. In today's world, the concept of literacy requires expansion to also include other competencies necessary for future living. Reading and writing are certainly basic and important literacy skills, but there are other, equally important areas that are prerequisites for future living. Competency for future living requires many types of knowledge, skills and attitudes that are not adequately focussed on in the school curriculum. Most schools have not systematically attempted to develop a more comprehensive program for a future living education.

A major goal of schools should be to develop *self-directed people with knowledge, skills and attitudes for fully functioning future living*. Self-directed people are those who believe that they can have some control over their own lives and who have learned knowledge, skills and attitudes helpful for full future functioning. They have a knowledge base for citizen involvement, for dealing with everyday issues and problems, and for personal growth and development. They can think and reason, make decisions and solve problems, work with others, communicate adequately, and reflect on and assess their own lives. Future living attitudes include a "scientific" attitude—for example, looking for evidence to support conclusions, keeping an open mind, questioning ideas, allowing dissent.

Self-directed people represent "ideal types" who can direct their own lives and fully function both in the present and the future. Such people can adapt to as well as change situations and events. They have a set of knowledge, skills and attitudes that aid them in choosing future lifestyles and in determining their futures. Schools can play a major role in educating for future living by providing knowledge, teaching skills, and fostering attitudes for future living competence. Schools need to develop a systematic framework, one that can be used to develop self-directing people through a systematic program of instruction for future living. This paper will focus on knowledge, skill and attitude frameworks for future living instruction, and how they might be incorporated into the school instructional program.

PROVIDING KNOWLEDGE FOR FUTURE LIVING

A fundamental, sound knowledge base is a critical component of a future living education. Knowledge for future living can aid the citizen in influencing political decisions. Whom to vote for, what letters to write, what groups to join, what positions to take—these decisions depend on adequate knowledge. Since the future will be determined in part through the political arena, this is critical knowledge for future living.

Everyday living decisions also depend on knowledge. Complex career and consumer decisions are best made with knowledge of choices. Also, knowledge about psychological concepts and about self are helpful for personal growth.

Citizenship Knowledge

Future living will require active citizens who take part in decision-making processes. Active citizenship requires knowledge, and there are important areas of knowledge that will help citizens play a role in what happens to them in the future. Some areas of knowledge that are important for citizenship education are as follows:

1. *Science and technology.* Science and technology currently play too small a role in the education of our youth. It appears that society is often training scientific and technological illiterates. Part of the problem stems from rapid technological change that we as adults have not had time to absorb and learn about. Partly, the problem stems from an overemphasis on teaching concepts from the sciences (biology, physics, etc.) and a lack of emphasis on the role of science and technology in modern life. Science and technology knowledge is heavily related to critical future living issues, such as energy development, pollution, transportation, medical advances, and so on. Students should learn scientific and technological knowledge as related to future living problems, and these include the biological and physical sciences as well as

other areas. Students should be exposed to the workings of science and technology through, for example, tinkering with and understanding how some of our modern gadgets work. They should work with tools. They should learn about recent inventions, the effects of inventions, etc. Schools should much more systematically teach students knowledge about scientific areas and about technological advances.

2. *Democratic heritage.* Our democracy stresses the concept of human dignity and allows for personal participation in the political process. In a complex, industrial society, many people feel that they are limited in their ability to participate. It is possible, however, to influence public policy, and the ability to do so has long been supported by individuals and groups who participate on a regular basis. Students need to learn about democratic systems of government in a realistic way. They need to learn about dedicated political figures who have affected the course of events. They need to learn at an early age about rights and responsibilities, about local government, about power and authority, about our legal system, laws and changes in laws. As students get older, they need to learn about state and federal government and about the realities of poiitical participation.

3. *An interdependent world.* Information about an increasingly interdependent world is necessary for an analysis of future living issues. Technological advances have made travel to the farthest corners of the globe possible and changed perceptions of time and space. Industrial society has increasingly made for an interdependent world economy, in which goods and services are transported in ever increasing numbers. It is important to learn about people in other cultures and countries, their relations with us, economic resources and their distribution, and so on.

4. *Problems and issues.* Schools should systematically focus on problems and issues for the future. Knowledge about problems and issues can help students form opinions and points of view, justified with sound reasons and evidence. Information about the environment, about medical dilemmas (such as whether to spend a great deal of money for expensive equipment that may save some lives) about issues of war and peace, about computers, about energy questions, about issues of privacy and invasion of privacy, about government involvement in social issues, about dwindling resources, about problems of cities, and so on can be taught by direct discussion of issues. These problems and issues can be a significant source of curriculum and can change as the issues change.

Everyday Living Knowledge

Future living requires knowledge that will help in everyday living. Current trends suggest a future world that is more complex, with more choices and more daily living knowledge necessary. Basic survival information such as health care, first aid and cooking can help students with everyday living. Students have to make complex career and consumer decisions. What to do with leisure time is another important area of everyday living. The trend towards more contact with a greater variety of people requires better understanding of others. Finally, everyday living in the future will allow for greater choice among diverse lifestyles. Knowledge in all these areas will aid in future living.

1. *Survival information.* Many people, in this technological society, have moved away from learning and using basic survival information. Foods are bought prepackaged and frozen. Environments safe and secure from the ravages of nature are the rule. Hospitals are available by the touch of a dial. People, however, still find that basic survival information is important.

Survival knowledge includes learning about cooking and growing foods. It includes basic information about preventive health care and the human body. First-aid information is important and useful. Information about survival in natural environments is important.[7]

2. *Consumer and career education.* In an increasingly complex world, career choices become more complex. It is estimated that today's children will be changing jobs more frequently. There are more increasingly specialized jobs from which to choose. Thousands upon thousands of choices are available. Yet it is surprising how little students learn about alternative careers. Time and time again the author has spoken with teachers and children about careers and has been amazed at the lack of information children have about available career choices. It is extremely important that students have the opportunity to learn about a wide variety of careers and occupations—what people do, how they do it, what their lifestyles are.

Consumer information is also important. More and more we are being bombarded with multiple choices among foods, clothing, appliances, etc. Children are subjected to massive advertising campaigns designed to increase their consumption of nutritionally empty foods. Massive advertising occurs for cigarettes, color televisions, and so on. It is important for students to have knowledge that will help them make better consumer choices, including information about nutrition, harmful products, ratings of appliances, advertising techniques, and so on.

3. *Leisure time.* Knowledge of choices for leisure time activities is also helpful. Schools should help students learn enjoyable leisure time experiences that are also productive for growth and development. These include reading for pleasure,

arts and crafts projects, music, games, political activity, clubs, nature activities, sports, exercise and meditation, relaxation techniques, and so on.

4. *Alternative lifestyles.* It is important that students have knowledge of alternative lifestyles.[8] The future will probably provide students with greater options for future living. More people will be able to choose whether to live in rural, suburban or urban settings. They will have choices about what part of the country to live in. Many people may turn to other types of alternatives, such as communal life styles in cities and on farms, religious retreats, groups of families and friends that live in close proximity to one another and share enjoyable experiences.

Personal Growth Knowledge

Future living is enhanced when people feel confident about themselves when they are at high levels of personal self-actualization. While contributions to this state are primarily made on the affective level, it is also true that knowledge can aid in personal growth and development. For example, humanistic psychologists have developed a theory based on human needs and self-actualization.[9] Knowledge of human needs, the need for rest and activity, the need for safety and security, the need to belong and be loved, the need for self-esteem, and so on can help students analyze their own problems and deal with personal issues and crises. Transactional analysts have developed theoretical perspectives about human growth, focusing on the parent, adult, and child within us.[10] Books have been written to help children understand these concepts and apply them to everyday living.[11] Lawrence Kohlberg and others have focused on moral development and on stages of moral reasoning as part of the human development process. Students can learn about different stages of moral reasoning.[12] Knowledge of human psychology can aid students in their personal growth and development.

Personal growth is also enhanced when schools present a variety of case studies of individuals who exemplify our highest values. Maslow, for example, suggests that we can learn much about the best qualities of human beings through the study of "self-actualized" people, who exhibit traits associated with our highest values.[13] Political figures, people in many careers, educators, scientists, and others can be presented through literature, books, newspapers, and so on. Alternative life styles can be illustrated through such individuals. Thousands of individual examples are available, from famous historical figures to current men and women in all walks of life. Students can read and study about dedicated, honest, resilient men and women with the courage of their convictions.[14] Case studies are particularly important in developing personal control and caring attitudes (see attitudes section of this paper), exemplifying individuals whose actions made a difference in their own and other's lives and who showed care and concern for others. Case studies can also illustrate human qualities and skills such as perseverance, acceptance of failure, personal decision-making, human emotion, and the like that relate to future living.

SKILLS FOR FUTURE LIVING

It is not possible to know precisely how the future will develop, but each day people face problems and issues that require skillful solutions. Skills are also important in everyday living. We can predict a number of skill areas that are critical for future living—intellectual skills, action skills, technical skills and so on. For example, thinking, creative problem-solving and decision-making skills are critical for future living. People need to know "how to learn"—for example, how to find out necessary information, how to research, how to draw conclusions, and how to ask questions. Learning how to communicate with others through basic literacy skills and other self-expression skills is important. The continual ability to personally reflect on and assess one's own life in a complex world aids students in living full and effective lives.

Thinking, Problem-Solving and Decision-Making Skills

Thinking skills can be taught in many different ways. Taba and others have outlined many types of thinking skills that can be developed with children, among them classification skills for concept development, interpretation of data skills, drawing conclusions, applying generalizations, and so on.[15] Many curricula programs now stress the development of thinking skills, among them Taba's own social studies program.[16] Schools can stress helping children develop and use thinking skills on a regular basis.[17]

Students can also learn skills to aid them in creative problem-solving. Noller, Parnes and Biondi, for example, outline a five step creative problem-solving process:

1. Fact-finding: gathering and analyzing data in preparation for defining the problem.

2. Problem-finding: analyzing problematic areas in order to pick out and point up *the* problem to be attacked.

3. Idea-finding: idea production—thinking up, processing, and developing numerous possible leads to solution.

4. Solution-finding: evaluating potential solutions against defined criteria.

5. Acceptance-finding: adoption—developing a plan of action and implementing the chosen solution.[18]

Their program is designed to provide students with exercises that allow them to stretch their creative problem-solving muscles and practice using this five-step approach.

Decision-making skills are also important for future living. Practicing decision-making skills means looking at alternatives, consequences, values and different points of view. Decision-making case studies and dilemmas can be presented frequently to students. In studying the American Revolution, for example, students can be asked to make a decision in a hypothetical dilemma, in which a young boy has to decide which side to support. Other historical periods can focus on dilemmas that make history relevant for future living. Future studies courses can also focus on current problems and dilemmas requiring thought and decision. Many materials have been designed to help students focus on learning decision-making skills.[19] Other sources, such as those for value clarification, also have developed ways for schools to focus on decision-making skills.[20]

Research Skills

It is not difficult to imagine citizens of the future making complex decisions and acting on them, whether through their vote or through more direct action. Making such complex decisions, however, requires them to be able to find and translate information into a usable structure. While it is possible that retrieval information systems will be easier to use in the future, research skills will still be needed to be able to collect appropriate and accurate information. Students, therefore, should learn to conduct research and learn the skills for research, including using library catalogues, outlining information, using a variety of sources, checking on the reliability of information, evaluating information, and so on.

Relating and Interacting Skills

Schools can facilitate interaction skills by promoting classrooms in which students practice such skills. Many teachers use a technique called classroom meetings to help students learn to interact with each other. Classroom meetings are large group meetings in which students have a chance to listen to each other's problems, to think and reason together, to solve problems together. Often classroom meetings involve problems of human relationships, such as problems on the playground, classroom problems and so on. This technique, practiced regularly, can help students learn to relate to each other.[21]

Group process and group dynamics activities are also helpful. Many techniques have been developed to help students learn about human relationships. Small group activities in which students work together on tasks and then analyze their relationships can help students focus on relating issues and problems. Specific tasks can help students explore feelings of trust and mistrust,[22] intergroup conflict,[23] unequal power,[24] and other concepts and issues. Issues in solving conflicts peacefully and skills in practicing peaceful conflict resolution can be explored.[25] Parent and Teacher Effectiveness Training approaches provide a conceptual model for learning how to listen to others, for learning how to solve problems to the mutual satisfaction of all concerned. These can be taught to students as well as adults.[26] These skills, coupled with an understanding of similarities and differences between many different kinds of peoples and cultures, can provide a basis for tolerance and acceptance of others and open the way toward more positive interactions and relationships with others.

Communication Skills

There are many skills under the heading of communication skills that are useful to learn for future living. Basic communication skills, such as reading, oral expression, comprehension and writing are in this category. However, basic listening and discussion skills are also important. Schools can focus on ways that students can argue rationally with each other, such as through the ability to examine one's own and other's arguments. Students can learn to arrive at consensus and clarify issues, rather than argue and debate with the idea of "winning" the argument.[27] Schools ought to spend more time having students practice discussion skills, learning to focus on differences and disagreements and learning to work together to brainstorm alternative solutions to problems.

Students can also learn many forms of self-expression designed to communicate ideas and feelings. It is important for students to learn skills related to self-expression through many mediums, such as painting, clay, weaving, and so on. These skills as forms of self-expression are important to *all* ages, and we should not abandon them in schools.

Personal Reflection and Assessment Skills

It is important for students to learn personally to reflect on and assess their lives on a regular basis. It is often taken for granted that people know how to do this, but there is much training and education that can help people learn these skills. Personal reflection and assessment skills can be explored in school settings.

Many specific skills fall under this category. For example, it's useful to help students learn how to set goals and focus on actions necessary to attain those goals.[28] Goal setting can focus on feelings of success and failure, on small steps necessary to reach goals, on goal alternatives, on long range and short range goals and so on.[29] Other skills include becoming aware of and learning to focus on one's talents, strengths and values.

Technical Skills

The world revolves around technology and it appears that trend will continue. Technological developments in computers, mass production and automation, new forms of energy, electronics and communications are continuing and accelerating. Skills in working with different forms of technologies are thus useful and important.

Technical skills provide students with the means to work with the technological products of the society. Such skills are many and varied, and may include the ability to repair household items, television sets, cars and the like as well as the building of solar energy devices, new homes and computers.

This is one of the most neglected areas of the school curriculum. This writer learned very few technical skills in school, and certainly very few related to new technologies. These important skills are still neglected. The school curriculum should include the learning of varied technical skills. Young children, for example, should learn to work with simple tools. Older students can learn about simple electronic items, how they work, precautions to take with them, and even how to make simple repairs. Students can learn about the workings of such important, complex items as computers and automobiles. They should learn about energy, including new, alternative forms of energy production, and the skills of producing simple energy devices.

DEVELOPING ATTITUDES

It is important for schools to help develop certain attitudes for future living. First, schools should help students develop a most important attitude—that they can have some control over their lives, that they cause things to happen that affect their lives. This attitude is important if students are to act so as to help create changes in the world that will benefit themselves and others. Second, students need to develop a "scientific" attitude about the world around them. A scientific attitude includes, among other things, searching for truth, questioning conclusions, and developing a favorable attitude towards intellectual endeavors. Third, students need to develop an attitude of self-acceptance and self-growth over time. They need to see themselves as capable and lovable individuals with human frailties and human strengths. They need to accept the fact that they will always be growing and searching. Fourth, students need to learn to think about both the present and the future as well as the past. They need to be willing to speculate about the future and see such speculation as worthwhile and important. Finally, they need to develop a "caring" quality. They need to learn to care about others and themselves.

"Personal Causation" Attitude

There is a basic underlying attitude called "personal causation" that is important for future living.[30] People with this attitude believe that in many situations they can control what happens to them. It is a personal feeling that one can act to change situations for one's own self-fulfillment. Many people who have this attitude do not necessarily always find themselves in situations that they can control. But with this attitude they are able to accept frustration and even failure and still expect that changes can or will be made. Many people who lived in and survived concentration camps in Germany did so because they were able to feel in control of their internal situation to some extent and inwardly maintain a degree of integrity and self-respect.[31] Many well-known political and religious leaders, educators, scientists and businesspeople believe that they can personally cause things to happen and act accordingly. Many others act in similar ways in their everyday lives, their careers, their lifestyles. People with this attitude are persistent and do not readily accept failure. They have goals. Often they have faith in others and a positive view of themselves and others. They believe that their actions, over the long haul, can influence the course of events that affect their lives.

The importance of this attitude cannot be stressed too strongly. It is assumed here that people can significantly affect future events and therefore future living. If we hold the basic attitude that we cannot change the course of events, then our attitude produces a self-fulfilling prophecy. We do not act to change the course of events, and therefore events do not change. This does not mean that the course of events changes easily, simply because we believe we can change it. Rather, the assumption is that the effects of many will make many changes that will affect our future lives. It is when we believe we can act to affect our lives and the future that changes are most likely to occur. Changes are not likely to occur if we do not act because we believe there's no hope of change. The "personal causation" attitude is especially important in a democratic society such as ours where options for change are open to us both as citizens and in our everyday lives. Countless individuals have developed personal and social goals and made decisions that have affected political and social events and have developed new ways of living and being.

This attitude is developed in schools when knowledge and skills are taught that foster self-directed learning and when schools allow students to feel as if they have some control over what happens to them. Schools can create personal causation climates that in the long run develop personal control attitudes and appropriate skills and knowledge. This climate occurs when students participate in school decisions. The structure and boundaries for students are developed as the student's abilities to take charge of their own learning are assessed and evaluated. The greater the abilities of students to take responsibility for their own learning, the greater responsibility that is given to them. The more schools are able to do these things, the greater the likelihood of developing a personal causation attitude.

The Scientific Attitude

The scientific attitude involves a commitment toward truth and democratic methods. The scientific attitude is antithetical to authoritarian values. It supports free, open inquiry, tolerance of difference, objectivity, the search for evidence, and flexibility—values that are encouraged and supported in a democratic society.[32]

Implicit in the process of science is an emphasis on the dignity of man. The scientific process values dissent and difference among reasonable people. It presupposes that, in the search for truth, differences in conceptions and theories developing over time will occur. It implies that, rather than destroying those who disagree with each other, the more natural and preferable course is to perform further experiments, collect greater evidence, and dialogue and communicate.

The scientific attitude includes a healthy skepticism about theories and ideas about man and nature. It attempts to focus on concepts and theories and raise questions about them looking towards experiment, observation, and mental acuity as ways to further truth. It accepts questions, problems, dilemmas and ambiguities as natural, positive phenomena, and supports the search for tentative hypotheses through reason and evidence. It often assumes failure and frustration will come before success, and accepts the fact that knowledge can only be built over time.

With a scientific attitude, generalizations are questioned. People try to come to conclusions carefully, objectively. They work cooperatively with others. They look at others as friends and allies, ready to help in the search for truth. They agree to disagree. Some of our fundamental Constitutional rights are basic to the scientific attitude, such as the right to dissent, to speak freely, and so on.

Schools can help foster scientific attitudes by encouraging

rigorous intellectual thought. Schools can respect the right and integrity of people to think and believe differently from each other, encouraging humane discourse and cooperative learning. Students can be encouraged to disagree and dissent with each other and the teacher provided they can develop arguments with evidence for their positions. Teachers can create questions and dilemmas as starting points for learning, and encourage experimentation and observation. Multiple resources illustrating different points of view can be used. The history of scientific discovery can be incorporated into the school curriculum to trace differences in points of view and the use of scientific method over time.

Self-Acceptance and Self-Growth

There is a special attitude toward oneself that is critical for effective future living. It combines self-acceptance with an attitude of self-growth. This combination helps people feel confident and capable, more relaxed, and more accepting of strengths *and* weaknesses. This is in contrast to a person with a negative self-concept. This person does not like himself. Much of his or her energies focus on self-blame and doubt. He or she may also continually blame others for things that happen.[33]

The self-accepting attitude is important for future living. It enables individuals to concentrate on situations and events, rather than on themselves. It enables a person to live through difficult times in which he or she may be blamed and criticized for his actions. Self-accepting people are also more likely to be able to concentrate on developing ideas, skills and attitudes important for future living.

An attitude of self-growth implies that people have a view of a changing self over time. While they accept themselves, they also see themselves as "improving" in many different ways. They are open to learning new skills and attitudes. They are willing to learn how to handle situations in new ways. They are willing to explore diverse career goals. They are willing to explore new ways of relating to people. They accept the fact that they will change as they pass through different stages of their lives.

Schools can help foster attitudes of both self-acceptance and self-growth. Using esteem and growth building activities and experiences along with positive feedback and positive expectations can foster both attitudes.[34] Fostering successful learning and individualized learning approaches takes into account differences among students. Teacher considerations of student needs and other individual student factors can foster self-acceptance and self-growth.

Present and Future-Oriented Attitude

Schools have had a tendency to develop a "past," rather than a present or future attitude. For example, much of what students learn in social studies is in the form of historical knowledge. As Toffler says, when history reaches the present, learning stops.[35] Generally, there is little that students do in school to help them focus systematically on the present and the future.

However, it is important that schools spend much more time developing a present and future attitude towards learning. The school's purpose, in my view, is to prepare students for future living, and part of skillful future living is the ability to focus one's mental energies on both the present and the future. This does not mean that schools do not teach about the past, but only that the past, when taught, be used as a vehicle to deal with present and future issues.

Caring

Finally, an important attitude to develop for future living is caring about others.[36] The caring quality is similar to a sense of "mutuality," a higher order stage of development.[37] Individuals with the caring quality have a basic sensitivity and understanding of others. They can empathize with the feelings and needs of others. They can act to help others.

PATTERNS OF INSTRUCTION FOR FUTURE LIVING

Some fantastic visions of schools for the future have been developed. Computerized instruction and technological devices suggest many ways to revolutionize learning.[38] Other visions include significant institutional changes in schools, such as eliminating the school as an educational institution[39] or making the school a more comprehensive educational institution.[40] However, these visions may blind us to the necessity of focussing on and carefully thinking about the knowledge, skills, and attitudes that are most helpful for living in the future effectively. While there are ways that technology and institutional changes can aid in learning, it is more important to develop patterns of instruction that can effectively help children develop competencies for future living. Quality instruction does not depend on major new innovations, but rather on dedicated teachers and school personnel who, themselves, focus on ways to develop an effective instructional program. The traditional school model is appropriate for an effective future living education program, although modifications may be helpful and useful. It is important for schools to first clarify what and how to teach as they think about changing the institutional structure of schools and/or using new innovations.

This paper suggests that schools should focus on knowledge, skills and attitudes that are important for future living. Instruction should aid the student to become more self-directing and more fully functioning. Future living literacy means that school focus on developing competencies so that students can become active citizens, make everyday living decisions, and reach their personal potential. There are many types of instruction that can aid the student as he or she faces the future, and many have been suggested here. Chart I outlines and reviews the knowledge and skill areas and attitudes suggested as critical for future living. The chart suggests that knowledge, skills and attitudes are intertwined in complex ways, and that developing curriculum programs and instructional techniques based on this model is a complex process. The model can serve as a starting point for exploring school curricula and instructional practices designed to enhance future living.

In order to implement a complex future living program, it is imperative that school districts clarify their goals and develop clear and systematic programs. This author's observations indicate that generally schools do not systematically design instruction for future living. Schools can and should begin to conceptualize their future living programs by establishing goal priorities and then deciding in what ways goals can be implemented at different grade levels and in different classrooms. Goals should be general and specific, maximizing ways that the achievement of goals can be measured.

For example, assume that a school district agrees that educating self-directed people for future living is an important general goal. Also assume that the district agrees with the general competencies suggested here in the knowledge, skill and attitude areas, and has developed specific objectives around these. One way to proceed is to develop planning charts for knowledge, skills and attitudes to be developed, similar to chart II. In chart II each knowledge area is listed separately, alongside grade levels. Next to each grade level the school personnel place those curricula programs or classroom practices that will be used to develop the knowledge areas. Some programs may be used for more than one area. Thus the school district may be using, or wish to use, a social studies program that includes many of the future living knowledge areas. The chart would list, for each grade level, the curriculum under the knowledge areas covered. Other school and classroom practices and experiences would also be listed in appropriate knowledge areas. Although not every knowledge area would be covered at every grade level, it would be expected that

Chart I
A Matrix Summarizing Knowledge Areas, Skills, and Attitudes for a
Future Living Education

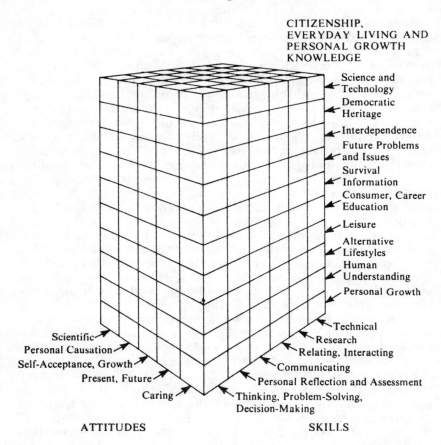

CITIZENSHIP,
EVERYDAY LIVING AND
PERSONAL GROWTH
KNOWLEDGE

Science and Technology
Democratic Heritage
Interdependence
Future Problems and Issues
Survival Information
Consumer, Career Education
Leisure
Alternative Lifestyles
Human Understanding
Personal Growth

Technical
Research
Relating, Interacting
Communicating
Personal Reflection and Assessment
Thinking, Problem-Solving, Decision-Making

Scientific
Personal Causation
Self-Acceptance, Growth
Present, Future
Caring

ATTITUDES   SKILLS

Chart II
Sample Planning Chart
Knowledge Framework

Science and Technology	Democratic Heritage	Inter-Dependence	Problems and Issues	Consumer Career Education	Leisure	Alt. Life-styles	Hum. Under-standing	Personal Growth

every knowledge area would be covered by the time a student reaches the twelfth grade. There may also be areas of overlap and repetition designed to reinforce specific knowledge, skills and attitudes or to teach different and more complex viewpoints at different grade levels.

In completing this chart, the school and school district can assess how its program focuses on future living knowledge. Similar charts for skills and attitudes do the same. As a result of this assessment, a school or school district can determine whether changes should be made in the curricula and instructional program so that other areas should be developed. Changes can also be included in the plan.

Once decisions are made about the knowledge, skills and attitudes to be explored at different grade levels, and about the general curricula and instructional patterns to be used, a more detailed plan can be developed for each grade level and/or each teacher (see chart III below).

The detailed plan does not necessarily include a daily plan or even a weekly, monthly or yearly plan, but indicates some of the curriculum areas and classroom practices that will be used to develop knowledge, skills and attitude competencies. The grade level plan includes specific indications of how teachers will develop competencies over time, and ways that these competencies will be assessed. These grade level plans, along with a general school overview, can be collated into a comprehensive school district plan. The comprehensive plan should include a general rationale, goals and objectives, a description

Chart III
Grade Level Plan
Grade _____

1. General description of goals, objectives, and competencies:
   (related to general plan for future living)
2. Brief description of program and assessment techniques consistent with above:
3.

Activities and/or patterns of classroom life and/or curriculum	Knowledge Area	Skills	Attitudes
Social Studies (sample)	*Community*: careers, lifestyles, government and laws, transportation, technology, services to others	Developing questions, collecting information, drawing conclusions, classifying	Present and Future; Caring About Others; Scientific Attitude

of an overall future living program, an overview of a K-12 curricula and instruction planning sequence, and specific plans for each grade level. The comprehensive plan should be assessed, reviewed, and updated periodically, and assessments made on a regular basis as to whether students are in fact learning what they are expected to learn in a school for future living.

It is better if future living assessments and programs are developed as part of a comprehensive, systematic school or system-wide future living plan. However, sometimes it is necessary for an individual teacher, working alone or with several others, to assess and plan for future living knowledge, skill and attitude programs. Essentially this requires analysis of school and community committments, focusing on ways they can be adapted and modified to better fit a future living program. Charts I and III provide potential guidelines for developing specific teaching plans. An individual teacher may also wish to act as a catalyst for a district-wide future living education assessment, using chart II as a guide.

SOME FINAL THOUGHTS

There are several important ideas that should be considered when developing a plan for future living education. First, certain types of knowledge should be emphasized, and schools should determine if their programs are geared to future living knowledge. Does a school, for instance, spend time focusing on citizenship knowledge? On everyday living knowledge? On personal growth knowledge? Are such areas as science and technology, career and consumer knowledge, alternative lifestyles, and so on included in the instructional program? These are several examples of the many questions that can be asked by educators as they explore whether their schools adequately promote knowledge for future living.

Second, a school district should determine whether there is strong enough emphasis on skills and attitudes for future living. Often schools purport to emphasize skills and attitudes but actual practices are inconsistent with future living skill and attitude goals. For example, many schools suggest that they promote thinking and problem-solving, but one is hard pressed to find examples of students using a variety of thinking skills, solving complex problems, and making decisions. Both curricula programs and classroom instruction can directly promote such goals. Another example is found in schools where children have little opportunity to relate to and interact with each other, yet this is often considered an important school goal. It is paradoxical that often teachers will tell me that they cannot allow children to interact with each other.

How are they going to learn? A program that helps students to relate is most called for when students do not know and/or do not use relating skills.

Schools can also promote the development of skills and attitudes that gradually allow students to take greater responsibility for their own learning and become self-directed learners. Schools promote this development when they emphasize contract learning, learning centers, small group experiences, learning packets, and so on. Non-graded schools also promote greater independence and responsibility. The gradual development of self-directed learning is successful when in high school most students can work independently, with teachers acting as facilitators of learning. Of course not all students will be ready for this type of learning in high school, and close monitoring of students can determine whether students need more or less guidance. Unfortunately, most school districts do not operate on this increased self-direction premise. High schools generally seem to emphasize teacher-centered learning, negating the self-directed learning approach. It is helpful to develop a systematic plan that enables students over time to use their thinking, problem-solving, decision-making and other self-directed skills and attitudes and learn on their own, with the help and guidance of the teacher, as they progress through the grades. For example, an interdisciplinary, thematic approach in high schools might help to make a less fragmented program and allow for self-directed skill and attitude development.

Third, schools can organize their programs to be consistent with their students' stages of development. For example, the elementary grades can focus on providing background knowledge, skills and attitudes prerequisite for advanced work. During the middle school-junior high school years, when students are dealing with questions of self-identity and can do more formal, advanced thinking, it may be appropriate to emphasize personal growth, reflection and assessment issues through moral dilemmas, career questions and lifestyle issues. In the high school years more abstract themes, questions and issues relating to political issues and involvement, interdependence, and future studies can be studied.

Fourth, schools should emphasize active, experiential real world learning. Students should experience as much as possible in the real world as they learn knowledge, skills and attitudes for future living. Experiments, simulation games and role play, field trips, audio-visual experiences, interviews, speakers, camping trips, and internships are examples of such experiences relevant for future living. A greater experiential, real world emphasis will significantly aid in developing future living education.

Assessment and monitoring of student competency progress

is an important technique for the success of a future living program. A competency based mastery approach, in which students are continually evaluated and assessed in formal and informal ways, can provide the backbone for a successful school experience.[41] Schools can plan to assess student competencies and place students in appropriate learning experiences. The last year or several years in school can be devoted to many types of experiences that are designed to use, reinforce and reemphasize skills learned earlier. For example, students can develop independent projects around a strong future living interest (e.g. careers of the future, technology, inventions, etc.). They can focus on relevant problems and simulation experiences related to future living. Questions and problems can be raised by the students and explored together. Field experiences can be developed to allow students to live in different settings in the "real world"—occupational settings, alternative living settings, and the like. Students can focus on the concept of future living skills and assess whether they feel prepared for future living. Future studies courses can intensify their experiences. Small group and individual conferences can help teachers assess student progress.

Plans such as these do not develop overnight. They may take years to develop and may cost money. But schools have the opportunity to develop such plans at relatively low cost. Summers are ideal for thinking about future living education goals and plans without the harried schedules of the school year. Teachers could be hired at relatively minimal cost to focus on these issues. School districts adjacent to each other can pool their resources to fund such planning. With such plans, teachers could clarify their own goals and see how their classroom program fits with a school and community conception of important elements for future living. It would become easier for schools to portray their goals and plans to the public, and would help schools and school districts continually clarify what they are doing and why. Mastery of these knowledge and skill areas, as well as the development of appropriate attitudes, could be monitored and progress reported.

It is not the intention of this paper to argue that schools should be the only institution responsible for future living learning. Other institutions, such as the home, religious institutions, social agencies, also have a role to play. It is suggested that there are areas important for future living, and that schools have an obligation to determine what role they can play in preparing their students for future living. A carefully developed school program outlining the school's responsibilities and goals can help to clarify what roles different institutions must play in future living education. Schools must play a major role in that preparation, given the time and the resources devoted to schooling in our society. A carefully developed school program outlining the school's goals and responsibilities may take years to develop, but would be well worth it. The resources of state and federal governments should be marshalled in an effort to help with this task. All would benefit, and progress could be made toward a quality future living education for all.

NOTES

1. For example, see Herman Kahn, et al. *The Next 200 Years: A Scenario for America and the World*, New York: William Morrow and Co., Inc. 1976.
2. A pessimistic scenario is presented in Donella H. Meadows, Dennis L. Meadows et al., *The Limits to Growth*, New York: The New American Library, 1974 (second edition).
3. The case for a simpler, voluntary lifestyle is presented by Duane S. Elgin and Arnold Mitchell, "Voluntary Simplicity: Lifestyle of the Future" in *The Futurist*, Volume XI, No. 4, August, 1977, pp. 200–209, 254–261.
4. See "Education for a World in Change: A Working Handbook for Global Perspectives," an entire issue of *Intercom*, #84/85, New York: Center for Global Perspectives, 218 East 18th St., New York, N.Y. 10003.
5. See Jib Fowles, "The Impending Society of Immortals," in *The Futurist*, Volume XII, No 3, June, 1978, pp. 175–184.
6. Edward Cornish, "Towards a Philosophy of Futurism," in *The Futurist*, Volume XI, Number 6, December, 1977, pp. 380–383.
7. See Fred Harwood and Elliott Seif, "Coping with the Here and Now: Teaching Survival Skills To Urban Students," in *The Instructor*, December, 1973, pp. 46–48; see also the Scout Skill Book series, North Brunswick, New Jersey: Boy Scouts of America 1976.
8. See, for example, Patrick Rivers, *The Survivalists*, New York: Universe Books, 1975; alternative lifestyles have also been explored in newspaper articles and magazine sources.
9. To explore human needs and self-actualization, see, for example, Abraham Maslow, *Motivation and Personality*, New York: Harper and Row, 1970 (second edition); see also Frank Goble, *The Third Force*, New York: Pocket Books, 1971.
10. See Thomas Harris, *I'm OK—You're OK: A Practical Guide to Transactional Analysis*, New York: Harper and Row, 1967.
11. See Alvyn M. Freed, *T.A. for Tots and T.A. for Kids*, Sacramento, California: Jalmar Press, 1974.
12. For a summary of stages of moral reasoning and examples of dilemma situations for teaching purposes, see Ronald E. Glabraith and Thomas M. Jones, *Moral Reasoning*, Minneapolis, Minn.: Greenhaven Press, 1976.
13. Examples of self-actualized people and their characteristics are found in Maslow, *Motivation and Personality*, Chapter 11.
14. See, for example, John F. Kennedy, *Profiles in Courage*, New York: Pocket Books, 1957; also Margaret Truman, *Woman of Courage*, New York: Bantam Books, 1977.
15. See Hilda Taba, et al., *Thinking in Elementary School Children*.

Cooperative Research Project No. 1574. San Francisco, CA.: San Francisco State College, 1964; see also Norman E. Wallen, et al., Teh Taba Curriculum Development Project in Social Studies, Menlo Park, CA: Addison Wesley Publishing Co., 1969.

16. *The Taba Social Studies Program* (curriculum materials for the elementary grades), Menlo Park, CA.: Addison Wesley Publishing Co.

17. Many sources are available for helping teachers stress thinking skills such as classification, interpretation, etc. See, for example, Louis Raths et al., *Teaching for Thinking: Theory and Application.* Columbus, Ohio: Charles E. Merrill Publishing Co., 1967.

18. Ruth Noller, Sidney Parnes and Angelo Diondi, *Creative Action-book*, New York: Charles Scribner's Sons, 1976.

19. There are many sources for information on decision-making skills and materials. See, for example, Dana G. Kurfman, editor, *Developing Decision-Making Skills.* Washington, D.C.: 47th Yearbook of the National Council for Social Studies.

20. For example, see Louis Raths, Merrill Harmin and Sidney Simon, *Values and Teaching, Second Edition.* Columbus, Ohio: Charles Merrill, 1978.

21. See William Glasser, *Schools Without Failure.* New York: Harper and Row, 1969.

22. See David and Frank Johnson, *Joining Together: Group Theory and Group Skills.* Englewood Cliffs, N.J.: Prentice-Hall, 1975; p. 186.

23. *Ibid.*, p. 187

24. *Ibid.*, p. 218

25. For conflict resolution information and ideas, see Barbara Stanford, editor, *Peacemaking: A Guide to Conflict Resolution*, New York: Bantam Books, Inc., 1977.

26. See for example, Thomas Gordon, *Parent Effectiveness Training (P.E.T.)* and *Teacher Effectiveness Training (T.E.T.)*, New York: Peter Wyden and sons

27. See, for example, Donald Oliver and James Shaver, *Teaching Public Issues in the High School*, Boston: Houghton Mifflin Co., 1966; see also Fred Newman, *Clarifying Public Controversy*, Boston: Little, Brown and Co., 1970.

28. See, for example, Richard DeCharms, "From Pawns to Origins: Toward Self-Motivation," in General Lesser, ed., *Psychology and Educational Practice*, Glenview, Illinois; Scott, Foresman, 1971; see also Alfred S. Alschuler, *Teaching Achievement Motivation: Theory and Practice in Psychological Education.* Middletown, Conn. Educational Ventures, Inc., 1970.

29. *Ibid.*

30. For a technical, extensive discussion of personal causation, see Richard DeCharms, *Personal Causation: The Internal Affective Determinants of Behavior.* New York: Academic Press, 1968.

31. See Victor Frankl, *Man's Search For Meaning: An Introduction to Logotherapy*, part I, Boston: Beacon Press, 1963; see also Bruno Bettelheim, *The Informed Heart: Autonomy in A Mass Age*, Glencoe, Illinois: Free Press, 1960.

32. See Jacob Bronowski, *A Sense of the Future*, Cambridge, Mass.: The MIT Press, 1977.

33. See Harris, *I'm O.K.—You're O.K.*
34. See William Purkey, *Inviting School Success: A Self-Concept Approach to Teaching and Learning*, Belmont, California: Wadsworth Publishing Co., 1978; see also Jack Canfield and Harold C. Wells, *100 Ways to Enhance Self-Esteem in the Classroom*, Englewood Cliffs, N.J.: Prentice-Hall, 1976.
35. Alvin Toffler, *Future Shock*, New York: Random House, 1970, p. 374.
36. A caring curriculum was recently discussed by Claude Lewis, "Learning to Care," in the *Philadelphia Bulletin*. Wednesday, May 31, 1978, p. B9. He described a curriculum developed by Dorothy Kobak, a psychiatric social worker for the New York City Board of Education.
37. See Erik H. Erikson, *Childhood and Society*, Second Edition, New York: W. W. Norton, 1963. A recent discussion of mutuality and maturity can be found in David C. McLelland et al., "Making It To Maturity," in *Psychology Today*, June, 1978, pp. 42–53, 114.
38. See, for example, Philip Kotler, "Educational Packagers: A Modest Proposal," and Peter H. Wagschal, "Illiterates With Doctorates: The Future of Education in an Electronic Age," in *The Futurist*, Volume XII, No. 4, August, 1978, pp. 239–242, 243–244.
39. See, for example, Ivan Illich, *DeSchooling Society*, New York: Harper and Row, 1971.
40. For example, see Edward G. Olsen, *The School and Community Reader*, New York: The MacMillan Co., 1963 (especially section 8); also Maurice F. Seay and Associates, *Community Education: A Developing Concept*, Midland Michigan: Pendell Publishing Co., 1974.
41. See Benjamin S. Bloom, *Human Characteristics and School Learning*, New York: McGraw-Hill, 1976; see also Benjamin S. Bloom et al., *Handbook on Formative and Summative Evaluation of Student Learning*, New York: McGraw-Hill, 1971.

LEARNING TO LIVE IN A GLOBAL VILLAGE

Gerald L. Kincaid

The celebration of our nation's 200th birthday brought to mind Benjamin Franklin's famous statement: "Yes, we must all hang together or, assuredly, we shall hang separately." It would seem as appropriate to address Franklin's statement to all of the nations of the world today as it was to the thirteen colonies 200 years ago. But educators need to answer this question: "Do we have the capacity to become world citizens when we are still struggling to become local and national citizens?"

H. G. Wells once said that "Civilization is a race between education and catastrophe." At this moment, education seems to be losing that race. But this is not a doomsday prophecy. On the contrary, the writer considers himself to be a pessimist with hope. Education can win that race, if (and it is that "if" being considered in this paper) alternatives are developed.

Abraham Lincoln once said: "If we could know where we are and whither we are tending, we could better judge what to do and how to do it." Lincoln's statement could be amended to read: "If we could know where we are and why, whither we are tending and why, and where we want to go and why, then we could better judge what to do and how to do it." In order to consider where we are, attention is given to two broad areas of the total situation: 1) the nature of our society, and 2) the nature of the individual human.

THE NATURE OF THE AMERICAN INDUSTRIALIZED SOCIETY

Trend analysis may help develop some important extrapolations about the future. The transition from an agrarian to an industrialized urban society has created a movement:

from independence to interdependence
from wholeness to specialization
from community decision making to anonymity in planning
from belongingness to alienation

As specialists, adults have organized into special interest groups which became interdependent but in constant conflict. If Haim Ginott's assessment is valid, i.e., that dependence breeds hostility,[1] then the development of increasing dependence upon other groups may provide us with some clues for understanding why we are seeing an increase in hostility in our society. It seems that such hostility and alienation have risen to dangerously high levels in recent years—as indicated in the following Harris Poll:

	1966	1976
Adults who feel left out of things	9%	42%
What I think doesn't count	37	64
Rich get richer; poor get poorer	45	77
People in government don't care what happens to me	26	61
People with power take advantage of me...(In 1971)	33	62

Along with the increases in alienation, there has been a rapid disintegration of the family. Today, there is:

an increase in the number and percentage of unwed mothers;

an increase in the number and percentage of divorces by couples with children;

an increase in suicides by children during the past 20 years: has doubled for ages 10–14; has tripled for ages 15–19;

an increase of crimes by children: armed robbery, rape, and murder up 100% in 10 years, assault on teachers up 77% from 1970–73;

an increase in white-collar and nonviolent crimes.

Many people, however, seem to feel impotent about solving the problems of alienation and crime, including the terrorism that is being used as a weapon by alienated groups. Indeed, it appears that the industrial society has developed a number of dilemmas about which participants seem to feel impotent.

SOME DILEMMAS ABOUT WHICH WE SEEM TO FEEL IMPOTENT

1. Interdependence requires trust and cooperation; present vested interests produce distrust and conflict.

2. There is a need to reduce consumption of non-renewable resources, but that would increase unemployment.

3. Inflation should be reduced; but, under our present system, that would cause unemployment.

4. Rising unemployment and inflation.

5. There is a need for economic equity and justice for the "have-nots;" but, under the present system, that could

reduce the "haves" to a level that could be disastrous for the total society.

In short, it appears that the American society has been traveling down a dead-end road at a rapidly increasing pace. Its leaders and their advisors seem to be impotent in bringing about major changes in direction or for selecting any new roads to travel. The blind are leading the blind. Why? Perhaps it is because our industrialized society has been operating on an unstated value system that has included:

1. Valuing things (property) over people
2. Valuing quantity (more) over quality (better)
3. Valuing competition over cooperation
4. Valuing specialization over wholeness

Operating on such a value system, both leaders and followers seem to have become locked into the status quo for an extended period of time. Yet during that period, many have talked about the virtues of honesty, truthfulness, integrity, and loving thy neighbor as thyself. This has not been common. As the British economist Lord Keynes said in 1930, "For at least another hundred years we must pretend to ourselves and to everyone that fair is foul and foul is fair; for foul is useful and fair is not. Avarice and usury and precaution must be our gods for a little longer still. For only they can lead us out of the tunnel of economic necessity into daylight."[2] In short, he seems to have said that the road to heaven is paved with bad intentions—that our golden rule must be "do the other fellow before he does us." So we have accepted the assumption that humans can be expected to perform at their best only when they can anticipate gain. The "profit motive" provides the ultimate stimulus for maximum productivity, whether in business, industry, government, or in education.

Certainly the evidence supporting the notion that humans are, by nature, selfish, greedy creatures seems overwhelming. To question that assumption would seem to border on lunacy. In *Zen and the Art of Motorcycle Maintenance*, Persig talks about fixing his motorcycle. But a stuck screw keeps him from getting at the part that needs fixing. Until he can get that screw unstuck, there is no way of repairing his cycle.[3] It is suggested that the individual human being is the stuck screw in our society—stuck with being a selfish, greedy creature that has our industrial society locked into a series of dilemmas.

HUMAN NATURE—BASIC NEEDS

What has been referred to as human nature could more appropriately be termed human behavior. The author prefers to define human nature by focusing on those characteristics that are unchangeable regardless of changing conditions. In his book, *The Next 10,000 Years*, Adrian Berry bases his projections on the continuation of the selfish, greedy characteristics of humans—that "human reaction to stimuli will remain constant."[4] Although Berry does project the survival of the human species during the next 10,000 years, the picture he projects is neither credible nor desirable to this reader.

However, if people can shift the focus away from the overt behaviors of humans that Berry and others have labeled "human nature" and take a careful look at the basic needs of humans, it is possible that we can develop a more accurate identification of the basic unchangeable characteristics of humans that we would be more justified in calling "human nature." Also, those characteristics will provide a basis for inventing a desirable future.

The author would agree with Maslow's hierarchy of human needs.[5] At the base, Maslow identifies the physical needs for survival, including food, clothing, shelter, sleep, reproduction, and health. Then he identifies love, recognition, and self-actualization as the basic emotional needs for maximum self-fulfillment. Maslow overlooked one other very important emotional need. As gregarious creatures, humans not only need others for love and recognition, they need to be needed by others. Thomas Huxley once observed that "not to be needed is the greatest shock the human system can sustain."[6] Being needed at a very early age may have been one of the most important factors that sustained young people while they were growing up during the rugged days of early agrarian society. Conversely, not being needed, sometimes until adulthood, may be the most important factor that burdens our youth in today's society. What are the implications of these basic human needs for the family, for our schools, for the world of work, for government, for our total society?

When basic physical or emotional needs are not being met, or are being threatened, individuals are likely to exhibit fears through behaviors often labeled as selfish or greedy. Perceptions of a strong threat to physical or emotional security may create reactions which range from flight to fight, from withdrawal to physical attacks against the source of the perceived threat. When someone challenges a cherished belief held over a period of time, emotional security may be threatened to such an extent that we either withdraw, by physically walking away or by refusing to listen, or we attack.

In March of 1933, during that fearful period when the stock market had collapsed and banks were closing all around us, Franklin D. Roosevelt made his famous statement that: "All we have to fear is fear itself." It is possible, however, that fear may be the basic cause for most negative-aggressive behaviors—from anger and hate to crimes of physical violence, those behaviors that have been attributed to selfishness and greed and to the evil nature of humans. These assumptions concerning fear and the results of fear[7] provide a basic explanation for why many behave as though selfishness and greed are basic to the nature of humans, for we have been surrounded by threats to our physical and emotional security to such an extent that we have been unable to attend to our basic physical and emotional needs.

HUMAN NATURE—BASIC POTENTIALS

Human potentials might also be considered as a part of human nature. And if educators can help develop those potentials to the fullest, then it may be possible to overcome many perceived threats to our physical and emotional security:

1. *Humans possess a high degree of curiosity.* We want to know. In *Your Most Enchanted Listener*, Wendell Johnson said: "The average 4-year-old asks 400 questions a day in the heroic effort to get the world inside his head."[8] Traditionally, however, schools have ignored that curiosity and have tried to get the child to answer school questions, about which the child may have little or no curiosity at that moment—questions which the child is not ready to pursue. It might be more profitable, as well as more humane, to focus our energy on helping the child find answers to his or her questions, and to learn how to ask better questions. Again from Johnson: "The wise man knows what the questions are; if then, we insist on answers we can trust, we shall become wise in finding them."[9]

2. *Humans possess a high potential for learning and learning how to learn*—as demonstrated by the research reported by Benjamin S. Bloom in his book: *Human Characteristics and School Learning.* . . . Bloom concludes that about 95% of our students have about equal capacities for learning anything taught in our schools when appropriate learning conditions are provided for each student.[10] If Bloom's conclusion is valid, then educators have a real challenge. For, then, world citizenship might become a real possibility—answering a question raised earlier. That conclusion, of course, presents a threat to some cherished notions about the normal distribution curve as it has been applied to student capacities for learning.

3. *Humans possess a high potential for creativity.* No matter how primitive the tribe of people studied by anthropologists and linguists, each tribe was found to have invented a very sophisticated language system for communicating

with each other about their world as they perceived it. Americans have underestimated the power of creativity in learning. At a conference on creativity several years ago, S. I. Hayakawa observed that all real learning involves a creative act on the part of the learner. And when engaged in a creative act, the heartbeat increases. Learners become oblivious to hunger and to the passage of time. And the energy released is comparable to that in the fight-flight situation when the emotion is fear. But in the creative act, the ultimate emotion is joy. In his Creativity booklet, published by Kaiser-Aluminum, Don Fabun stated that "The creative person is a perpetual child. Tragically, most of us grow up."

4. *Humans possess a high potential for self-reflection*—the potential to reflect on why they see things as they do, to reflect on why their perceptions differ from the perceptions of others, to reflect on the limitations of their experiences—so they can determine what new experiences may be needed in order to continue their learning about themselves and the universe surrounding them.[11] This potential may be the most important and the least developed in all of us.

Curiosity, learning capacities, creativity, and self-reflection, all need to be enhanced to the maximum if each person is to become a crew member of spaceship earth, rather than being a mere passenger.[12] Instead of focusing attention on the selfish, greedy behaviors of humans, people in education can shift their attention to meeting the basic human needs and to developing the basic human potentials for creative learning. It may then be possible to learn how to live in a global village before it is too late.

DEVELOPING NEW MYTHS

There is a need to face up to the enormity of the problem involved if society is to develop a new set of myths—as Robert Theobald suggests in his book: *Beyond Despair*—a new set of myths (assumptions) that are appropriate for today and tomorrow.[13] For the new myths may be diametrically opposed to some of our most cherished assumptions that form the basis for our current behaviors and practices. If applied to our unstated values, listed earlier, it could mean valuing *people over things, quality over quantity, cooperation over competition, wholeness over specialization,* etc.

Bloom deals with the problem of changing myths (or beliefs) about learning potentials. He says that "Research, lectures, and injunctions to the teachers to have greater faith in the learning potential of their students are not very effective.

Each teacher can and will change his or her beliefs in the learning potential of their students *only* by discovering this in the classroom."[14] Bloom committed the error of overgeneralization by using the word "only." There is often agreement that obtaining first-hand evidence in the classroom would be an appropriate way for a teacher to change his or her convictions on this issue. On the other hand, Bloom ignored the reflective capacity of humans, including teachers, which enable participants to arrive at convictions through a careful examination of past experiences.

For example, when this writer took chemistry in high school, he concluded that he did not have the capacity to learn chemistry. This conviction was discarded early during the first college course in chemistry. Reflecting on that experience and on other similar experiences of myself and others, it was not difficult to accept, tentatively anyway, Bloom's research and conclusions about learning potentials. Also, reflecting on those experiences helped to create an appreciation for the importance of providing learning experiences appropriate for each student's background—so that he or she would have enough success to develop a positive self-image about his or her capacity to learn whatever needs to be learned.

Certainly, the need for specialization in today's technological world is so obvious that it would seem ridiculous to spend any time discussing the pros and cons. Sometimes, however, the obvious needs to be re-examined. Isaac Goldberg once said: "Man pays for his specialization. In his attempt to conquer the part, he loses contact with the whole; and, bereft of this sense of entireness, he is left to contemplate, rather uneasily, a sheaf of brilliant fragments."[15] That statement points to another kind of dilemma that our industrial society has been facing for many years. John Gardner alluded to that dilemma several years ago when he said: "We have reached the point in our specialization when there is no one left to deal with the problems that cut across specializations."

Should specialization be considered as an "either-or" situation? Rather than condemning specialization, would it be preferable to consider overspecialization at too early an age. In his book, *The View from a Distant Star*, Harlow Shapley argues that one should not specialize before graduate school, so that the specialization can be viewed more intelligently.[16] But today, in effect, we start kids specializing as soon as they enter school by breaking all of their learning into fragments—one period for reading, one for writing, one for arithmetic, etc. Then at the secondary level, the student has a different teacher for each specialty, with no connections made among them. Is it any wonder that so many students end up with intellectual indigestion?

APPLYING NEW MYTHS

If, in another perspective, schools were organized around basic human needs and potentials, starting at the elementary level, so that 95% of the students maintained a positive self-image about themselves and their capacity to learn, imagine the quantity and the quality of learning that would take place with that many productive learners stimulating each other on a cooperative basis! Imagine the fulfillment of the human emotional needs for love and recognition, and the need to be needed, when the excitement of creativity through interaction has replaced the fear of failure! Imagine the productivity that would result from the absence of all the negative-aggressive behaviors that are caused by the fear of failure! Imagine the time that would be saved when each student is so engaged in the creative process of learning and of helping other learners that discipline problems no longer exist! Imagine the atmosphere that would prevail when each student regularly experiences love and recognition and being needed by others! Can we imagine the outcries of exultation at success, ranging from Eureka! and Hallelujah! to "God damn, I did it!"

Can we imagine the kind of society that might develop if teachers, students, parents, grandparents, and other taxpayers were to join together in a joint enterprise to explore where they are, whither they are tending and why, and where they want to go? As Bloom points out, in essence, success not only breeds success and the ability to tackle tougher problems, regular success provides a form of immunization against emotional illness—just as regular failure leads to emotional illness.[17]

Now "come back to earth" and consider some of the consequences of such utopian dreams. If we were to develop an educational program along the lines suggested, that focused on meeting the basic human needs and that developed fully the human potentials identified, would we not create some other dilemmas even more devasting than those already mentioned? There are some possible dilemmas.

First, much has been written about many people who are already suffering from being over-educated. Many college graduates, some with advanced degrees, have been unable to obtain jobs commensurate with their educational attainments, resulting in considerable frustration, unhappiness, even depression. If 95% of the students were to develop their learning potentials to the point suggested, would not society be overwhelmed by millions of frustrated, unhappy, depressed people? Wouldn't mental and emotional illness increase dramatically, instead of decreasing as Bloom suggests?

It is suggested that the emotional problems referred to are not the result of over-education, but the result of over-training or over-specialization. James Jelinek, in the *1978 ASCD Year-book*, makes an important distinction between education and training. He says: "Any response built into the structure of the learner, if it cannot be changed by him, is a dangerous response to acquire. The trained person is forever the slave of the trainer."[18] Too much of what has been going on in colleges and universities should be called "training," not "education." Graduates have not developed their creative learning poten-tials. The fully developed, creative learner, on the other hand, can convert any job that needs doing into a creative enter-prise—the tougher the problem the greater the joy in solving it. Also, each creative learner can become a functioning citizen of our global village.

The second major dilemma concerns the idea that students who grow up in a loving, cooperative atmosphere, where ev-eryone succeeds, will be woefully inadequate to cope with a ruthless, dog-eat-dog, do the other fellow before he does you kind of world when they leave school. It is, perhaps, this sort of view that led Robert L. Heilbroner to his pessimistic con-clusions in his book: *The Human Prospect*. At the end of Chap-ter 4, Heilbroner says: "A failure to recognize the limitations and difficulties of our capacities for response would only build an architecture of hope on false beliefs."[19]

That attitude, it seems to me, provides one of the greatest obstacles to the development and the utilization of our crea-tive human potentials. When accepting any specific limitation of one's ability to do something, one may say: "It can't be done." Consequently, there is a self-fulfilling prophecy. In re-sponse to the dilemma of "raising lambs for the wolves," it is suggested that while raising the so-called lambs, it would be necessary to involve the so-called wolves (the adult world) in the process from the very beginning—thereby civilizing the wolves.

The following is a brief scenario of such a process, of how it might proceed, taking note of Heilbroner's final chapter in the last edition of his book on "What Has Posterity Done for Me?" He concludes that chapter with the hope that *future genera-tions* will discover "the transcendant importance of posterity for them."[20]

A SCENARIO

This scenario is based upon the belief that the time is now for parents, grandparents, and other taxpayers to be involved in working, learning, and planning with educators and stu-dents in order to develop a better future for themselves and posterity.

We had a year to get ready to open a new school—an alter-native school, if you please—that would guarantee success for every student enrolled. We sent personal letters to the parents, grandparents, and other taxpayers in the school community that read something like this:

Dear Parent/Guardian:

We, the staff at the Global Village School, are planning to open the school next September. We will guarantee that every child enrolled will succeed in all of his or her school work and in life after school. In order to succeed in reaching that goal, we will need your help. In fact, your help will be so important that we don't think we can succeed without it. We urge you to come to the first planning meeting on _____. We need your help in deciding how the school should be organized, what should be learned, and how the school should operate. Please check the above date on your calendar. We are looking forward to working with you at that time.

At the first meeting, those attending were seated in small groups, with a staff member acting as recording secretary. After each subgroup had time to get to know each other, they listened to a moving speech by Dan Fader, which he concluded by urging that "caring work" should go on in every classroom—where the students are divided into pairs or threes; the students are required to look after each other so well that the one being "cared for" does as well or better than the one doing the "caring work."[21] Each subgroup then discussed the following questions:

1. What do you think Fader meant by "caring work"—in the nursery school? in the ghetto? in middle-class society? in the classroom?
2. What would we need to do to practice "caring work" in this group? Should we?
3. Can you think of anything that anyone, a child or an adult, has said or done that made you feel good—or that made you feel important?
4. Did it make you want to do your best?
5. Do you think such things should be said or done often in school?
6. Do you think such things should be said or done often outside of school?
7. What could we do to make it happen more often?
8. How do you feel about this meeting? What could be done to make it better next week?

A report was prepared from the records of each subgroup and sent to those who attended and to those who missed the first meeting.

Second Meeting:
"What Do You Do When You're Mad?"—a song by Ruth Bebermeyer—was played.[22] Subgroups discussed the following questions:

1. What do people say or do that makes you mad?
2. Who are the people who make you mad? Older? Younger? Same age? In authority? Subordinate?
3. What do we do when we're mad? What do we want to do? What should we do?
4. Why do people do or say the things that make us mad? How often do you suppose that person has a hurting heart, as the song says?
5. If we were to talk some more, as the song says, what could we talk about that might help?
6. What have we learned about anger and how to deal with it?
7. What should happen in school? Out of school?

Again, a report was prepared and sent to the participants, etc. As the meetings progressed, the discussions gradually moved from "affective-cognitive" topics and questions to those that were more of a "cognitive-affective" nature.

At Meetings # "N," subgroups worked on the following questions:

1. What are the most important problems facing us in today's global village?
2. Which of these problems seem most threatening to our physical survival? Our emotional survival?
3. Which problems seem to be most basic—that must be solved before we can solve other problems? Which must be solved at the same time?
4. What attitudes and values seem to be basic to any one of the problems identified?
5. What do we need to know? What do we need to be able to do to solve any one of the problems identified?
6. Should the major goals for our school include the abilities, attitudes, and values identified?
7. What factors might inhibit or squelch the development of the abilities, attitudes and values identified?
8. What are some factors that might help develop them?
9. What would we need to do to support the positive factors and to eliminate the negative factors?

After a long series of such meetings, the Global Village School had begun to evolve. The parents, grandparents, and the taxpayers became more and more creative learners. Their fears of giving up old ideas and of creating new ideas gradually diminished. Attendance at the meetings increased as time went by, as the participants gradually developed a stronger and stronger self-image, a feeling that they were important, that they were good learners, that they had someting to con-tribute, and that involvement in real learning stimulates ex-citement and joy.

They decided that to help each kid find answers to his or her own questions and to learn how to ask better questions would require a great deal of planning time by the school staff. They decided that the staff should have a minimum of one day out of every five days to get ready for the next four days, that the staff should not work with the kids for more than four days each week. They invented various strategies for taking care of the kids on the planning days, including learning and work experiences that would produce a feeling of importance.

They decided that the school curriculum would need to be very broad—that it should include:

1. Learning to understand self and others; learning how to learn as a creative enterprise, both individually and co-operatively.
2. Learning about their total environment—their global vil-lage, including its renewable and nonrenewable re-sources.
3. Learning to become responsible crew members of their spaceship earth; not passengers.

They decided that the learning atmosphere must be creative and cooperative, that students and staff would need to coop-erate vertically and horizontally, that a trusting relationship was imperative. They recognized how their own initial fears and distrust had diminished as the series of meeting pro-gressed.

Since representatives of the mass media were members of the planning sessions, news about what was going on soon spread throughout the city. Also, members of the planning sessions did lots of talking. Although there were many skeptics at first, curiosity would not be denied. By the time the school opened, a year after the first meeting, other school commun-ities in the city were asking for help in reorganizing their schools. They had no trouble getting volunteers from the ini-tial planning sessions to help them develop and carry out similar sessions.

By the end of the Global School's first year, the school and the city were getting national attention. By the end of the second year, they were getting international attention—not just because of what was happening in the school, but because of what was happening in the total community. Business, industry, and the city government discovered that to really improve the effectiveness of their organizations, they, too, needed to develop the creativity of their employees. They, too, started moving toward a four-day work week for their employees, with the fifth day used for developing the creativity of their employees at all levels. They began to involve their employees more and more in decision-making. There was a remarkable improvement in the quantity and quality of employee productivity.

By the end of the third year, even China and Russia began making inquiries. By the end of the fourth year, the U.N. was becoming a more effective organization, since all governmental organizations were discovering that effective government was possible when the creative learning capacities of its members were fully developed and used. By the end of the fifth year, some major steps toward disarmament were underway, with the savings to be used to help undeveloped nations become more self-sufficient, and to resolve the resources-pollution problems of our global village.

At last, world peace was more than a fleeting dream. For the creative human potential was at last being released from the cold grip of fear. Nothing succeeds like success—especially when we shift our focus from the selfish, greedy human behaviors that have blinded us to the basic human needs and potentials. Can we imagine such a future? Where *do* we want to go?[23]

The time is now! The future is here! Our posterity is us!

This is only a synopsis of a book by the same title, with only the salient points presented here. In the book, the author is attempting to elaborate on the major premises of this paper.

NOTES

1. Haim G. Ginott, *Between Parent & Teenager*, Avon, 1969, p. 36.
2. E. F. Schumacher, *Small is Beautiful*, Harper & Row, 1973, p. 24.
3. Robert M. Pirsig, *Zen and the Art of Motorcycle Maintenance*, A Bantam Book, 1974, pp. 272–281.
4. Adrian Berry, *The Next Ten Thousand Years*, A Mentor Book, 1974, pp. 32 and 62.
5. Abraham Maslow, *Motivation and Personality*, Harper, 1954.
6. John W. Gardner, *Excellence*, Harper & Row, 1961, pp. 182–3.
7. Bonaru W. Overstreet, *Understanding Fear In Ourselves and Others*, Collier Books, New York, 1951.
8. Wendell Johnson, *Your Most Enchanted Listener*, Harper & Brothers, 1956, p. 9.
9. *Ibid.*, pp. 42 and 48.
10. Benjamin S. Bloom, *Human Characteristics and School Learning*, McGraw-Hill Book Company, 1976, pp. 208–16.
11. J. Samuel Bois, *The Art of Awareness*, W. C. Brown Company Publishers, 1966, pp. 153–177.

12. Paul R. Ehrlich and Richard L. Harriman, *How to Be a Survivor*, Ballantine Books, 1971, p. 19.
13. Robert Theobald, *Beyond Despair*, The New Republic Book Company, 1976, pp. 23–25.
14. Benjamin S. Bloom, "New Views of the Learner," *Educational Leadership*, April, 1978, pp. 563–576.
15. F. K. Berrien, *Comments and Cases on Human Relations*, Harper & Brothers, 1951, p. 36.
16. Harlow Shapley, *The View from a Distant Star*, Basic Books, Inc., 1963, pp. 142–155.
17. Bloom, *op. cit.*
18. James John Jelinek, "The Learning of Values," *Improving The Human Condition*, ASCD, 1978, p. 223.
19. Robert L. Heilbroner, *An Inquiry Into The Human Prospect*, W. W. Norton & Company, 1975, p. 124.
20. *Ibid.*, p. 176.
21. Speech by Daniel Fader (Professor, Dept. of English, Language and Literature, University of Michigan) presented at the NCTE Convention, Chicago, Ill., Nov. 1976.
22. From her album "I Wonder," Community Psychological Consultants, 1740 Gulf Drive, St. Louis, Mo., 63130.
23. Alvin Toffler, *Future Shock*, A Bantam Book, 1970, p. 478.

PREPARING FOR TOMORROW'S WORLD: AN ALTERNATIVE CURRICULUM MODEL FOR THE SECONDARY SCHOOLS

Louis A. Iozzi and Janey Cheu

INTRODUCTION

Curriculum change in American education has, on several occasions, been compared to a slowly swinging pendulum. Just as a pendulum oscillates back and forth, the topics, courses, strategies, and ideas prominent at various times in the history of education often fade into the background only to return again at some later time. Sometimes these "innovations" from yesteryear appear in slightly altered form. More often than not, however, they reappear essentially unchanged.

The slow oscillation of this swinging pendulum is frequently altered by well intentioned educators attempting to resolve current crisis situations. This is evidenced by the introduction into the curriculum of a plethora of mandatory courses, focusing on specific problems. For example, several years ago, it became apparent that experimentation with and the use of dangerous, habit-forming drugs was becoming an extremely serious problem. Education responded by requiring all students—and teachers for that matter—to participate in drug education courses. In retrospect, one can seriously question how successful we have been. Did we treat the symptom or the cause?

Among the other more recent examples for education of a "response to crisis" nature are environmental education, energy education, sex education, and death education. Most recently, the holocaust is being promoted for inclusion in the ever expanding school curriculum. Over the years, education has responded to crisis situations which span the spectrum of scale from purely local concerns on through the national curriculum efforts in the sciences, mathematics, and other areas so prominent during the 1960s.

Today's popular movement commonly known as the "back to basics" movement exemplifies the "pendulum" idea and "response to crisis" solutions. Even a superficial glance at the history of education reveals that, at various times, the "basics" were emphasized. So today, the swing of the pendulum has returned. Moreover, this movement has gained momentum, acquiring "crisis" proportions. Who here has not heard the cries that: "Johnny can't read." "Jane can't write." "Scores on the SAT's are dropping." "Taxes are too high; cut out the frills in education."

This is not meant to discredit such noble educational efforts, nor is it an attempt to minimize the important necessity for education to respond to the needs and demands of the times. It would seem, however, that through more, adequate forward-looking educational planning, many of the crisis situations that are encountered might be more easily avoided.

Without belaboring the point, it is well known that American education has for years been criticized for not preparing youth adequately for the future. Many have argued the point, but few have articulated it as well as Marshall McLuhan when he commented that, in education, Americans are racing down a high speed superhighway—looking in a rear-view mirror.

Education of the "pendulum" variety relies on the past; education of a "response to crisis" nature emphasizes, at best, the present. Effective educational planning for the future demands that educators have a clear image of what they would like that future to be. Thus, the kind of educational approach presented in this paper looks to and prepares students for a preferred but constantly changing world—a world in which events can only be partially anticipated.

THE NEXT QUARTER CENTURY AND BEYOND

Why has education to date not been very effective in preparing youth for the situations they might encounter in the future? While many possible reasons might be cited, it is suggested that some of the most notable are the following:

- Not knowing with a high degree of certainty what changes will occur.
- The rapidly increasing rate at which change takes place.
- Present events may or may not have a major impact upon life in the year 2000 and beyond.
- The methods, strategies and techniques employed in futuristics are largely unfamiliar to educational planners and decision-makers.

If the above highly simplified suggestions are at all reasonable, it is clear that teaching which emphasizes recall of specific knowledge, facts, and subject matter is simply not sufficient; nor is this learning technique of enduring significance. An education of this type becomes rapidly obsolete—often before the student has an opportunity to master the subject matter. There are statistics which show how rapidly specific information and knowledge are accumulating. In many instances, such information is too specialized and too rapidly outdated for an inclusion in futures oriented curriculum. Alvin Toffler has over the past decade addressed this issue many times. Certain trends, events, and research can provide important clues, however, for helping us to prepare our students more adequately for tomorrow's world.

Shane summarized the views and forecasts of a distinguished international panel of educators and leaders identifying the important developments which will likely have a significant impact on future events. According to this panel, the next quarter-century and beyond will bring about:

1. A continued acceleration in the rate of change.
2. Greater complexity of life because of new technological breakthroughs.
3. The end of the hydrocarbon age.
4. A need to reassess our present concepts of growth.
5. Continued crowding, over-population, and persistent food shortages.
6. Continued pressure for human equity in all areas.
7. Increased demands from less developed countries for a new economic order.
8. International disagreement and conflict.
9. Changing concepts of work and leisure.
10. Increased governmental debt and capital deficits.
11. Governance problems and threats to freedom.
12. A post-extravagant society (the good old days are gone).[1]

Others including Schwartz, Teige, Epstein and Harman have developed more elaborate and detailed lists of future developments and/or crises to which present day youth will have to respond. For our purpose, however, Shane's summary is quite adequate.

Careful inspection and analysis of the above list reveals that there is a need to cultivate the development of certain kinds of process skills in our youth. It is possible to surmise with a degree of certainty that students need assistance in developing highly flexible and generalizable skills to cope with a rapidly changing world. More specifically, educators must place an emphasis on the development of problem-solving, decision-making, and a variety of analytical or critical thinking skills.

Further review and analysis of the literature in the field of futuristics provide further information as to the kinds of issues that will very likely be prominent in the year 2000 and beyond. These issues include but are not limited to:

Food allocation
Energy allocation and depletion
Advances in biomedical technology
Social unrest and conflict
Environmental quality and modification
Application of existing and emerging technologies
Mental health
Natural resource use
Transportation
Science/technology/society conflict
Land use

Underlying all of these issues are concerns for and about equity, justice, affiliation, property, life, governance, truth, law, individual rights, et cetera. To be considered valid, any curriculum model designed to prepare today's students for the future must necessarily include a moral/ethical dimension.

The intent here is not to identify "specifics" but rather the broad issue areas that will become prominent over the next quarter century and beyond. This perspective is useful because it serves to acquaint the curriculum developer and the student with the general context in which the student's problem-solving and decision-making skills will be applied.

THEORETICAL RATIONALE

The staff at the Institute for Science, Technology, and Social Science Education view education for tomorrow's world as development of those skills necessary for complex problem-solving and decision-making. Moreover, because the dimension of values has such significant ramifications, projected future issues will be, in large part, moral/ethical issues cast in a scientific, technological, and social context.

The goals of development should contain the following components:

- Increased skills in dealing with problems containing multiple interacting variables.
- Increased decision-making/problem-solving skills incorporating a wider societal perspective.
- Increased critical thinking in the evaluation of consequences and implications of alternative actions.
- Increased knowledge of the broad issues emerging and projected for the next quarter century and beyond.

The question, then, is how to best approach the development of more complex and comprehensive problem-solving capabilities. What is the most appropriate approach, particularly in the area of values?

While there are several approaches to values education, the more encompassing approach is the cognitive-developmental approach offered by Lawrence Kohlberg. Kohlberg's ideas are derived from the philosophic position of Dewey and Piaget. The emphasis here is to help individuals grow intellectually and morally. This is perhaps a more functional approach than arbitrary indoctrination of values as used in "character" or "socialization" education or taking a "values relativity" stance, typically employed in the more common values clarification approach.

According to Kohlberg, development of reasoning from childhood to adulthood is viewed as progression through a series of stages. At each successive stage, one's concerns take on a broader perspective. Stages are not skipped nor does regression occur. That is, each stage is characterized by a very different way of perceiving and interpreting one's experiences. At Kohlberg's Stage "2", for example, "right" and "wrong" is judged in terms of satisfying one's own needs and sometimes the needs of others if it is convenient to do so. Stage "3" type of reasoning centers around maintenance of approval in one's own social group. The orientation is towards conformity to group expectation. At the higher principled stages, reasoning takes into account concerns for the welfare of others in a broader context, and includes concerns for human dignity, liberty, justice, and equality—those very same principles on which our Constitution is based.

Kohlberg's cognitive moral/ethical development theory is an extension of Piaget's intellectual development theory. Development is viewed not as mere accumulation of information, but changes in thinking capabilities—the structures of thought processes. In the course of development, higher-level thought structures are attained, and result in the extension of an individual's social perspective and reasoning capabilities. Applying higher levels of thinking to problems results in problem solutions that have greater consistency and are more generalizable.

Typically, this developmental approach has been employed successfully in the social studies education context, but may be readily and usefully adapted to any program in which societal issues are an important concern.

THE SOCIO-SCIENTIFIC REASONING MODEL

Combining the authors' own philosophy, ideas, and research with the theories of Piaget and Kohlberg, the socio-scientific reasoning model has been developed. Socio-scientific reasoning, as defined here, is the incorporation of the hypothetico-deductive mode of problem-solving with the social and moral/ethical concerns of decision-making. This model has served as a guide in the development of a series of educational materials to help students advance to higher levels of thinking and reasoning capabilities. Moreover, it is highly flexible and readily adaptable to other curriculum development efforts.

The basic assumption of this model is that effective problem-solving requires simultaneous development in the realms of logical reasoning, moral/ethical reasoning, and critical thinking. Pure objective scientific thinking cannot be applied in the resolution of most of the projected future conflicts without regard to the impact of those decisions on human needs and human goals. A technological solution, for example, may be, after critical analysis, feasible and logically consistent. From a societal perspective, however, one must question whether or not it should be applied. How to best prioritize our needs and evaluate trade-offs with a concern for the needs of future generations involves logical reasoning and critical thinking, but now with an added dimension—a social moral/ethical reasoning dimension.

Hence, this model consists of four interacting components (see Figure I): cognitive development (A) is based on the theories of Piaget, while moral/ethical reasoning (B) relies strongly on Kohlberg's ideas. The aspects of critical thinking (D) upon which our model relies most heavily are generating hypotheses, judging the reliability and the adequacy of data and data sources, deductive logic of an "if-then" nature, and the adequate identification of valid and non-valid assumptions. Since component (C), knowledge of the problem issue, will vary, so too will the concepts vary accordingly. For example, the problem issues and concepts could deal with environment, bioethics, or any other topic one chooses to investigate.

Each component of this model is not seen as a totally sepa-

Figure I
The Socio-Scientific Reasoning Model
Increased Complexity

A = Cognitive Development (Piaget)
B = Moral/Ethical Reasoning (Kohlberg)
C = Knowledge (of Problem Issue)
D   Critical Thinking
         (1) Hypothesis Testing
         (2) Judge Reliability/Adequacy of data and sources
         (3) Deductive logic (if-then)
         (4) Identification of valid/non-valid assumptions

rate and distinct entity. Rather, each component interacts with and has an effect on all other components. Thus, cognitive development has an effect on moral/ethical reasoning. These interact with critical thinking which in turn interfaces with knowledge and all other components.

While each stage reflects a distinctly unique mental capability for problem-solving, development progresses in a continuous spiraling process. In this process there are, however, leaps and halts. Fixation at any stage is possible.

The goal is to help all students to "spiral" or progress through the stages and to achieve their "more adequate" or higher potential.

This model responds to the need to stimulate upward progression. Research assessing development in Piaget's cognitive and Kohlberg's moral/ethical stages reveal that people do not advance at a consistent rate. Often, particularly at the upper levels, we find low rates of advancement or fixation at a given stage. For example, research findings indicate that about 50 percent of late adolescent and adults are formal logical thinkers, while only about 10 percent of the formal thinkers reason at Kohlberg's principled moral/ethical level.[2] These findings further suggest that although reasoning in the moral/ethical realm is dependent on cognitive development, it does not necessarily develop in a synchronous manner.[3]

CURRICULUM STRATEGIES TO PROMOTE UPWARD PROGRESSION

The application of our socio-scientific reasoning model centers on identifying those learning experiences important for assisting students to advance through the stages. In addition, this model will also help curriculum developers determine the type of activities appropriate for different students at different grade levels, with different needs. Implicit in the stage theory is that at each stage there is a characteristic form of thinking capability upon which experiences and information are interpreted and acted. An example of those strategies and activities which we consider appropriate for secondary school students is found in Figure II.

The strategy underlying all of these activities is that of creating disequilibrium. According to Piaget, it is only when disequilibrium is created that active restructuring of thought processes takes place, leading to movement to the next higher stage. Restructuring occurs when internal disequilibrium is felt by the individual. New experiences and inputs, which are not readily comprehensible to the individual, challenge his/her existing mode of thought by revealing inadequacies or inconsistencies in that problem-solving strategy.[4] Arrestment at a given stage is partially explained by the developmental theor-

Figure II

Module	Knowledge	Critical Thinking	Moral/Ethical Reasoning
Beacon City: A Land Use Simulation*	X		X
Bioethics, Dilemmas in	X	X	X
Environ. Dilemmas: Critical Decisions for Society	X	X	X
Energy: Decisions for Today and Tomorrow	X	X	X
Future Scenarios in Communication	X	X	X

(* – Field test duration—2 weeks)
X = pre-post test difference significant at .05 level or higher

ists as the lack of opportunities that create conflict or dissonance which place the individual in a position where he/she
needs to reassess his/her particular mode of thinking. Perhaps,
as Clive Beck points out, the reason why people do not develop
morally is because they have not had the opportunity to en-
tertain alternatives—their imaginations have not been extended.[5]

The following have been identified as some of the basic elements needed to provide experiential opportunities that would
promote development toward higher levels of reasoning:

• Exposure to alternative viewpoints
• Taking the perspective of others
• Examining and clarifying one's own ideas
• Examining the consequences and implications of one's
  own decisions
• Defending one's position

One educational activity incorporating these elements is the
classroom dilemma discussion, an activity most commonly employed by Kohlberg and his colleagues. We have, however,
modified and extended this approach to encompass more critical analysis and evaluation of information and data, as well
as employed other formats such as role playing, simulations,
and future forecasting and analysis methodologies.

Our approach focuses on dynamic student-to-student interaction with the idea that, within a heterogeneous classroom,
there is a diversity of stage reasoning models. Through discourse, students are thus exposed to divergent viewpoints and
different levels of reasoning. Students taking different positions will question and challenge "why" a particular stance is
held. In the course of discussion, students will reflect on their

own thinking, clarify their arguments, and evaluate the adequacy of their reasons. The emphasis is not on the desirability or value of one position over the other, but the reasoning given in support of the arguments. In a heterogeneous group, the students thus encounter higher levels or + 1 reasoning.

Effective discussion, however, cannot take place in a vacuum. Needed also is a knowledge base or context from which students can begin to analyze and evaluate information. With information which they have extracted and synthesized, additional ideas and rational arguments can be developed for discussion. For curriculum materials, we have created problem situations in a variety of contexts which, according to scholars in the field of future studies, will probably be prominent in the next quarter century and beyond. This adds another perspective to the dilemma problem—that which elicits scientific logical reasoning in addition to moral/ethical reasoning—but in a futuristic context.

Included in each curriculum module are several types of extension activities. These serve as mechanisms for students to put some of the ideas and judgments that have emanated from the discussion into larger structural frameworks. They also provide students with opportunities to project into the future, to think beyond their own immediate experiences and to consider the impact of different decisions on future society.

CURRICULUM MATERIAL BASED ON THE SOCIO-SCIENTIFIC REASONING MODEL

The curriculum materials produced by our institute exemplify the flexibility, adaptability, and effectiveness of the sociscientific reasoning model in curriculum development efforts. The materials are "free standing" modules that can be used in a number of different courses in a variety of ways. This circumvents the problems often encountered when implementing new courses of study in the existing, highly structured school programs. Moreover, it illustrates our belief that decision-making for the future requires a transdisciplinary approach. Future issues of prominence will impinge upon nearly every subject area of study.

Typically, each module can be conducted within a 4 to 6 week period. To date, we have produced 10 modules, and by the end of the current school year, four additional modules will be available. Modules for the senior high school level are:

Dilemmas in Bioethics
Environmental Dilemmas: Critical Decisions for Society
Beacon City: A Land Use Simulation
Technology, and Society: A Futuristic Perspective
Future—New Jersey: The Quality of Life

Food—Dilemmas and Critical Decisions
The Rights of the Environment: A Social Dilemma

For the junior high school, the modules are:

Energy: Decisions for Today and Tomorrow
Perspectives on Transportation
Future Scenarios in Communications
Coastal Decisions: Difficult Choices
Space Encounters
Technology and Changing Life Styles
People and Environmental Changes

The modules range on a continuum from those which are highly structured sequentially to those which contain discrete, independent activities. The modules for the lower grades tend to be more structured with subsequent activities building upon skills learned in prior activities.

All the modules, however, are related by a common thread. They provide meaningful experiences for students which stimulate an internal personal sense of conflict and expose them to higher level reasoning in the context of emerging future issues. As indicated, this process can be effected using a variety of educational techniques, provided that they are appropriate for the unique thought structures of different cognitive levels and offer opportunities for students to reflect upon the adequacy of their own thinking. In addition, all modules relate existing and emerging conflict issues at the interface of science, technology, and society.

ASSESSMENT OF THE SOCIO-SCIENTIFIC REASONING MODEL

Initial field tests of our first five curriculum modules involved more than 3,000 New Jersey school children in grades 7 through 12. The results of these field tests, which included pre- and post-test scores and other data on both experimental and control groups, indicated that exposure to these curriculum materials produced increases in knowledge content, critical thinking skills (*Cornell Critical Thinking Test*) and moral/ethical reasoning.[6] Papers and research reports dealing with the specific results achieved, using each module tested to date, are in preparation. It is anticipated that these reports will be available for distribution in 1979.

CONCLUSION

The socio-scientific reasoning model which has guided our curriculum development efforts is an effective and relevant model for educating youth for tomorrow's world. The developmental perspective offers several important dimensions in curriculum development. Emphasizing simultaneous development in the intellectual and moral/ethical realms, this curriculum approach may better prepare students for decision-making about present issues as well as issues projected to be of major importance in the next quarter century and beyond. Through understanding the ways that students structure information at their different thinking levels, we can then develop those instructional materials that will help advance their thinking.

We are thus confident that application of this model is most appropriate for promoting one of our major goals: effectively preparing youth to function in an increasingly changing and complex world—tomorrow's world.

NOTES

1. Shane, Harold G. *Curriculum Change Toward the 21st Century.* Washington, D.C. National Education Association, 1977.
2. Kohlberg, Lawrence. "The Cognitive Approach to Moral Education," *Phi Delta Kappa, 56:* 670–70, 1975.
3. Tomlinson, Keasey, Carol and Clark B. Keasey. "The Mediating Role of Cognitive Development in Moral Judgment." *Child Development, 45,* pp. 291–298, 1974.
4. Piaget, Jean. "Piaget's Theory," in P. H. Mussen (ed.) *Charmichaels Manual of Child Psychology,* New York: Wiley, 1970.
5. Beck, Clive M. *Ethics.* Toronto: McGraw-Hill, 1972.
6. Rest, James. "New Approaches in the Assessment of Moral Judgment." In Thomas Lickoma (ed.) *Moral Development and Behavior: Theory, Research and Social Issues,* New York: Holt, Rinehart and Winston, 1976.

COMMON CHARACTERISTICS OF UTOPIAN AND FUTURISTIC MODELS OF SOCIETY

Hans Joachim Harloff

Perhaps the most fundamental form of education is that which shapes an entire cultural system for the individual by forming a new community structure. Both futurists and utopians have proposed such profound educational shifts. How do their ideas compare?

First, some definitions. The concept "utopia," unfortunately, has been divested of its original, purely positive, meaning; frequently it has even been turned into the opposite. By the use of the term "utopian," the ideas of political opponents are frequently relegated into the realm of dreams and vain hopes. But this trait of non-realizability cannot be found in the writings of Sir Thomas More, the originator of the concept "utopia." According to More, utopia is, rather, a state of ultimate perfection in regard to political, legal, and social conditions. It is the society of reason, which More contrasts to the social structures prevailing at the beginning of the 16th century, which he conceived of as being ruled by selfishness and greed. Utopia was the ideal that the rulers of his time were to put into practice. The misunderstanding (i.e., the criticism of non-realizability) was brought about in part by More himself, for he chose the word ou-topos = nowhere; but by this he meant *nowhere realized* and not *nowhere possible*.

A worse misunderstanding is that "Dystopias" such as George Orwell's *1984* or Huxley's *Brave New World*[1] or apparent fools' paradises such as Gilgamesh's *Dilmun* or Lucian's *Island of the Blessed* were called utopias.[2] Some authors (e.g., Doxiadis) have therefore thought to replace the concept utopia by the term "Entopia."[3]

The best way to use the term utopia is to signify a society of reason and humanitarianism, which unfortunately can be implemented only over the resistance of ruling political and economic interests. Utopia might be what Todd and Wheeler call a "fountain of hope, guideline for political action, embodiment of reason, solution of social problems, road to happiness, the ideal towards which we must strive."[4] In this sense, the beginning of Utopian literature is frequently seen in Plato's *Republic* or even earlier; the old testament and in particular the five books of Moses can be conceived of as the first model of a utopian society.

Futuristic societies are those societies which, in the opinions of social scientists, will come about because they are inevitable. A secondary meaning refers to societies which come about if humanity is to be saved from certain doom. But it should be emphasized that societies that will or must come about, simply because they are projections of prevailing trends, are of relatively little importance to us. They are merely of peripheral interest, since in the case of societies there is no such concept as "must come about." This author believes that all conditions of society are man-made and can be shaped or fashioned almost at will. Hence, the free-will conception of history (people themselves draw the blueprint for ideal societies and to subsequently put them into practice) is the most valid position to take. But determination has its place, in the sense that the awareness of historic trends permits one to see where history would go if not consciously molded.

Because of the widely prevalent misunderstanding of "unrealizability," it cannot be emphasized strongly enough that utopias, as we have defined them here, have often been realized. Although most of them have been short-lived, there were and are others that have had long-term success. Examples are the Israeli kibbutzim, the Herrnhuters, and the Hutterites (the last two, however, because of their extraordinary economic successes, have frequently been considered political/social dangers).[5] Today's commune movement can be perceived as the beginning of an international utopian network, with the goal of creating a world-wide humanitarian order and the corresponding transformation of industrial societies.

COMMON TRAITS OF UTOPIAN SOCIETIES

Proposals for utopian societies are so numerous that it would be no easy task to compare them all, especially since their traits are so widely divergent. Yet, in the case of many of these draft proposals, one can find astonishing correspondences which up to now have not been given sufficient recognition.

Common Characteristics:

1. In size, individual communities of utopian societies usually encompass somewhere between one hundred and one thousand people (one thousand being just about the upper limit). Skinner's *Walden Two* and Steve Gaskin's Farm have

one thousand inhabitants (but not its practical realization at Twin Oaks).[6] As a rule, however, one to three hundred people constitute a community. A Hutterite communal farm, for instance, consists of 120–130 individuals and, in case of further growth, divides into two separate communities.[7] Most of Fourier's phalanxes had hardly more than one hundred inhabitants, although according to Fourier's and his student Brisbane's plans, these groups were to encompass 1,600 and 400 members respectively.

2. Utopian societies, as a general rule, consist of subsistence communities. This, for instance, is true of Plato's Republic and of Jewish communities that put into practice the commands of the Torah. Nature is not to be exploited any more than are human beings; but enough will be produced to satisfy the physical needs of all.

3. Beyond satisfaction of material needs, the members of utopian societies have, as a rule, a common goal which aims at the realization of certain internal and/or external conditions. This goal differs fro utopia to utopia, but is agreed upon within any single utopia.

4. In virtually all utopian communities, means of production are commonly owned. Plato's *Republic* is the one well-known exception. But Sir Thomas More's *Utopia*, Skinner's *Walden Two*, the kibbutzim, the Amana communities, the Hutterites, *Oneida*, and social-reformative utopias of Robert Owen (New Harmony), Charles Fourier (phalanxes) and Etienne Cabet (Icarian movement), the Shakers, Rappists, Herrnhuters—all practice in general common ownership of, or at least common control over, means of production.

5. In most utopias, communal living prevails (i.e., the individual or the individual family has only one room to itself and otherwise uses the communal facilities, such as the communal bath, kitchen, dining halls, etc.).

6. In many utopias, children form their own sub-society. This applies not only to Skinner's *Walden Two* and to the kibbutzim,[8] but also the Hutterites, the Perfectionists of Oneida, or the Owenites in New Harmony. In substantially weakened form—but particularly admirably—special children's communities are found in Huxley's *Island*. There, on the average, twenty couples form a MAC, a mutual adoption club. Each couple adopts the children of all other couples and the children move back and forth at will among the homes of their parents and of their numerous adoptive parents.

7. Affection of people for one another/love is the supreme law in utopian societies. As is well known, the commands of the Torah were summarized by Christ as follows: "Do unto others as you would have others do unto you" (book of Matthew, chap. 7, verse 12); and before, in chapter 5, verse 4 ff, the command to love is explicitly extended to enemies: "Love

your enemies; pray for those who persecute you." Not all utopian societies have such high demands for their members, but all put the love of the community's inhabitants for one another over and above material possessions. Derived from this, the spiritual and emotional wellbeing of all and the development of each personality is given priority. War, aggression, or even competition of the members of the same society among one another are rejected.

8. As a general rule, utopian societies are based on equality of all members and are democratically organized. Positions in society are distributed irrespective of race, sex, and—within limits—also age. Naturally, there are some exceptions here. For example, the expertocracy in Skinner's *Walden Two* is not democratic (and was not incorporated into the realization of his utopia at Twin Oaks).[9]

9. The organization of work and its practical applications are also liberal, human and democratic. As a rule, there is no separation between mental and physical labor, and no alienation. People can realize themselves in their work, or, at least, work is a useful contribution to the life of the community. Monotonous and strenuous activities are carried out by most or all of the population and are not imposed on a socially discriminated group or class.

10. Among the members of a community of a utopia, these characteristics result in a strong feeling of unity. In the case of actually existing utopias, this cohesion, to be sure, is in part brought about by the ultimate acceptance for membership of only those persons who can be well assimilated into the existing community.

DRAFT MODELS OF FUTURISTIC SOCIETIES

The models conceived by futurists are not completely uniform either. Some advocate zero or even negative rates of economic growth for industrial countries so as to save raw materials for future generations and for less developed countries.[10] In opposition, there are others who maintain that economic growth in advanced industrialized countries is the only remedy for the economic problems of the Third and Fourth World. In these advanced countries, it is asserted, only high growth rates will provide the means that would enable industry to shift to production procedures not harmful for the environment.[11]

This is not the place for an extensive discussion with the growth fetishists. Yet three important counterarguments should be repeated:

—Precautionary motives alone should command that further growth be foregone (what would happen if "human

ingenuity" did not discover, on time, substitutes for exhausted raw materials?);
—Recycling does not solve, but merely postpones, the ex-
haustion of raw materials;
—Finally, the fact that matter is finite contradicts any possibility of unlimited (progressive) growth.

In this connection, it is more important to point out that
even without raw material shortages and without any obligation to consider the needs of poorer countries, citizens of
advanced industrialized nations ought to change their life
styles. Symptoms such as drug abuse and alcoholism, juvenile
and child delinquency, and organized gang-terrorism leave no
doubt that our society is sick. In most cases, it is not worry
about future generations nor concern about developmental
opportunities of poorer nations that drives hundreds and thousands of young people into alternate subcultures; the motivation is rather stress, strain and alienation in an automated
job environment, as well as the emotional frigidity and agres-
siveness of people in our anonymous metropolises.[12] Our society is characterized by lack of love and the transfer of all
difficult problems to heartless institutions. Addicts are
handed over to detoxification centers, the sick and the dying
to hospitals, the old to old age homes, the mentally ill to psychiatric wards, the law violators to penal institutions.[13] In
other words, wherever people are in need, our society fails; by
means of modified application of force, it tries to lead deviants
back unto the path of "virtue" (i.e., assimilation), or it excludes
them all together from participation in public life.

As compared to this, what are the model societies that futurists recommend as a remedy? The new society that uses
resources sparingly and thereby gives due consideration to
future generations and the needs of less developed countries
can be outlined in the following headings:

(1) quasi-village units
(2) communal living
(3) striving for self sufficiency/self reliance and renunciation of excessive consumption
(4) small nets
(5) quartic sector/sector D
(6) intermediate technology/soft systems

In part, the concepts embodied in these recommendations
overlap. They paraphrase mutually complementary aspects of
one and the same vision of the future, in which merely the
emphases are shifted.
(1) Quasi-village units: In the past it has been suggested

that today's predominantly urban populations be transferred
to quasi-villages (100–300 persons in a compact building structure).[14] Cost and raw material savings in construction and
maintenance of living quarters speak in favor of such a measure. More important, however, are psychological reasons:

—Only in a small unit of maximally 300 members can persons as individuals get sufficient attention and consideration from others, and develop enough self respect to be
happy. Only in such communities can they conceive of
themselves as irreplaceable.[15]

—Only in such a small unit of 300 persons can a new environmental consciousness be developed (i.e., a feeling of
responsibility for the "neighborhood," for the municipality
and for yet larger entities).

—Only in such a small community can sufficient "social control" prevail to exert moral pressure on those who want
to gain advantages from the community, but do not want
to assume any responsibilities.

—Only the small unit can grant to all the right to participate
in decision-making.

—Only the small unit is flexible enough to be able to coor-
dinate the job assignment of all according to their individual desires and to the communal needs.

In this connection, it must be noted that, in accordance with
recent ecological findings, the dispersion of all people into
quasi-villages over the entire arable land no longer seems
necessary. Computations show that, if we shift to nutrition
predominantly from plants alone, the population of not-too-
densely populated cities—such as, for instance, most American
cities—can be fed from the area of the city.[16] This does not
mean that we can surrender the concept of the quasi-village;
rather, these small units must then be created within the city.
So that the positive psychological effects discussed above can
materialize, the advent of these communities must be supported by means of corresponding physical structures.

In any case, we find that on this important point regarding
the size of the individual communities, there is complete
agreement between futurist and utopian social proposals.

(2) and (3) Communal living, striving for self sufficiency/self
reliance, and renunciation of excessive consumption: Futurists suggest that the individual small community by itself or
in association with neighboring units be as economically independent as possible (i.e., that it produces virtually everything necessary to sustain life).[17] In the long run, this will
probably be possible only with a smaller consumption of goods

than prevails today in advanced industrialized societies. But this does not necessarily mean a lower living standard.

In this connection, mounting criticism of equating a higher gross national product with higher living standards or, even worse, with higher quality of life, must be noted. And, it must be considered that in communal living the individual (or the individual small family) has access to many more durable and semi-durable consumer goods than in individual single dwelling or small family homes. Finally, one thought should still be added that appeared in the writings of Skinner and subsequently, in somewhat modified form, was taken up by Schumacher, Galtung and Wirak, Illich, Friedman, Binswanger et al.: A society based on the selfprovisioning of communities needs no banks, insurance companies, advertising, hardly any transportation system, hardly any automobile industry, no cosmetics industry, no bars or taverns, no public administration. Moreover, there would be no unemployment.

Hence, a much greater labor force potential would be at society's disposal to produce the really useful and necessary goods for daily needs. The possibility can, therefore, not be excluded that these things necessary for everyday life would be available to a greater extent than today, even if they were produced with intermediate technology (see below) and with less labor time inputs.[18] So, in regard to the points on survival community and communal living, we find a far reaching correspondence with utopian social proposals.

(4) and (5): From the headings, "small nets" and "quartic sector" one can easily establish a connection with what in the case of utopian communities has been termed the command of love. In the case of the concept of "quartic sector," Friedman points to the fact that, in our industrialized, capitalistic societies, there exists a form of value-creation that is economically invisible since it does not take place via the market.[19] The corresponding performances are not paid for. The activities of the housewife or the house owner who himself repairs his roof is one example. In the futurist society of small self-sufficient communities, most productive activities are those of the quartic sector type. Individuals work for themselves and for the members of their own commune or community. The alienated production of commodities is thus replaced by the production of necessary goods for community needs. Not the drive for profits, but love, a feeling of responsibility, and a striving for self-realization are motives for such production. The same idea is contained in the concept "small nets," as developed by Rusterholz, Geissberger, and Binswanger. Here, however, the old neighborhood concept stands more strongly in the foreground. 15-20 families—as a rule living close to one another—combine by reason of mutual attraction to a "kinship by choice family"

(a small net). This community reduces their dependence on public services by undertaking care of themselves, (for example, care for the sick and the old, education, and the organization of recreational activities).

(6) Intermediate technology/Soft systems: By "intermediate technology" is meant that the members of the futurist society in their production of goods take advantage of a simple technology (i.e., work-facilitating tools rather than automated equipment or other heavy machinery). The society of the future, with its goal of conserving resources, will in its economic activities make increased use once again of the factor of production labor, and less use of man-made ("hard") energy and machines.[20] Instead of alienated, industrial mass production there will be production of individual pieces or of small series, in which the personal efforts of the direct producer will again become visible. Still, this will not lead to the burden of hard physical labor, since heavy and boring activities will be performed by groups.

Thus, in regard to the organization and execution of work, there exists a far reaching correspondence between futurist and utopian social proposals.

The three remaining common characteristics of utopian societies which can be compared to futurist societies are political organization (equality of members), ownership of the means of production, and the common goal of a community (apart from communal provisioning). As to the first two points, there is no substantial agreement among futurists themselves. However, the majority are closer to ideas of socialism (market socialism) and direct democracy than capitalism (whether of the free-market or the centrally controlled state-capitalist varieties), so that even here similarity with utopian models of society can be noted.

As regards common goals within individual communities (apart from problems of communal living and provisioning), the views among futurists agree with one another only to a limited degree. Frequently, this issue is not discussed at all. One interesting proposal that was made by Lynch can be mentioned. He wants intentionally to leave strips of uninhabited land ("waste" land) between settled territories, to be placed at the disposal mainly of newly forming groups. In this manner, new ways for people to live together could always be tried out; or likeminded people—irrespective of what kind (Lynch, apart from ethnic groups, mentioned hobby photographers, homosexuals, and members of radical religious sects)—who for the long run are integrated into other groups, can meet temporarily so that they can dedicate themselves fully to their common interest. This proposal for institutionalized free areas is impressive because it opens the society of the future to innovations and gives more room for the development of individual interests than would be the case with narrower exclusive ties to one's own small community.[21]

PURPOSE OF THIS COMPARISON

In summary, futurist and utopian societies are very similar to each other. Does this correspondence prove anything? Probably not. Why, then, should these comparisons be made? The answer is that we cannot wash our hands of the future. The reader might surmise that if the society of the future and the ideal societies of utopian thinkers correspond to each other, then we need to do nothing but wait for the future, in order to reach the "promised land." Unfortunately, it is not that simple: the societies of the future outlined here do not come by themselves. On the contrary, great efforts on our part and on the part of future generations will be necessary to commit us to new lifestyles proposed here.

Moreover the comparison demonstrates that, if we begin today to work on the society of the future, then we must start basically by building a society of equals, brethren, and free individuals, such as mankind has dreamed about since time immemorial. We start to put into practice what two centuries of industrialization/technicalization and human striving for material possession and well-being has temporarily obscured. This shift will require a tremendous educational achievement. But where better than in institutions like education and the family can such achievements be initiated?

NOTES

1. Lasky, H. *Utopia and Revolution* (London: MacMillan, 1977).
2. Todd, I., & Wheeler, M. *Utopia*. (New York: Harmony Books, 1978) and Skinner, B. F., Foreword In K. Kinkade, *A Walden Two Experiment: The First Five Years of Twin Oaks Community* (New York: William Morrow and Co., 1973).
3. Sommer, R. *Personal Space: The Behavioral Basis of Design* (Englewood Cliffs, N.J.: Prentice-Hall, 1969) p. 146.
4. Todd, I., & Wheeler, M. *Utopia* (New York: Harmony Books, 1979) p. 7.
5. Ungers, L., & O. M. *Kommunen in der Neuen Welt* (Koln: Kiepenheur und Witsch, 1972.)
6. Kinkade, K. *A Walden Two Experiment—The First Five Years of Twin Oaks Community* (New York: William Morrow and Co., 1973), and Bott, G. *Das Geheimnis der Zwillingseic* Film Uber Die Versuche Anders zu Leben. KDR-TV broadcast, January 22, 1978.
7. See Ungers, L., *Kommunen in der Neuen Welt*, passim.
8. Moos, R., & Brownstein, R. *Environment and Utopia: A Synthesis* (New York: Plenum, 1977), passim.
9. See Kinkade, K., and Bott, G.

10. See Meadows, D., Meadows, D., Zahn, E., & Milling, P. *Die Grenzen des Wachstums—Bericht des Club of Rome zur Lage der Menschheit.* Stuttgart: Deutsche Verlags-Anstalt, 1972; Jungk, R. *Der Jahrtausend-mensch—Bericht aus den Werkstatten der Neuen Gesellschaft* (Munchen/Gutersloh/Wien: C. Bertelsmann, 1973); Goldsmith, E., Allen, R., Allaby, M., Davoll, J., & Lawrence, S. *Planspiel zum Uberleben—ein Aktionsprogramm* (Munchen: Deutscher Taschenbuch Verlag, 1975); Goldsmith, E. "Entindustrialisierung—unsere uberlebenschance," In *Die Tagliche Revolution-Moglichkeiten des Alternativen Lebens in Unserem Alltag* (Frankfurt a.M.: Fischer Taschenbuch, 1978); Galtung, J., & Wirak, A. *Human Needs, Human Rights, and the Theory of Development* (Oslo: Professoratet i konflikt-og fredsforskning, Papers no. 37, 1976); and Harloff, H. J., "Zukunftige Mobilitatser-Fordernisse Westlicher Industrienationen." In D. Mertens und M. Kaiser (Eds.), *Berufliche Flexibilitatsforschung in der Diskussion, Materialienband 2: Sozialstrukturelle Bedingungen und Gesellschaftliche Auswirkungen von Beruflicher Flexibilitat* (Nurnberg: Institut fur Arbeitsmarkt und Berufsforschung der Bundesanstalt fur Arbeit, 1978).
11. Bundesministerium fur Wirtschaft. *Mehr und Sichere Arbeitsplatze Durche Wachstum* (Bonn-Duisford: Referat Presse und Information, 1977); Friedrichs, G. *Technischer Wandel und Beschaftigung* (Bonn-Bad Godesberg, 1977); Beckerman, W. *Two Cheers for the Affluent Society* (New York: Saint Martin's Press, 1974) and Kahn, H. S. in W. L. Oltmans (Ed.), *On Growth* (New York, 1974), pp. 313-325.
12. Bahr, H. E. "Liebe, Gluck: Zunehmende Verlassenheit—Neue Solidaritat," in H. E. Bahr and R. Grondemeyer (Eds.), *Anders Leben—Uberleben* (Frankfurt, a.M.: Fischer Taschenbuch Verlag, 1977b), and Altman, I. The Environment and Social Behavior (Monterey, Calif.: Brooks & Cole, 1975), p. 41, 160-164.
13. See Rusterholz, H., "Kleine Netze (I)." In *Die Tagliche Revolution: Moglichkeiten des Alternativen Lebens in Unserem Alltag* (Frankfurt a.M.: Fischer Taschenbuch, 1978).
14. See Goldsmith, E., Allen, R., Allaby, M., Davoll, J., & Lawrence, S. *Planspiel zum Uberleben—ein Aktionsprogramm* (Munchen: Deutscher Taschenbuch Verlag, 1975). See also writings of Lynch and Harloff.
15. Bahr, H. E. and Galtung, J. "Weltproduktion fur Grundbedurfnisse," in H. E. Bahr und R. Gronemeyer (Eds.), *Anders leben—uberleben* (Frankfurt, a.M.: Fischer Taschenbuch, 1977).
16. See Vogtmann, H. (Director of the Forschungsinstituts fur Biologischen Landbau, Oberwil, Schweiz). Assertions in a letter in which he refers to Hoffman, *Garten Organischvd.* 1, 1976.
17. Goldsmith talks about ten "neighborhoods" of 500 people each forming a municipality of 5000 inhabitants.
18. Skinner, B. F. *Walden Two.* New York: MacMillan, 1976. (Originally published, 1948).
19. Schumacher, E. F. *Die Ruckkehr zum Menschlichen mass-alternativen fur wirtschaft und Technik* (Reinbek bei Hamburg: Rowohlt, 1977), passim.
20. See Lovins, A. B. *Soft Energy Paths: Toward a Durable Peace.*

(Harmondsworth: Penguin Books, 1977); Schumacher, E. F., Dickinson, D. *Alternative Technologie: Strategien der Technischen Veranderung* (Munchen: Trikont, 1978); Harloff, H. J. and Prokol-Gruppe-Berlin. *Der Sanfte Weg—Technik in Einer Neuen Gesellschaft.* (Stuttgart: Deutsche Verlags-Anstalt, 1976).

21. Lynch, K., "Grounds for Utopia," in B. Honikman (Ed.), *Responding to Social Change.* (Stroudsburg, Penn.: Dowden, Hutchinson, and Ross, 1975).

COMPUTER CONFERENCING: ITS USE AS A PEDAGOGICAL TOOL

Richard B. Heydinger

For the past few years computer conferencing has been heralded as a new form of communication. Its advantages and disadvantages have been discussed, and evaluations of computer conferences have been conducted.[1] Yet only passing reference has been made to the potential which this new form of communication offers for expanding educational opportunities. With the use of computer conferences, "class" meetings can now become time free and space free. Course discussions may literally continue twenty-four hours per day, seven days a week, in any location with phone service. With the continuing interest in external education, individualized instruction, and interdisciplinary course work, computer conferencing offers some significant advantages for expanding educational opportunities. Although the applications of this new form of communication as a pedagogical tool are only at the trial stage, some speculations can be offered on its effectiveness. For some situations computer conferencing can be a powerful device for facilitating communication; yet there are also many barriers to the effective and meaningful use of conferencing in a "conventional" teaching-learning situation.

This paper examines those factors in support of conferencing and those factors inhibiting its growth in light of experiences at the University of Michigan with CONFER, a computer conferencing system developed at the Center for Research on Learning and Teaching (CRLT).[2] For the past three years Karl Zinn, a research scientist at CRLT, and Robert Parnes, the designer of CONFER, have been instrumental in introducing Michigan faculty to the potentials of computer conferencing. Since CONFER first became operational on the Michigan terminal system three and one half years ago, over 100 faculty members have been introduced to CONFER with approximately fifteen of them using CONFER in at least one of their courses. Currently on the Michigan system there are over twenty computer conferences at various levels of activity.

Although some of this article is speculative, much of it is based on the experiences at the University of Michigan.[3]

WHAT IS COMPUTER CONFERENCING?[4]

To take part in a discussion on a computer conference, a person enters her/his message via a computer terminal into a software system which sorts, stores, and selectively transmits these messages as determined by the sender. Messages may be sent to one, some, or all conference participants. Thus, in the context of a traditional course, students can communicate with one member of the class, with only the professor, or with the entire class; and this may be done either anonymously or with the author of the message identified. A complete transcript of the conference is maintained and available to any conference participant upon request. To facilitate conference interaction, discussion items are cross-referenced and may be grouped according to an agenda. This feature allows participants to recall and trace the development of selected topics across the life of the conference. Because the conference is accessed through a time-shared computer system, participants may catch-up on the discussion whenever and wherever it is most convenient for them.

Figure 1
An Example of CONFER

Below is a sample of an interaction on CONFER. All names are fictitious. Because space does not permit, lengthy discussion items are not shown.

To access a CONFERence the user must sign-on to the system, just as one logs onto any computing system. After signing onto the conference, CONFER reminds the user of any personal items that she/he has posted for this particular date (see 1). Next, the user is "introduced" to new conference participants (2). Then, any new responses to public items which have been posted since the last sign-on are noted (3). The user is told what public items have not been reviewed by this user (4) and what private messages are waiting (5). This user chooses to display the private message and responds to it; then checks the responses to an item which she/he had entered previously. The session is concluded by displaying the descriptors of those public messages not yet seen (6).

```
     CONFER II (11/78) - DESIGNED BY ROBERT PARNES
     CONFERENCE FOR CRLT:ORGANIZER
1    REMINDER FOR 11/19/78
     CONTACT PR REGARDING EDUCOM CONFERENCE
     OK? TO DELETE REMINDER: no
2    NEW PARTICIPANTS
     SMYTHE, FRED   00:59   11-16   K556:FLG
     In School of Education. Long Time Fan of CONFER.
     Winston, Gerald   12:58   11-17 XS45:MESSAGES
     Computer Addict........Hi, I'm Back on CONFER (This time on my own
     $$)
```

3 NEW VOTES ON ITEMS:
    10   44   49   50   51   52   53   67
THESE ARE NOW THE * ITEMS
4 LAST ITEM IS ITEM 77
LAST YOU HAVE SEEN IS 74
5 LAST MESSAGE IS 1
DO NEXT? message 1
1 LINES=8 21:08:49 11-19-78
MESSAGE FROM HAYES, DON 12:27 11-18-78 K034:MF
Meeting in my office is set for Friday (11/24/78). I assume that you have
ride from airport.
ENTER FORWARD, REPLY, DELETE, OR IGNORE: reply
ENTER YOUR MESSAGE: TERMINATE WITH $ENDFILE.
I shall get to your office on my own. I shall look in CONFER on
Wednesday (11/22/78) for an agenda for the meeting. Happy Thanks-
giving.
   cc: Brandon $ENDFILE
TO EDIT COPY OF MESSAGE ENTER E:
OK? TO SEND TO HAYES, DON: ok re:meeting is set - no ride
MESSAGE SENT
ENTER RECIPIENT (OR PRESS RETURN): Brandon
OK? TO SEND TO BRANDON, TOM: ok re:meeting in DH's office
MESSAGE SENT
ENTER RECIPIENT (OR PRESS RETURN):
ENTER FORWARD, REPLY, DELETE, OR IGNORE: delete
DELETED
DO NEXT? votes on item 10
ITEM 10 21:19 11-19-78 14 LINES
HEYDINGER, RICK
CENTRALIZATION VS. DECENTRALIZATION OF ADMIN COMPUTING
   AS IT RELATES TO PLANNING
VOTES/FEELINGS
The U of Mich seems to be on the threshold of dealing with this
problem through networking to decentralize the power of the
mainframe host (and its load!) at the computing center to remotes in
indiv. depts. At least they have started. (Bill Winston)
I'm worried about decentralization thru minis because of potential
compatibility and definition consistency problems. Don't you think
registrars will be enticed to develop their own stats to counter those
of the controller's? (Joe Jones)
GIVE YOUR CURRENT FEELINGS AND/OR VOTE ON ONE LINE
6 DO NEXT? describe items 75-77
ITEM 75 15:06 11-15-78 28 LINES PRIME=50
BROADWATER, DOUG
ANOTHER CHANGE TO THE VOTE FACILITY
ITEM 76 12:21 11-16-78 20 LINES PRIME=62
NOWLIN, JOHN
HOW TO GAIN MORE ACCESS TO THE CONFER FORMATTER
ITEM 77 16:08 11-17-78 33 LINES
STRENG, JOEL
INVITATION TO OBSERVE (IN PERSON) THE MID-EAST
SIMULATION GAME BY CONFER

"Electronic mail," which has been widely discussed in the computer and data processing literature, is similar to computer conferencing in that both are message switching systems. However, there are major distinctions between these two new forms of communication[5] and to understand fully the potential which computer conferencing offers education, the differences between these systems must be understood. Electronic mail is a person-to-person communication system. It is designed for *private*, usually two-person exchanges. Copies of transmittals may be easily routed to other users; however, the system resembles a highly sophisticated telegraph. It is not intended that all users of the mail system will communicate with each other simultaneously. Usually, there is no common interest or topic drawing the users of a mail system together.

In contrast, computer conferencing systems are designed to promote *public* communication. Their use facilitates simultaneous communication with *all* members of a conference in order that information may be shared. Although CONFER (as well as other computer conferencing systems) has the capability to send private messages to one or more individuals in the conference, users are most often interested in sharing their insights or comments with all members of the conference. This capability is analogous to the public statement in a face-to-face meeting. Yet computer conferencing adds new dimensions to the usual characteristics of public communication. It is these characteristics of conferencing which give it significant potential for educational use.

Pessimists concerned about the creeping technocracy which characterizes our society should rest assured. Computer conferencing cannot supplant the richness of face-to-face contact between teacher and students. In fact, it is not even a reasonable proxy. Although it can complement the pedagogical process, computer conferencing will not take the place of the lecture, the face-to-face discussion, the blackboard, the textbook, the hands-on laboratory, or the audio-visual aid which is so useful in teaching. Instead, computer conferencing should be

Figure 2
A Summary of CONFER Commands

SUMMARY OF CONFER COMMANDS
A list of CONFER commands that you can enter at DO NEXT follows. Enter the command followed by ? to get more information about each one. You may ⟨ATTN⟩ this printing at any time.

Item output commands.
ITEM   — displays descriptor, text, references, votes, and
                          gets your vote.

DESCRIPTOR — displays descriptor and references.
VOTES — lets you see the votes on an item, and gets your vote.

Item input commands.
ENTER — Lets you enter an item into the conference.
UPDATE — lets you update an old item and enter the updated item into the conference.

Item classification commands.
FORGET — lets you tell CONFER which items you want ignored for your conference activity.
ORGANIZE — lets you create and destroy categories, categorize items and make a selected category the * items.
AGENDA — lets you see the agenda categories and make a selected category the * items.
WHICH — lets you search the conference for a specified character string and make the items having it the * items.

Message related commands
MESSAGES — lets you process messages transmitted to you or stored in a message file.
TRANSMIT — lets you transmit messages to others.

Other useful commands
STOP — terminate the current CONFER session.
BRIEF — lets you view and change your brief notice.
PARTICI-
PANT — lets you check on conference activity of participants and display their brief notices.
NOTICES — lets you view notices from the conference organizer.
REMIND — lets you enter and view postdated reminders to yourself.
? — gives you this printout.

Special purpose commands
COIN — lets you join another conference.
= — lets you change conference IDs.
@ — lets you assume an alias ID.
KEEP — lets you save the text of an item, message, or reminder entered at the previous DO NEXT?
$ — lets you enter an MTS (rather than CONFER) command.
MTS — lets you return to MTS.

Except for STOP and MTS, which must be spelled out, you may use just the first letter of each of the commands at DO NEXT? At any time when CONFER prompts you for input (except when there is a ">" in the left margin), you may enter 7 to receive assistance from CONFER.

seen as a new and different form of communication, one which can greatly facilitate student-faculty interaction in selected situations.

USES OF COMPUTER CONFERENCING

As our experience with conferencing grows, most likely we shall conclude that computer conferencing has limited use in the conventional classroom. It seems to have the greatest potential for non-traditional forms of pedagogy (such as self-paced instruction) and for the non-traditional clientele (such as those who cannot travel to a campus). Yet conferencing potentially has a variety of other applications as well. Although the instructional experiences with conferencing to date are limited, the following uses have either been demonstrated or seem plausible.

Computer conferencing offers the opportunity to break down the geographical barriers of the classroom. Although other forms of technology (such as television, radio and even printed material) can be transmitted directly to the student, at present none of these are interactive. Computer conferencing offers students and faculty an opportunity to interact regardless of their location. For example, if a statewide communication system were available, students from across the state could register for the same course and participate in ongoing "classroom" discussions.

Even more exciting is the possibility of involving outside experts directly in course discussion. For example, a Washington politician could become an adjunct faculty member in a political science course by spending a half hour each day at a terminal in her/his Washington office. For advanced level courses, expert faculty members from other institutions could be called on as resources. For example, by using CONFER, a political science course at the University of Michigan entitled "War in World Politics" involved several senior professors who would not ordinarily have attended classes and several scholars on the topic who were not located in Ann Arbor. Thus, *computer conferencing offers the potential for overcoming the geographical barriers which today prevent many exciting educational adventures.*

Computer conferencing offers the potential for more flexible, more responsible management of a course. A number of courses at Michigan, including the course just previously mentioned, used CONFER to "hand out" assignments, modify the course syllabus, and advise on procedural problems such as the availability of library materials. The capability for easy communication between class meetings offers other advantages, too. For example, in a Law School course entitled "Information Systems and the Law," students were requested to enter their responses to discussion questions on CONFER prior to the next class meeting. In this way, the professor was able to gauge the nature of the problems which students were encountering and prepare the next classroom lecture accordingly. Thus, *computer conferencing allows a course to become a more dynamic learning experience based on the evolving needs of the students.*

Because a computer ("that mathematical machine") is the communication facilitator, most faculty who have not tried computer conferencing assume that topics in the natural sciences are best suited for conferencing. Experience has shown, much to the surprise of those involved, that topics such as policy analysis, literature, and philosophy are enhanced with this computerized communication system. Because the discussion is not bound by the constraints of class meeting time, the subtleties and nuances of a topic may be thoroughly debated. Because all discussion items are entered via a keyboard, students must focus their thinking before "jumping into" the discussion. With the debate being recorded verbatim, the student may trace the major tenets of an on-going interaction. For example, this capability might significantly enhance the learning of an introductory philosophy student who is groping to understand the difference between existentialism and pragmatism. Thus, *conferencing is not limited to the discussion of narrowly defined topics or topics in the natural sciences; early evidence in course use indicates that conferencing may be more useful for discussing topics in the humanities and social sciences.*

The dialogue of a computer conference can also be used to develop course projects. For example, in the course on law and information systems the students use CONFER to state "publicly" the topic which they intend to develop into a term paper. Students are encouraged to react to each others' topics and suggest additional resources or refinements. Obviously, conferencing can only facilitate this interaction; the motivation to interact must still be present. In a similar way, students could also be requested to keep journals or diaries relating to the course and enter these into the conference. For example, students might be asked to enter "the most interesting thing learned this week." Group projects (which are frequently course requirements) can also be enhanced by using conferencing. Team members can communicate easily with one another to develop their topic, agree on a division of labor, or schedule face-to-face meetings. If the team wishes to collect reactions from other class members, conferencing can facilitate this process as well. In all of these examples conferencing facilitates increased interaction and enriches the educational process. Thus, *conferencing facilitates repeated communication amongst students, their peers, and the professor.*

With an increasing emphasis placed on interdisciplinary skills and interdisciplinary courses, computer conferencing offers some significant advantages. Interdisciplinary courses could now involve a large number of faculty from many different departments. For example, a course on the ethics of death and dying could include faculty members from the medical school, law school, and the departments of religion, philosophy, and physiology without requiring them to leave their office, except for their scheduled lectures. This notion need not be confined to the single campus. With the advent of conferencing and nationwide microwave and packet switching networks, courses on esoteric topics can be organized. For example, an advanced level graduate seminar which might only attract one or two students at one institution could be offered simultaneously at a number of institutions with many professors acting as resources. The classroom could be literally nationwide with students receiving credit at their home institution. EDUNET[6] and communication networks such as TELENET are taking this dream and translating it into a reality. Thus, *computer conferencing can significantly expand the resources available for a single course; it is particularly attractive for the interdisciplinary course and the advanced level graduate seminar which can substantially benefit from a mix of resources.*

Computer conferencing offers the possibility for overcoming one of the most troublesome problems facing both individualized and external education, namely "the lonely learner syndrome." Some recent research has shown that students in individually paced, computer assisted courses are *less* likely to complete course material than students placed in the traditional classroom format.[7] Experience with a totally self-paced, four-year liberal arts curriculum also documented a high rate of non-completion.[8] With conferencing, each student could regularly communicate with a faculty member and promptly receive reactions. Frequent dialogue between faculty and students can eliminate this feeling of isolation and can motivate the student to persevere. Through these communiques, the professor could modify course assignments and point students to resources which will meet their individual needs.

Although the telephone offers a similar opportunity, there are some critical distinctions between these two forms of communication. With conferencing both faculty and student enter messages in their own real time, thus giving each party more flexibility. Conferencing also forces students to write-up their inquiries, thus requiring them to think through the exact question which is troubling them. Not only is this process a valuable pedagogical spin-off from conferencing, but with a more focused question the faculty member may be able to respond easily and efficiently. Conferencing may also be less threatening to the student than a phone call. The shy student may carefully compose her/his inquiry allowing plenty of time to overcome nervousness. And, of course, the telephone will always be available to those who prefer it or for those discussions which require dialogue without interruption.

If the technology of conferencing were combined with other instructional technologies, its advantages for both indidivualized and external education might become even more significant. For example, in their own homes students might view a discussion via video disc. Then, by signing on to the course conference the student could react to the material and direct any questions to the faculty member who "teaches" this course. By combining conferencing with existing forms of individualized instruction, students could study at their own pace and place; yet they need not do this in isolation. Thus, *conferencing facilitates individualized education and offers a partial solution to the problem of the lonely learner.*

Conferencing might also augment the student advising which requires interaction with a number of different faculty members. For example, students who design special majors may ideally require advising from two or three faculty members. Conferencing permits faculty members from a variety of different disciplines to discuss and react to the curriculum plan of a student with a specific career interest. At Michigan, CONFER is also being used as the primary communication device for a doctoral advising committee. If a particular question on the thesis research arises, the doctoral candidate may direct the question to a specific faculty member while simultaneously notifying others of the concern. Messages may be easily posted notifying committee members of progress on the thesis. In this way, doctoral committees which rarely come together may stay in touch with the student, offer insights, and enrich the research. Thus, *conferencing offers some unique potentials for enhancing the effectiveness of student advising.*

Conferencing also offers some communication alternatives which may not be immediately obvious. For example, students have at their disposal a vehicle for making anonymous comments to other students and/or the instructor. This permits students to provide candid feedback on a specific lecture or to react to the overall direction of the course without fear of reprisal. This anonymity has unique potential for psychology and sociology courses in which students might share their own intimate experiences. Gaming and simulation exercises which might be difficult without guaranteed anonymity can now become an integral part of a course. For example, a major component of an undergraduate political science course at Michigan is the play of the Mid-East Simulation Game. In this game, CONFER is used for all diplomatic communiques which are not face-to-face, thus increasing the feel of simulated distance and adding one more dimension of reality to the game. A student at Michigan even conducted his dissertation research exclusively on CONFER by organizing a simulation game which included ten participants who did not meet face-to-face until the game was over. The transcripts from this "conference" formed the raw data for his dissertation on bargaining behavior. *Because conferencing permits anonymous communication, it significantly expands the types of pedagogical activities which could be a part of a course.*

This list of possible applications demonstrates that computer conferencing could have an important role in the future of education. The teacher-student relationship might take on some new dimensions, and communication in a variety of educational settings could be enhanced. However, conferencing is not a panacea. Experience with the traditional course has demonstrated that this new form of communication has a number of obstacles which must be addressed before a computer conference will be successful as a pedagogical aid.

OBSTACLES TO THE USE OF COMPUTER CONFERENCING

These obstacles are not put forth as an argument against the use of computer conferencing; rather they are stated to warn potential users and to suggest some hypotheses which researchers might investigate.

A Need for a Conference. If conferencing is to be successful, there must be a reason for people to confer. Students must not only be motivated to interact with each other but there must be a topic to discuss or business to transact. Experience at the University of Michigan has demonstrated that if students have frequent classroom meetings, the need for conferencing diminishes. If a course meets three times a week, there is little reason to log on to the conference. Even if a class meets infrequently, but students study or congregate in the same place, a bulletin board may be a more effective means of communication than a computer conference. If an objective of the course is to introduce students to the use of conferencing, a number of techniques have proved effective for ensuring high student use. One professor gave out all assignments on CONFER, thus forcing students to enter the conference periodically. Another faculty member indicated that a significant portion of the course discussion would be taking place on CONFER. These strategies may insure high usage, but they also can create an aritficial need for conferencing. Thus, *before deciding to use conferencing, a faculty member should be able to demonstrate the need for utilizing this communication me-*

dium. Without this, the other factors inhibiting conferencing will prevail and the conference will be an empty one.

Faculty Reluctance. One of the greatest barriers for student use of conferencing is a reluctance on the part of faculty to try out this new form of communication. As with any pedogogical innovation, the resistance to change is high. The use of conferencing requires rethinking the organization of the course. In many cases, the faculty member must learn new skills, such as how to interact with a computing system. As might be expected, the earliest adopters of conferencing are those who have had experience with computing. The most effective users of CONFER seem to be those faculty who comprehend the *use* of computing and the man-machine interface; they are not necessarily the most sophisticated users of computing. Thus, *once the cost and access barriers have been eliminated, faculty reluctance may be the greatest barrier to the widespread use of conferencing.*

Access. Students using conferencing frequently encounter two access problems: the availability of terminals and signing-on to the system. On most campuses, student terminals are located only in computer labs and a few other user areas. In an ideal situation, each student would have their own terminal, just as they do a typewriter or calculator. In reality, students must travel to the terminal and sometimes make reservations in advance or encounter long waiting lines. Once the student sits down at the keyboard, she/he may be interacting with this foreign beast in the presence of many other students, all of which can be an intimidating experience.[9] The spontaneous interaction which can be so beneficial to the educational process is inhibited.

The second access barrier involves the "handshaking operation" with the computer system. On most large systems, the student must first identify the type of terminal, perhaps access a network, then access the computer system, and finally sign on to the conference itself. Although this straightforward procedure requires no more than thirty seconds and five responses, it can be frustrating to the student who has little familiarity with computing systems. Thus, *system access can be a severe obstacle and one which can inhibit the curious student.*

Computer Phobia. Although many of today's students have had some experience with computing, a significant number still have had little experience and fear a machine which talks back to them. For the student who has no typing skills or is frustrated by using a keyboard, it will be difficult to be an active participant in a computer conference. Also, although today's computing and communications technology is vastly improved, unforeseen problems do occur (such as communication errors and system crashes). Although these are rare, it is inevitable that they will happen at the time the uninitiated conferencing student is working on the system. *When taken together, these factors can result in an uncomfortable feeling or phobia toward conferencing. For those students who are wary of this new form of communication, this can swing the balance in favor of not using the system.*

Introduction Time. As with any new skill, a certain introductory period is necessary before a person learns how to use conferencing effectively. A number of researchers have pointed to the fact that conferencing is most effective if it is used idiosyncratically. Each person develops her/his own style for entering and editing messages, the length of time spent at each sitting, the best time of the day to use conferencing, and the best method for composing messages. If computer conferencing is to be used in a conventional course format, time must be allotted to build-up students' skills in using the system. If time is not set aside, students may spend the majority of the course becoming familiar with the system; and it will not be until the final week of the semester that effective use of conferencing occurs. If one goal of the course is to introduce students to conferencing, this drawn-out evolutionary process may be acceptable. However, if the plans are to use conferencing throughout the course, special arrangements must be made for ensuring student familiarity with the system. Conferencing may be most effective in external programs in which this form of communication is the main point of contact between students and faculty. In these programs, students will anticipate the value of the time invested in learning to use the system. Thus, *computer conferencing would seem to be most effective if it is used repeatedly or employed in those courses which stretch across a number of semesters.*

Leadership. As with any effective discussion, a computer conference requires the time and energy of a good leader. A faculty member who organizes a conference must examine the structure of the course to determine which activities and which topics are appropriately handled via conferencing. The on-going discussion must be monitored to ensure that it is evolving in a manner which is consistent with the professor's goals for the course. The faculty member will set the tone for the conference. For example, if the professor puts forth ideas which are obviously extemporaneous and not highly polished, students will be encouraged to do likewise. If the conference is used to announce the location and time of a bull session at the local pub, students will envision a different use for the conference than if only course assignments are handed out, typed in syllabus format.

At times during the conference, the leader will most likely need to boost the morale of those who are intimidated by the conferencing format. Special sessions may be necessary to overcome these fears. Also, in contrast to the classroom situation in which discussion is limited to a fixed time period, the organizer of a computer conference is "on call" at all times. Although a faculty member may now choose when to interact with students, effective leadership requires frequent interaction and quick response to student inquiries. This unlimited set of office hours can cause a never-ending drain on a faculty member's time and energy. Yet it is obvious that this offers students and faculty an opportunity to interact continuously. This new format can only enhance the educational process. Thus, *for conferencing to be successful, professors must feel comfortable interacting with students on an ad-hoc basis. The successful conference will also require the faculty member to exert firm yet sensitive leadership to the evolving discussion. Many faculty may feel uncomfortable in this new role.*

Costs. Although the costs of communication and computing are plunging, the current cost of computer conferencing presents a significant obstacle for its use in the conventional course. Even though conferencing requires a relatively small amount of computer processing, file storage costs can be high; and charges for an entire conference involving twenty to thirty students can easily run into hundreds of dollars. This cost will increase if the users must pay network communication costs to access remote computing facilities. If additional terminals are rented or purchased to provide easy access to the conference, this will drive the costs still higher.

Presently, most departments do not allocate funds to cover such an array of course costs. If students find computer conferencing highly desirable, they may be willing to assume some of the costs (such as is currently done for labs, textbooks, and special enrollment fees). External[10] students who must usually study on their own and travel many miles to the campus may be the first to recognize the advantages of conferencing and pay for some of the costs. As costs for transportation continue to rise and computing costs continue to fall, conferencing will become increasingly attractive as an economical alternative for enriching the pedagogical process. In the interim, however, *the costs associated with computer conferencing remain a serious obstacle to its use as a course aid.*

Security and Anonymity. As stated previously, computer conferencing offers students and faculty the opportunity to communicate anonymously with each other. For example, students can evaluate a lecture, comment on the dynamics of the classroom, or critique the course readings without fear of reprisal. Yet this will only occur if students are confident that the faculty member does not have access to these confidential messages. Students must believe that only public "items" are retained permanently while "messages" are destroyed.[11] With the recent advent of bugging, snooping, and other electronic eavesdropping, building confidence that the system security cannot and will not be violated may be difficult. Further attention needs to be devoted to this problem, not only in the educational sector, but perhaps in professional communications as well. As the use of conferencing expands, protocols must be developed for the moral and ethical use of conferencing. Thus, *without guaranteed anonymity and security, the unique potential which conferencing poses for enhancing the educational process will be lost.*

The Advent of Extra Work. Although computer conferencing offers some significant advances for "interactive" education, it also could increase the volume of useless information which students and faculty must process. For example, volumes of mindless dribble which conference participants must review could become the main traffic on the network. Given today's frenetic environment, most people—including students—do not need to be bombarded by additional information. Instead, all of us need more time for quiet reflection and processing of our own thoughts. In the worst scenario, computer conferencing could offer students and faculty the opportunity to exchange trivial bits of information while they delude themselves into thinking that the educational process has been significantly improved. Thus, *at all times we must remain on-guard against conferencing creating an unnecessary and useless burden on our time.*

WHITHER COMPUTER CONFERENCING?

Give this inventory of applications and obstacles, what conclusions can be drawn for the future of computer conferencing as a pedogogical tool? From the limited experience to date, it is obvious that there are many significant obstacles to conferencing and that conferencing has only selective applicability. For most traditional college courses taught to on-campus students, conferencing might offer a few advantages, but nothing significant enough to justify its widespread use. The large lecture course which meets frequently and has little classroom discussion is not likely to adopt conferencing. With such a large number of students, no one would feel responsible for participation, the cost could become prohibitive, and the discussion would be diffuse.

Many pedagogical innovations are based on the assumption that the student is a zealous learner who is bridled by the current system. Conferencing offers an opportunity to test that assumption. If conferencing is available to students, they can continue discussions between class meetings, thereby enhancing their learning. Yet the majority of the students may have little desire to continue the discussion beyond specified class hours. Graduate courses where a high degree of interest may be assumed are more likely candidates for conferencing.

Computer conferencing offers significant and perhaps unique opportunities for expanding educational opportunities. Students who are prevented from fully participating in formal education may have access barriers eliminated or at least lessened. External education, whether it be in the form of continuing professional education or degree programs, would benefit substantially from the use of conferencing. Traditional courses that would find it advantageous to expand the variety of pedagogies or the mix of resources available to the students may find conferencing useful.

Those faculty who currently opt to teach new courses or experiment with new pedagogical styles will be the first adopters of conferencing. They are those most prone to innovation and they will find new applications which go far beyond those suggested in this paper. However, as long as the number of these faculty remains small and the number of institutions seeking new educational markets is few, the use of conferencing will be minimal.

Many of the current obstacles such as cost, accessibility, and computer phobia will undoubtedly disappear over time. After this occurs, the use of conferencing will be determined by the pressure which institutions feel to expand their educational resources and their clientele. With the developing technology and the tightening market for education, the prognosis points to expanded use in selected applications.

NOTES

1. Johansen, Robert, Jacques Vallee, Kathleen Spangler, and R. Garry Shirts, Consultant, *The Camelia Report*, Institute for the Future: Report R-37: Menlo Park, CA, February, 1977 and Johansen, Robert, Robert DeGrasse, Jr., and Thaddeus Wilson, *Group Communication Through Computers, Volume 5: Effects on Working Patterns*, Institute for the Future: Menlo Park, CA, November, 1977.
2. For readers interested in additional technical details on CONFER, write Robert Parnes or Karl Zinn, 109 E. Madison Street, CRLT, University of Michigan, Ann Arbor, Michigan 48109.
3. The author has participated in a number of computer conferences over the past eighteen months. The "findings" discussed in this article are a result of an evaluation project conducted by the author and through the author's ongoing use of conferencing.
4. The brief description given in this section is not intended to provide the reader with a thorough introduction to conferencing. Readers wanting more background on conferencing systems and their operations should see (Turoff, May, 1977, Uhlig, May, 1977, and Zinn, April, 1977).
5. Johansen, Robert, *Interpersonal Communication Through Computers*, Institute for the Future: Menlo Park, CA, May, 1978.

6. EDUNET is a national computer service network organized under the auspices of EDUCOM (the Inter-University Communications Council), Princeton, N.J. EDUNET facilitates the sharing of computer-based resources in all facets of higher education and research.

7. Alderman, Donald L., Lola Rhea Appel and Richard T. Murphy, "Plato and Ticcit: An Evaluation of CAI in the Community College," *Educational Technology*, April, 1978, pp. 40–45.

8. *College IV: The Evolution of an Experiment in Self-Paced Instruction*, Formative Evaluation Research Associates: Ann Arbor, MI, May, 1977, p. 28.

9. As computing becomes more prevalent at all levels of education, this obstacle will be minimized.

10. "External" refers to students who pursue their course work through external degree programs. Usually these students do not attend classes on the campus and frequently their academic calendar is negotiated.

11. In CONFER, a *message* refers to private exchanges which are sent directly to another conference participant. They do not become part of the permanent record of the conference; however, they may be saved by individual participants. In contrast, *items* are public entries into the conference, which become a permanent part of the conference record.

ETHNOGRAPHIC FUTURES RESEARCH AND ITS EDUCATIONAL POTENTIAL

Robert B. Textor

The purpose of this paper is to explain briefly a particular cultural and ethnographic approach to futures research, and then to examine the potential utility of this approach for educational purposes. Although this approach is still in the early stages of development, experience to date suggests that its educational potential is considerable. Indeed, so intertwined are the research and the educational effects of this approach, that it is sometimes difficult to disentangle them.

CULTURAL AND ETHNOGRAPHIC FUTURES RESEARCH

Cultural Futures Research (CFR) means cultural approaches to alternative futures. CFR focuses on alternative future *cultures* for a given society. A "culture" is conceived of as a set of standards for determining what is, what can be, how one feels about it, what should be done about it, and how one proceeds to go about doing it.[1] In short, a culture is a system of standards and meanings that can and often does serve to guide decisions and behavior. Since a culture is a system, if follows that any scenarized future culture must "hang together" as a system, and also that the process by which the present culture is seen as becoming the future culture must make sense in terms of what is known about processes of sociocultural change.

Ethnographic Futures Research (EFR) is simply the methodological arm of Cultural Futures Research (CFR). EFR stands to CFR in much the same relationship that ethnography stands to cultural anthropology. Ethnography is the method that one uses to study an extant culture, and EFR is here suggested as the method one might use to elicit, develop, or scenarize a possible future culture. EFR will be illustrated by referring to its use during 1977 to elicit scenarios from an opportunity sample of 25 civilian Buddhist intellectual Thais available for interview in California, with respect to alternative future cultures for Thailand as of the year 2000. Only the minimally necessary specifics will be presented, since details are available elsewhere.[2]

THE FORMAT OF ETHNOGRAPHIC FUTURES RESEARCH

EFR is based on open-ended and in-depth semi-structured interviewing. As in all ethnographic inquiry, the investigator starts with a tentative and flexible approach. He is alert to shifts in the direction and scope of the scenario that he is eliciting and is prepared to adapt his line of inquiry in response to initiatives taken by the interviewee. To a very considerable extent, the interviewer encourages the interviewee to "take charge" of the interview. At the same time that the investigator thus encourages spontaneity, however, he is also concerned with completeness, and comparability across interviews, which means that his interview must possess sufficient structure to insure that scenarios will cover pre-established broad topics which he deems to be analytically important, even in the event that a particular interviewee does not spontaneously bring up a particular topic.

As the EFR interviewing format has been developed to date, there are four elements in it. For clarity of explanation, let us assume that a male interviewer (myself) is interviewing a female interviewee.

The "How Do Things Happen" Question

The interview is begun with a broad question concerning "how things happen," in the judgment of the interviewee, which cause one future rather than another to transpire in the society under examination. In working with the 25 Thai interviewees, for example, the author chose to ascertain the extent to which Buddhist karma or Brahmanical "fate"—two causative mechanisms considered broadly valid in the traditional culture of Thailand—were seen as operating on the modern nation-state of Thailand. Since these interviewees were relatively Westernized intellectuals, it was of interest to examine the extent to which this kind of supernaturalistic thinking pervaded their speculations concerning social causation, and the extent to which a more naturalistic or modern stance was taken. On the whole, the 25 interviewees tended rather markedly to favor naturalistic explanations of *social* causation, although many of these same people gave evidence of depending partly upon supernaturalistic explanations with respect to their own *personal* lives. Among naturalistic stances, the principal types were a broadly political economy stance, and a stance viewing change as springing from the acculturative influence of foreigners, particularly Westerners.

Optimistic Scenario

The bulk of the interview was taken up by an optimistic scenario. This scenario posits a continuum of realistic or "happenable" future cultures for a country as of a particular time horizon—in this case Thailand as of A.D. 2000. This continuum stretches from Scenario 1, which is the worst possible (realistic) future culture for Thailand in the year 2000, to Scenario 100, which is the best possible realistic future culture for Thailand as of that year. The interviewee is told to regard alternative future cultures which are, by her own personal values, below scale position 1 or above scale position 100 as beyond the possible, hence disregardable. The interviewee is then asked to describe in depth her scenario at scale position 90— that is, a very good future culture, but not quite the best that could occur. Interviewees typically took at least an hour and a half to do this.

Pessimistic Scenario

The pessimistic scenario is defined as that which lodges at position No. 10 on the continuum—a very bad future culture, but not quite the worst that could occur. Interviewees typically took much less time spelling out their pessimistic scenarios and often found it convenient simply to say that it was something like a mirror opposite of their optimistic scenario.

The Imaginary Omniscient Clairvoyant Consultation

Finally, the interviewee was asked to imagine that she is now consulting a clairvoyant who has the ability to predict any aspect of the future with total accuracy. The interviewee is requested to specify the questions she would ask of such an omniscient clairvoyant, but there is just one catch: she has only five minutes to ask her questions and so must be careful to include all crucial questions within this brief space of time. The questions she asks thus presumably reflect her most important anxieties and throw light on the basic variables and contingencies in her thinking and planning. Incidentally, this exércise posed few difficulties for the Thai interviewees, whose culture includes a rich variety of divinatory rituals, and whose society includes numerous soothsayers, some of whose patrons belong to the modern educated sector. Results from the "omniscient clairvoyant" experience proved generally consistent with the optimistic and pessimistic scenarios. (Both the dual scenario and the omniscient clairvoyant items are adapted from methodological work carried out at the Institute for the Future and described by Amara and Lipinski.[3])

RECORDING AND RELIABILITY PROCEDURES

The recording procedure attempted to maximize the involvement of the interviewee in the actual recording process. This was done by means of a cumulative summarization technique, which is apparently new to ethnography. As the interviewee talked, the interviewer listened and made brief memory-jogging notes. Then, whenever the interviewee seemed to have rounded out her comments on a particular subject or domain, she was asked to pause and listen carefully while the interviewer dictated into a dictaphone a summary of what she had just said. She was urged to interrupt the summary at any point to make corrections or additions. As each summary was dictated, eye contact was maintained with the interviewee and the interviewer was alert for any non-verbal signs of dissatisfaction. These dictated materials became the protocol for the interview.

This policy of total openness and feedback served greatly to increase rapport and trust. Equally important, it seemed to increase the interviewee's *identification* with the research project, and her eagerness to insure that what went into the protocol was truly representative of her perceptions and feelings.

This approach also had a positive effect upon the quality of the interview—much different than would have been the effect of simply tape-recording the entire interview. The interviewer's knowing that in at most a few minutes he would have to summarize what the interviewee was saying, to her satisfaction, served as a goad upon the interviewer to listen carefully and creatively.

Early in each interview, it was indicated that the interviewee would be sent, by mail, a copy of the protocol as soon as it was transcribed—unless she objected, which few did. This was then done, enclosing a personal note urging her to write the interviewer, or telephone collect, if she had any corrections or additions. Interviewees seemed to appreciate this form of feedback, and the fact that none of them indicated any dissatisfaction was reassuring.

GENERALIZING PROCEDURES

The precise procedures used in summarizing the results of 70 hours of interviewing are described in other publications[4] and need not be detailed here. Suffice to say that the procedures are similar to, though perhaps a bit more explicit than, those which most ethnographers would use in preparing an ethnography about an extant culture. Just as the conventional ethnographer seeks to portray the regularities or patterning that characterize an extant culture, so the investigator engaged in EFR seeks to portray such patterning in one or more hypothetical future cultures. The question of how much "regularity" of interviewee response there must be before the ethnographer is entitled to say "This is a pattern" is one which has no standard answer. Most ethnographers handle this problem judgementally, and are not averse to using concepts like "dominant" and "alternative" patterns, where appropriate.

The common anthropological notion of patterning must somehow be brought to bear on the three basic considerations that seem to characterize all or much general futures research, namely considerations of the possible, the probable, and the preferable. In its present state of development, EFR makes a broad distinction between patterns of the imaging of alternative futures that appear to involve primarily the *cognitive* processes of believing, knowing and expecting—and patterns that appear to involve primarily the *evaluative* processes of judging and prioritizing on the basis of desirability, linked perhaps with processes of affective feeling.

Primarily Cognitive Patterns

In the Thailand Futures Study, it was found convenient to distinguish between consensually shared patterns involving a cognitive structuring of the basic alternative "paths into" the future on the one hand, and less basic, more focused "expectations," on the other. The former are "basic" in the sense that they are assumptions about the *limits* of possible variability. The latter tend to be forecasts dealing with variable possibilities *within* the limits imposed by the basic assumptions. Again, details appear in my other publications.

With virtual unanimity, the Thai intellectuals believed that there were, as of April-July 1977, only *two* basic paths into the future. Path One was the "conventional" path, led politically by military officers or their civilian agents. Path Two could be called the "jungle" path, led by leftists who, as of that time at least, lived in the jungles as insurgents. Most, but not all, interviewees preferred a hypothetical Path Three, a non-violent Buddhist Middle Way which would produce solid gains in terms of economic equity and personal freedom while avoiding large-scale bloodshed or civil war. Tragically, virtually none of the interviewees believed that Path Three was a viable one.

An example of an "expectation" is that a solid majority of the interviewees foresaw as virtually inevitable, or highly probable, a major civil war lasting many years and producing widespread social dislocation and bloodshed. For most, this was a decidedly pessimistic scenario—but it was the one that they perceived as the more likely. The pervasiveness and depth of this shared cognitive conviction were surprising to me despite my many years of having specialized on Thailand.

Primarily Evaluative Patterns

Evaluative patterns tend to be more stable than cognitive or expectational patterns. What an individual *expects* to happen is more subject to events beyond his control—such as the fall of a national cabinet—then is true with respect to what he, at bottom, *wants* for his society. In an attempt to specify the patterns of a consensually desired hypothetical future Thai culture as of A.D. 2000, I steeped myself in the protocols and isolated 12 value themes, each of which I expressed in the form of a normative proposition. The 12 propositions are as follows.

1. *Thailand must somehow preserve its national independence.* To the reader from a powerful nation, who has not done research in the Third World, it is difficult to overstate the sense of dependency that many of the Thai intellectuals expressed. They simply did not see their nation as being the master of its own fate, in the sense that Americans, for example, *culturally* assume considerable national autonomy and scope for choice. They seemed, to this observer, objective about, and resigned to, the low power position that Thailand occupies in world affairs. Many felt a need for one or more allies among the great powers unless and until there is stable world peace, but few seemed to regard this as otherwise a good thing in itself, and some saw it as distinctly harmful. In the event that a full-fledged civil war breaks out, interviewees hoped that the great powers would remain neutral and, especially, that they would not become directly involved in a military way. The memory of deep American involvement in Vietnam, with its war-prolonging consequences, was clearly operative.

At the same time, however, interviewees hardly expected that the great powers would simply go away and leave Thailand alone. Thailand is an attractive market for manufactured goods. More important, Thailand and nearby countries have raw materials that industrial nations need, materials some of which will increasingly be in critically short world supply. Especially if new deposits of minerals are found—and a natural gas bonanza actually did begin in 1978—Thailand was seen as likely to have no other choice than continued intensive relations with the industrial world, capitalist and probably communist as well.

2. *Thai culture must be selectively conserved and revitalized.* Interviewees who spoke at all about Thai culture as a whole cultural system, spoke with deep feeling and pointed to a need

for preserving and enhancing those aspects of their culture which give uniqueness and beauty to Thai life and a sense of identity to the Thai people. Cultural dependency upon the industrialized West and Japan must, they felt, be reduced. Implicitly, cultural dependency was more likely to be decried when wrapped in economic dependency.

Selective cultural conservation was seen as a process that Thais must assertively lead and manage. For example, traditional *kreengcaj* (deference to one's seniors in the kin group) was seen as a custom that should be retained because it contributes to the integrity of the family. By contrast, such deference to one's seniors in a governmental hierarchy should be reduced because it contributes to rigidity, wrong decisions, and waste of national resources.

Radical and non-radical alike, devout and apparently otherwise, the interviewees were unanimous in contending that the religious aspect of their culture should be selectively conserved. Buddhism was seen as a unifying, identity-giving, and humanizing force of great power. However, some felt that certain divinatory or magical accretions to folk Buddhism ought to be eliminated.

On the whole, there seemed to be greater clarity about cultural items worthy of being discarded or resisted, than about items worthy of being somehow revitalized—but at any rate, there was no mistaking a pervasive yearning for an enhanced sense of Thainess through the revivification of cultural symbols, and a feeling that if this revivification required the use of governmental regulations or subsidies, well and good.

3. *Inequities must be redressed.* The interviewees shared the cognitive position that inequity is the root cause of political instability, and essentially took the functionalist position that no Thai government can remain stable unless it redresses inequities in a forthright and visible manner. Aside from this cognitive proposition, there was also the evaluative proposition, shared even by forecasters of distinctly privileged socioeconomic background, that the Thai social system is extremely unfair in the rewards it distributes, and that this is blatantly wrong. Virtually all optimistic scenarios called for reducing "the gap" between rich and poor. Virtually all pessimistic scenarios presumed a government that was unwilling or unable to reduce this gap.

One special form of social inequity was pointed up by both female and male interviewees, namely inequity as between the sexes. While the social position of the Thai woman has traditionally been high by general Asian standards, nonetheless the need for complete legal and social equality for women was an emphasized theme. Interviewees explained prostitution as stemming primarily from poverty, and under optimistic conditions forecasted its substantial reduction as poverty is eliminated. Radicals went further and forecasted its virtual prohibition.

Many of the intellectuals addressed the problem of inequality of educational opportunity as an institutional feature that tends to perpetuate inequities between classes, as well as between urban and rural Thais. While those who spoke to education issues were uniformly of the view that education has a contribution to make toward a more desirable Thailand, the current content of education was criticized as being often irrelevant to the country's real needs, and as perpetuating unneeded snob values and in effect blocking the social mobility of many Thais who under different conditions could make strong contributions to a better Thailand.

4. *Government must be made responsive.* With great regularity, interviewees cognitively took the position that a government must be responsive or it will be replaced by another that is. Evaluatively, a key theme was not that a specifically parliamentary-style system for insuring responsiveness is needed (though some called for this), but simply that *some* means must be found to insure that the government truly responds to people's needs. The social distance between the government in Bangkok and the ordinary peasant in the village was noted by several, and various forms of village democracy designed to give local people more control over their own lives were proposed in optimistic scenarios, by both radical and non-radical interviewees.

No optimistic scenario called for an indefinitely continuing domination of the political process by the military, and many called specifically for military officers to confine their concerns strictly to professional military matters, and to enjoy no greater political rights or powers than civilians.

5. *Corruption and favoritism must be drastically reduced.* This value proposition is one of the least surprising. Corruption and favoritism were portrayed as both indices and perpetuators of inequity and non-responsiveness. In optimistic scenarios both were forecasted as minimal by the year 2000, while in pessimistic scenarios the existing government was seen as based so heavily on these two social patterns as to be unable to bring about their fundamental reform.

6. *Freedom must be enhanced.* Forecasters used a variety of definitions of freedom. Most tended to emphasize personal freedom and civil liberties. The then-ruling Thanin Administration's policy of placing restrictions on professors' freedom to teach, and students' freedom to inquire, was seen as undermining the next generation's capacity for coping with national problems. Some radicals tended to emphasize what might be called cultural freedom under the guidance of a new socialist government, in which Thais would collectively make their own decisions concerning the national future, would avoid exces-

sive consumerism, would bring an end to political-economic-cultural dependency, and would jointly decide how national resources would be utilized and divided. When probed, such interviewees conceded that the ideological tutelage called for by their optimistic scenarios would probably result in a diminution of "psychic" freedom—e.g., the individual farmer's freedom to decide whether to go to work or take the day off.

7. *Violence must be minimized.* The crucial subject of violence has been discussed above in its cognitive aspects. Suffice here simply to add that the avoidance or minimization of violence was a fundamental value proposition among the interviewees, even those who desired radical social change. Since there was a rather strong tendency to regard the insurgents as the more likely winners of the political struggle in the long run (regardless of personal preference), there was also a tendency to prefer that, however the struggle for power might be settled, it be settled quickly, so as to minimize loss of life.

8. *Disorder, even if nonviolent, must be minimized.* Traditionally, the Thai people have placed a strong positive value upon situations of all sorts that are neat and orderly (*riabrauj*). All else equal, the interviewees expressed a preference for social order, and this preference tended to apply even among some who would bring to an end the elaborate deference traditionally required of juniors in a hierarchical structure. It might incidentally be noted that the preservation of something like the existing order of things is in fact very much in the career interest of most of these intellectuals, who, as returning graduates of respected colleges and universities, will stand to benefit from the existing credentialistic prestige hierarchy.

9. *The population must be limited.* Interviewees of every political persuasion were aware of Thailand's high current rate of population growth, and eager to use the educational potential and technical capacity of the government to promote smaller families. The sample evidently did not include a single demographic chauvinist.

10. *The natural environment must be preserved.* Interviewees considered it imperative that action be taken to preserve the environment, giving such examples as the need to reduce air and water pollution, and to curb erosion through scientific forestry policies. The extreme air pollution and traffic congestion of Bangkok were frequently cited as examples of an inadequate national ecological policy.

11. *The economy must grow.* The intellectuals saw much greater chances for accomplishing social equity programs in an expanding economy than in a stagnant one. Many pessimistic scenarios included stagflation resulting from the flight of private capital, stemming in turn from lack of investor confidence due to political instability. Even radicals supported

economic growth strongly, though in a context of economic and cultural independence from foreign countries, especially capitalist ones. It was generally believed that Thailand's high population growth rate and strong built-in demographic momentum constituted further imperative reasons for stimulating economic growth.

There was a general tendency, though, to prefer agricultural over industrial development, and to prefer industries linked to Thailand's natural comparative advantages, over industries located in Thailand simply because Thai wages are low.

12. *Stringent governmental controls must be imposed upon the economy.* There was consensus that a *laissez-faire* economy would not, under Thai conditions, be an equitable economy, and that it would also result in unwanted social distortions, such as too much consumerism and cultural dependency. The need for strong, rational, responsive, corruption-free controls upon the economy was taken as almost axiomatic, and some forecasters went further in varying degrees, advocating government ownership of various economic facilities.

Moving farther from the *prima facie* approach, one can, of course, adduce more general value orientations, and proceed to explore value trade-offs. Four very basic such value orientations can be addressed (order, growth, equity, and freedom), and then tradeoffs can be analyzed by taking these a pair at a time, combinatorially. This analytical method provides a useful insight into the policy implications of the protocols. For details, see Textor 1978.

ETHNOGRAPHIC FUTURES RESEARCH AND FUTURES EDUCATION

As an anthropologist-educator, I have been especially concerned with the possible educational effects or implications of EFR. These implications have outdistanced my original expectations. In addition to EFR's being an effective way of educating oneself with respect to culture and its potential, EFR also, willy-nilly, serves as a powerful educational stimulus for the interviewee. Training students to conduct their own EFR seems to have similar stimulating effects on them. These two educative effects will now be explored.

The Interviewee as Educatee

The Thai intellectuals generally seemed nervous or uncertain at the beginning of the interview, but after about ten or fifteen minutes they began to show signs of enjoying themselves, and, by the end of the interview, typically, they would thank the interviewer, adding a comment such as: "This is a terribly important topic but no one has ever sat down with me before to help me examine it systematically." In short, it seems that "education" had taken place in the quite literal sense that EFR had helped to "draw out" ideas and values which had previously been implicit rather than explicit—or, in other words, that tempocentrism had been reduced. By starting out defining the interviewer as the educatee, two educatees were produced: interviewer and interviewee. Inadvertently, this technique creates new futurists, of a sort.

Totally to my surprise, these new quasi-futurists went one step further. A few weeks after interviewing commenced, a group of them started, completely on their own initiative, to conduct informal half-day seminars for themselves and other Thais on selected aspects of Thailand's future—complete with moderators, resource persons, and organized discussion formats. The discussion was lively and informed, and there was an obvious relationship between the content of the EFR interviews and the content of these meetings—though it was also not surprising that some "dangerous" points of view expressed in the interviews went unstated in these seminars.

Since Thailand, like most Third World nations, is quite steeply hierarchical in its social structure, the fact that these 25 people, most of whom will join the intellectual or technocratic elite of their country, have had their consciousnesses raised through EFR is significant. While Thailand, being a relatively small and weak nation, is by no means fully in charge of its national destiny, nonetheless, if it should come about that this type of futures research-cum-futures education can be made a regular part of the educational processes in Thailand, the intellectual leadership of that nation could come to play a stronger role in shaping the nation's future. Thus, EFR, along with other techniques, conceivably could make a modest contribution toward the kind of "anticipatory democracy" which many futures researchers favor.

The Student Ethnographer as Educatee

It has long been my approach in teaching a variety of anthropology courses to treat my students as quasi-ethnographers, to offer training and guidance, and to expect them to do their own field interviewing on a subject of their choice and produce a mini-ethnography. Accordingly, I found myself quite naturally using EFR in teaching or co-teaching classes on cultural futures research. Here once again no formal evaluational data exist, but the EFR experience seems to have been highly stimulating and helpful to my students. Two classes have so far been instructed, with membership in each case including both undergraduate and graduate students. One class did a composite EFR term paper on "Brazil 2001," while another class examined "Sweden 2005." In the first case, none of the students was specialized on Brazil, spoke or read

Portuguese, or had ever been to Brazil. In the second case, similarly, none was specialized on Sweden or spoke Swedish. In both cases, students were powerfully "turned on," after an initial learning period characterized by diffidence and anxiety. The big triumph was when the student "brought home" his first successful EFR interview and shared results with his peers. The quality of their results, too, has been impressive. In the Brazil case, a professor of Brazilian history has judged the joint term paper publishable, and expressed pleasure at its essential accuracy and insightfulness.

FINAL REMARKS

It seems clear that CFR and EFR have a strong educational potential, strong enough at least to justify continued development of this general approach, as well as more formal evaluation of its educational effectiveness. In addition, there is a broader potential of this approach that should be mentioned here briefly, namely the de-ethnocentrization of futures research. To date, futures research has been the virtual monopoly of the industrialized nations of the First and Second Worlds.[5] This is understandable enough, if only because it is in these two worlds that the great majority of professionals are found, of the types that are likely to be interested in futures research. There are, however, two serious dangers inherent in this status quo.

First, there is the danger that futures researchers coming from modern, industrialized nations will simply assume that their particular ways of imaging the future are the correct and standard ways, and ignore the possibility that an equally able futures researcher enculturated in a non-industrial culture might come up with a significantly different set of lenses through which to view the future. Just as cultural anthropology studies cross-cultural differences in various peoples' "world views," so cultural futures research is needed to study cross-cultural differences in various peoples' future views. In short, CFR adds a cross-temporal dimension to cross-cultural research.

Second, there is the related danger of privilege. Although most futures researchers are probably egalitarian at the level of overt political philosophy, a continuation of the status quo in futures research could easily produce quite anti-egalitarian results. If, as is widely hoped, futures research in fact does prove capable of helping its practitioners and their clients cope with the future, then an industriocentric futures research profession could, and probably would, find itself being used to preserve and enhance the privileges of the already-privileged.[6]

Therefore, I hope for a time when cross-cultural variabilities in imaging the future will be widely understood, and when ethnographic techniques for studying alternative futures will be available to all the world's scholars. Since EFR requires no computers or battalions of interviewers and since the cost of training a person in EFR is extremely modest, perhaps it will become part of the "appropriate technology"[17] of futures research, suitable for adoption and adaptation by people throughout the world, whether or not they belong to privileged groups and establishments.

NOTES

1. Goodenough, Ward Hunt, *Cooperation in Change*. New York: Russell Sage Foundation 1968. Pp. 257–9.
2. Textor, Robert B., "Cultural Futures for Thailand: An Ethnographic Enquiry." *Futures*. October 1978. Pp. 347–60.
3. Amara, Roy, and Andrew Lipinski, *Linking the Corporation to the Future*. Menlo Park, CA: Institute for the Future, 1976.
4. Textor, Robert B., "Cultural Futures for Thailand: An Ethnographic Enquiry." *Futures*. October 1978. Pp. 347–60. 1965. *A Guide to Ethnographic Futures Research* (Preliminary Version, videotape training film, three reels). *A Handbook of Ethnographic Futures Research*. Forthcoming.
5. Masini, Eleonora Barbieri, "The Global Diffusion of Futures Research," in Jib Fowles, Ed., *Handbook of Futures Research*. Westport CN: Greenwood Press, 1978. Pp. 17–30.
6. Herrera, Amilcar Ol, et al., *Catastrophe or New Society?: A Latin American World Model*. Ottawa: International Development Research Centre, 1976. Jalee, Pierre, *The Pillage of the Third World*. London: Monthly Review Press, 1968. Tr. from the French.

III
SELECTED TOPICS IN EDUCATION

INTRODUCTION TO SECTION III
SELECTED TOPICS IN EDUCATION

Topics of special concern to scholars interested in the future of education are extremely diverse. Part of this diversity can be attributed to the nagging suspicion by many that *all* societal, individual, or global issues—educational or otherwise—have educational implications. Still another reason for the diversity is the inherent interdisciplinary nature of any study of the future.

One of the issues facing educators on a worldwide scale is the relationship of work to education. Some educators today would argue that education has been involved too much with job preparation, thereby subverting the "real" purpose of education: lifelong learning. Futurists such as Robert Theobald and Fred Best have argued that one's "work" must be separated from one's "job." Bertrand de Jouvenel, Willis Harman, and Walter Hack add that the future will require satisfaction of human needs—not just technological needs; they conclude that more generalists are needed, not more specialists.

The study of the future is not a discipline; by its very nature, it is interdisciplinary and problem/possibility centered. William Ashley and Constance Faddis offer suggestions in this section to help in the transition from industrial mindsets to postindustrial thinking in career education. Factors such as job satisfaction, adaptability, and individuality must be considered if this transformation is to be smooth. The authors are concerned with the transfer of skills and how educators, employees, career counselors, legislators, and researchers can aid in such a change.

Some readers may argue that Ashley and Faddis rely too much on the present structure of education and other social institutions in their approach, but it is the authors' contention that the need for new skills in an increasingly technological world will not disappear. They also believe that the transaction will be evolutionary and not revolutionary. Valuable insight is provided for those concerned with a "where we go from here" attitude rather than a stance of social reconstruction.

Arthur Wirth calls for the examination and re-evaluation of the "job efficiency" approach to work relations. He agrees with John Dewey: as long as priority is focused primarily on pecuniary gain rather than social utility, the intellectual and moral development of both workers and management will be one-sided and warped. Wirth believes that educational institutions have reflected the assumptions of the managerial center of society—reliance on "neutral" goals of improved efficiency (defined as increased measurable output). If this approach is continued, he believes the symptoms of alienation, lack of commitment, and other pathological behaviors will increase in all institutions of society.

Wirth advocates the study of the Scandinavian model known as the "sociotechnical" or "industrial democracy" design. This approach requires commitment, responsibility, and freedom for human choice. The model would, however, necessitate drastic changes in educational practices. The model suggests smaller learning communities within larger systems, collaborative learning, project-based thinking, and an educational system that allows for a full range of learning alternatives.

A more pressing issue concerning the future of education is examined by James Gelatt, who presents interesting insights into the future of special education. Population control, research, technology, networking, court litigation, and changes in teacher training programs are all suggested as areas affecting the improvement of the handicapped person. The author does, however, caution that public support of handicapped programs may wane. Questions such as "What is a productive life?" and "What is an equal education?" for these special populations must be addressed. Gelatt suggests that the general public may have other priorities, given limited tax bases, than exceptional children. The author concludes that maybe we shouldn't ask whether handicapped children are human persons, but rather, what kind of care should we give them in order for us to be human.

A final issue centers on educating for futures thinking. Anyone who has tried to "teach about the future" understands the perils, inconsistencies, frustration, and insecurity of the undertaking. Basil McDermott suggests that much more often than not, the future is more "believing is seeing" rather than the converse. He contends that the problem of "futurizing" is often related to the knowledge being used. Although he does not use these particular terms, the author believes futurists spend too much time on substantive and process problems rather than address the conceptual framework underlying these problems.

McDermott concludes that futures researchers should focus
on the ignorance of our knowledge rather than on the chas-
tisement of the world for being wicked or callous. Increased
specialization has caused "ignorance" from loss of total perspective, and therefore, the author feels that control of our
destiny is often based on illusion. McDermott calls for a "second education" that requires a considerable amount of "unlearning" and re-evaluation of assumed knowledge. His analysis is a plea to remind the reader of the dangers of
speculation, assumption, and ignorance.

OCCUPATIONAL ADAPTABILITY AND TRANSFERABLE SKILLS: PREPARING FOR TOMORROW'S CAREERS

William L. Ashley and Constance R. Faddis

JOB MOBILITY: LIFE IN THE FAST LANE

Predicting the future is a game played—for fun or necessity—by just about everyone, from occasional readers of newspaper astrology columns to government officials charged with anticipating and planning for the future needs of the nation. The one thing they can all depend on is what Alvin Toffler calls "the roaring current of change, a current so powerful today that it overturns institutions, shifts our values and shrivels our roots. Change is the process by which the future invades our lives. . . ."[1]

Most of us spend a large portion of our lives engaged in some sort of work, whether as employees or employers. In American culture, we usually even introduce ourselves by stating what we do. But that, too, is changing, because "what we do" is increasingly in flux.

Occupational mobility is becoming the rule for many people in the American labor force, where it was once the exception. A century ago, most people worked in some aspect of agriculture, but industrialization, and now automation and computerization, have had drastic effects on the redistribution of labor. By the year 2000, more than 90 percent of the labor force in western cultures could be employed in services industries.[2] While urbanization in the Third World is expected to slow as those countries' planners turn back to subsidizing growing more of their own food,[3] mobility of the work forces there will continue to be a fact in either direction.

Occupational mobility is any move from one job to another. This includes all changes, from a lateral transfer within the same firm (e.g., from forklift operator to crane operator) to major career changes (e.g., a garment cutter finds her job mechanized and starts a new life in the theatre). Any of these job changes can include major and/or minor differences in knowledge, job skills, environment, context, and expectations. From this perspective, mobility also includes voluntary and involuntary movements, mid-career occupational change, school-to-work or home-to-work transitions, within-industry transfers due to elimination or restructuring of previous jobs or the creation of new ones, and the vocational rehabilitation of handicapped workers.

According to *Forty Million Americans in Career Transition*, written by the College Board in 1978, 36 percent of the U.S. population between the ages of 16 and 65 are currently either in "actual" career transition (e.g., unemployed and looking for work) or in "anticipatory" career transition (e.g., dissatisfied with their current job and considering a change). Occupational mobility has become a significant feature of American life, and its frequency is expected to increase in the future.

Over the next 30 years, the Western labor market will continue to shift away from a demand for craft or blue collar workers to more white collar workers and non-domestic service workers. By the year 2000, as little as two percent of the American labor force could be required to turn out all necessary manufactured goods.[4]

Increasing automation and computerization will play roles in occupational shifts, but so will changes in social and organizational structures. In the short run, say in the next 10 years, the influx of women and minorities into previously white-male dominated occupations will have considerable effects on the markets for those occupations. A surplus of highly educated workers is already glutting some fields. Persons in middle management positions will probably spend more of their time managing "by exception," that is, when the computer breaks down, or when a change in rules is needed.[5]

The typical bureaucratic pyramid of today's organizations may also be on its way out. According to an article in *Personnel Journal*,

> Temporary task forces capable of rapidly solving problems may be the organizational form that will gradually replace the present inflexible bureaucratic pyramid. Such task forces will be composed of specialists who possess the diverse skills required to respond to changing conditions and problems.[6]

Other factors could have enormous effects on the availability and variety of future job openings. The proposed decrease of work hours ("the 4-day week") would entail hiring more persons to perform the same labor in some industries, and would free people to pursue more leisure activities or education (and thus expand the market in those areas). Job-sharing, whether by choice or necessity, would create much the same situation. The idea of gradual retirement, in which a person may work fewer and fewer hours or may do less complex tasks over the years of employment, opens a similar can of worms. These kinds of adjustments to traditional work structures may be necessitated by a future scarcity of jobs, as well as by a rise in non-money rewards as an important new job value.

The May 1978 issue of *Psychology Today* was devoted to an assessment of emerging job values, and revealed a significant shift away from the traditional attitude of one career, one employer, work-for-the-money. Among the findings was that only 17.6 percent of the workers answering the national survey "strongly agreed" that they were satisfied with their jobs.[7] Herbert Greenberg, president of Marketing Survey and Research Corporation, claims that 80 percent of American workers are doing jobs for which they are not suited, and calls this "misemployment" a greater tragedy than unemployment.[8] In addition, the *Psychology Today* survey found that the lower the status of a job, the greater is the worker's expectation that he or she will change jobs in the next five years (e.g., 59.7 percent of semi-skilled or unskilled workers). Yet even among the highest status group measured (professionals), over 25 percent expected to change jobs within five years.

The implications are obvious. G. Lowell Martin sees workers becoming "more cosmopolitan and less loyal to an individual employer or company."[9] And a shift away from money as the most important job value is reducing workers' willingness to stay in employment situations in which the work, the environment, or other non-money rewards seem inadequate. For many, mobility is an attractive alternative, for others an unpleasant necessity, but that it has become a fact of American life is reflected in the success of such self-help-in-job-changing books as Crystal and Bolles' *Where Do I Go from Here with My Life?*, Lathrop's *Who's Hiring Who*; and Bolles' *The Three Boxes of Life and How to Get Out of Them.*

EDUCATION: COPING WHEN THE FLOOR TILTS

We have seen that the labor needs of industry are changing as industry itself evolves, and the perceived job needs of individuals are changing as attitudes toward the world of work also evolve. What are the implications of these changes in work? Will workers have what they need to cope? What will it mean if industry doesn't have enough, say, craftspersons tomorrow? How shall we redistribute the wealth, resources, and privileges, both on the level of the individual worker and a worldwide scale? How can workers and industry meet each others' needs in a future where rapid change is the new law of the jungle?

Alvin Toffler, in *Future Shock*, offers a solution to too-much-change-too-fast: a "prime objective must be to increase the individual's 'cope-ability'—the speed and economy with which he (sic) can adapt to continual change."[10] Toffler's "cope-ability" is what we call adaptability, and it is becoming an important survival skill in a new age of work. Those who learn to become adaptable, who acquire occupational skills that will not become obsolete, who develop the ability to adapt what they do know and to learn what they don't, will survive, cope, and flourish in the midst of change. They will need to be, in effect, specialized generalists. But where will these workers come from? It is apparent from the current condition of the labor market, unemployment, and misemployment that occupational adaptability is not an innate characteristic of workers. How can adaptability be acquired?

Is Education the Agent for Dealing with Change?

Over the last 10 years, schools have been charged with a great many functions besides teaching the three R's. According to O'Toole, ". . .society has attempted to utilize the schools as levers to correct nearly every evil known to humankind."[11] But it has become clear that education, by itself, in the public or private sector, cannot accomplish the complete socialization and occupational preparation of students. Acquiring knowledge and skills is the primary focus of the educational process, yet significantly large percentages of persons leaving the schools are functionally incompetent. Not only are they unable, for example, to balance their checkbooks or read a loan agreement, they are unable to get or keep a job that meets their needs. Also, where education has managed to prepare students successfully for work, the tendency has been to maximize the graduate's utility to his or her first employer, with little consideration for the graduate's (or society's) long-range needs.

Educational accreditation in specific skill areas is currently one of the most powerful determinants of who gets what jobs, but it does not guarantee job satisfaction or competent performance. In addition, increasing mobility and the evolving labor scene may require people to be trained and retrained a number of times in their lives. This has important implications not only for *what* people learn in schools, but how well they learn how to learn; that is, how adaptable and confident they are in facing new learning situations. Psychologist Herbert Gerjuoy of the Human Resources Research Organization is quoted in *Future Shock* on this subject:

> The new education must teach the individual how to classify
> and reclassify information, how to evaluate its veracity, how to
> change categories when necessary, how to move from the con-
> crete to the abstract and back, how to look at problems from a
> new direction—how to teach himself. Tomorrow's illiterate will
> not be the man (sic) who can't read; he will be the man who has
> not learned how to learn.[12]

Of course, schools can't be expected to prepare students for
all unknown future contingencies. Yet it does seem reasonable
to expect them "to help students develop their individual attributes, potentials, or capacities to levels of proficiency useful
in a wide range of situations."[13] An education geared to facilitating adaptability will develop students' ability and confidence to transfer school learning to life applications. The capacity to transfer may be the most powerful one a person can
possess.

RESEARCH: HANG ON, HELP IS ON THE WAY

Issues of occupational adaptability—patterns of job mobility, the transferability of skills, the transfer of learning to
application, teaching for transfer, and the concept of adaptability itself—are among the research concerns of the National
Center for Research in Vocational Education. Under the spon-
sorship of the National Institute of Education, the Transferable Skills project, started in 1976, is continuing a broad range
of programmatic research. Earlier project activities explored
aspects of the current state-of-knowledge, and resulted in a
number of publications and products that are helpful in gain-
ing a better understanding of occupational adaptability and
transferable skills.

The project's current activities, building on earlier findings
and ideas, are aimed at three general areas of investigation
and development. A series of commissioned papers and symposia, along with the assistance of a panel of consultants, is
continuing to build an information and data base on various
aspects of occupational adaptability, occupational mobility,
teaching transferable skills, and implementation strategies
for educators and trainers. The first of the symposia, entitled
"Occupational Adaptability: Perspectives for Tomorrow's Careers," was held in Dallas, Texas, in December, 1978, at the
convention of the American Vocational Association.

Other current project efforts aim at examining the relationship between functional competencies and transferable skills,
and the relationship between transferable skills and job satisfaction. In addition, work is being done on a planning guide

for persons interested in understanding and facilitating adaptability in educational activities.

It would be useful, at this point, to offer some of our working definitions. We, the authors, view *occupational adaptability* as an individual's capacity to make behavioral adjustments in response to changing situational variables (such as job demands, performance contexts, and knowledge and skill requirements) in order to exhibit appropriate new or modified behaviors. Intrinsic to occupational adaptability is the ability to transfer or generalize from prior learning and experiences in order to reorganize skills, knowledge, and attitudes into new behaviors. Transfer is that "magical something" that is expected to happen in the gap between the occurrence of learning and applying what was learned in actual practice.

Part of any individual's ability to transfer skills, knowledge, attitudes, or any other developed capability or talent effectively, depends on his or her ability to learn from each new experience, and to adapt his or her performance continuously to meet the demands of new and changing situations. Adaptable individuals, it would seem, need to be proficient in a broad range of learning skills and approaches. Individuals differ in the ways that they learn, and some learn better in one way than in another. Also, some skills, information, and concepts are more easily learned when presented and practiced through a variety of approaches rather than through a single approach.

A third characteristic that seems to be consistent with the concept of adaptability is cognitive and psychomotor flexibility. The ability to detach or "un-hook" oneself from previous mental and psychomotor frames of reference, and quickly adopt new ones as the situation requires, is one example of flexibility. Another instance might be the ability to generate a variety of alternative approaches or solutions to a problem when the traditional ones are impractical or impossible.

In addition to the ability to transfer or generalize, to learn and relearn continually, and to implement cognitive and psychomotor flexibility, an individual needs to develop and be able to apply various occupationally transferable skills. What, then, are the transferable skills that have been identified and reported? With regard to the world of work, Robert Stump described them as "the skills and abilities which an individual brings with him/her from job to job, and which apply in each job." [14]

Douglas Sjogren reviewed a wide range of literature and research related to transferable skills. He used Kawula and Smith's generic skills classification scheme to determine which skills are highly transferable, and included skill information collected by the project from business and community representatives.

1. *Mathematics skills.* In the area of mathematics, the evidence seems to be that skills through what is usually regarded as first year algebra are transferable across many occupational situations. Skills at a higher order are certainly transferable but to a much more restricted range of occupations.

2. *Communication skills.* To have some reasonable range of occupational options, a person should have skills in verbal and nonverbal forms of communications, written expressions and comprehension, and speaking and listening. The level of development of these skills seems to be about what might be expected of a student in the secondary schools.

3. *Interpersonal skills.* There seems to be considerable overlap between this area and the communication skills area. Generally it would appear that a person should be able to carry on a conversation, give intelligible instructions to others, and generally be able to attend to others in a positive manner. The importance of interpersonal skills to worker success has been recognized increasingly in recent years to the extent that many organizations provide extensive educational programs in this area. This is an area, however, that has received little emphasis in the regular educational programs. Thus, it is difficult to say at what level of proficiency high school graduates could be expected to have developed interpersonal skills.

4. *Reasoning skills.* Estimation and information-seeking skills are important in this area and are given some emphasis in the schools. Other skills like setting priorities, determining alternatives, and planning are probably not emphasized as much. These skills do seem important, however, for a large number of occupations. Perhaps the current educational/training system does less in this area than in others.

5. *Manipulative skills.* In the psychomotor/sensory area the skills apparently transferable to a large number of occupations seems to be those of sensory acuity, manual dexterity, and coordination. Some of these skills may be more genetically determined than those in the other areas. Skills in this area are amenable to training, however, and this is another area in which our current educational and training programs may be somewhat deficient.[15]

In the authors' view, all skills are potentially transferable to some extent and on some occasions. However, there doesn't seem to be a single agreed-upon list of specific skills and characteristics that apply generally to most settings. No one as yet has produced a "cookbook" of "the best" transferable skills and how to develop them. Nor will having transferable skills guarantee adaptability, but we do think they will facilitate it.

TEACHING FOR TRANSFER: HOW LONG CAN YOU TREAD WATER?

Education should prepare students for work, or, borrowing from Marshall McLuhan, for "learning a living." We expect students to master learning skills and to transfer the use of such skills from the classroom to all future learning situations, on the job or elsewhere. We want what they learn—psychomotor, interpersonal, problem-solving, and basic skills—to transfer and be used in dealing with the complexities and changing demands of daily life and the world of work.

Unfortunately, there appears to be a lack of awareness on the part of both teachers and workers in regard to the concept of transfer. And while a few exemplary educational programs have made moves toward including transferability as an outcome[16] most curricula "only permit a sterile, pale, weak contact with the academic's reconstructions of reality. . . .Subject matter emphasis encourages active passivity, prevents transfer of knowledge, and fails to encourage active use of what is acquired."[17]

If occupational adaptability is a vital component of survival in a constantly changing world of work, acquiring transfer capabilities and transferable skills must not be left to chance. "Individuals are more likely to develop skills for occupational transferability when their educational programs include those skills as part of the explicit curriculum."[18] In other words, transferability must be taught as part of the learning continuum.

The important questions in teaching for transfer are not so much *what* skills are transferable, nor *whether* they are transferable. It has been the authors' finding that "all skills are potentially transferable to some extent and on some occasions."[19] We believe the important questions to be:

1. Which occupational skills should be taught to provide an optional preparation for employability, both for specific jobs and across a variety of jobs?
2. What are the optimal sequences for developing the skills that are components of adaptability?
3. What levels of abstraction are required to permit reasonably efficient transfer of skills to any given situation?
4. Which job behaviors are more adaptable to a training setting?

These more theoretical questions must also be addressed

with a view to important practical considerations. For instance, as technology advances and jobs are demolished in its wake, how can workers be recycled to jobs where they can perform? Who will initially fill the new jobs that are being created by the demands of society and science? How do we analyze the tasks and identify the transferable skills workers have that are the prerequisites for new skill acquisition? How do we teach such necessary but elusive transferable skills as decision-making, risk-taking, self-assessment, and the like? How do we test for transfer? How do we assess mastery of transferable skills necessary for job performance?

It's probably not possible to teach adaptability in one easy course or set of courses, as we would teach mathematics. Before a technology of teaching for transfer can be developed and adopted by teachers, the factors that influence transfer and the power each has must be determined and, where possible, defined. But we believe it is viable and practical to move toward developing a technology to teach for transfer, even at this early stage of turbulent theory.

In Teaching for Transfer: A Perspective, a work by Selz and Ashley, the two project authors offer a number of "how to" suggestions for teaching for transfer, based on the concepts just discussed. Briefly, the tactics include raising student awareness of transfer, transferable skills, and personal competencies; appropriate sequencing of tasks; appropriate degrees of practice for mastery in a wide variety of performance situations; and, reinforcement of correct applications of transfer and cue recognition in multiperceptual contexts.

These practical ideas could apply to any learning situation. They could be the basis for developing whole new curricula, or they could be incorporated into extant curricula to make them more relevant to adaptability. They would apply with equal validity to academic or vocational education, industrial training or retraining programs, manpower programs, study circles, day care centers, or continuing adult education. Regardless of what is taught, or where, or to whom, maximum positive transfer can and should be a conscious, deliberate objective.

Attention to adaptability and its components of transfer and transferable skills would have many advantages besides helping to match workers better to a fluctuating labor market. It could offer an answer to what Toffler called "a fight. . .between standardization and variety in the curriculum."[20]

Of course, teaching occupational adaptability and transferable skills is not a panacea. Adaptability has its limits, and an overemphasis on it in educational environments could run roughshod over many people, especially those with certain personality traits or physiological limitations. Nor could all transferable skills be taught to everyone. So what would the tradeoffs be? "The values and orientations of employers and the work environment itself determine to a great extent which skills can transfer and which cannot."[21] Factors such as union controls and fluctuations of the labor market can have appreciable effects on who gets jobs, and there are other non-skill-related barriers. Not all communities or individuals will necessarily view occupational adaptability as a valuable trait, either, particularly where communal attitudes value traditional or familiar work environments and social stability. And high occupational adaptability, if emphasized in isolation of other aspects of one's life, may produce undesirable side-effects, such as interpersonal ineffectiveness and the stress on the worker's family that frequent moves for jobs often entail. Occupational adaptability may *not* be for everyone.

On the other hand, adaptability empowers the individual. It is intimately linked to a person's perceptions of his or her extent of control over his or her life and work environments. Having transfer skills and transferable skills—and knowing one has them—can give "the individual person some tools by which he or she can begin now to change the system *at least as it affects his or her life.*"[22] Bolles calls work one of the three "boxes" of life, and reflects on an emerging (or possibly re-emerging) view of work as an aspect of the flow of life, not a separate entity with strict boundaries. As the world of work flows into life skills, perhaps the same can be said of adaptability, transfer, and transferable skills.

IMPLICATIONS: A JOURNEY OF A THOUSAND MILES. . . .

Between the efforts of exemplary educational programs, books by such authors as Crystal and Bolles, and the research begun by our project and others, some positive first steps have been taken toward introducing and developing the concept of occupational adaptability, at least in the United States. But what we do know, and what we've collectively or individually managed to develop and introduce, amount to no more than random pieces of an immense mosaic—we can only speculate on the patterns and messages of a picture that itself is constantly changing. As Crystal and Bolles pointed out, work—and consequently, occupational adaptability—flows through all aspects of our lives, with no true boundaries. Likewise, the flow and attitudes of the work force affect every aspect of human society, viewed from the perspective of any discipline.

The question then becomes, if there is so much that we still need to know and still have to do, what are the best directions in which to go next? Who has the capability/influence/responsibility to pursue the idea of occupational adaptability and make it a reality?

Five clusters of interest groups are in situations that would enable them to facilitate preparation of individuals for change: educators, employers, career counselors, legislators, and researchers. That's not counting the efforts of the individual him- or herself—the basic unit of change. What each of these groups could do to advance occupational adaptability will be discussed briefly in the hope that somewhere in here, you will recognize where *you* can help to get adaptability out of the theory stage and into the repertoire of the labor market, now.

1. *Educators.* This group includes teachers, trainers, school administrators and supervisors, and school counselors. All of them face the general accusation that education is not doing its job.

Assuming that educators choose to incorporate occupational adaptability (i.e., transfer and transferable skills) as an objective, what are the next steps? It's unlikely that an entire curriculum for occupational adaptability will be forthcoming from anyone in the immediate future; there are too many unanswered questions. For instance, "Critical decisions must be made about what is important for learning, what is merely 'nice to know,' and what is nonessential. Moreover, decisions about what is learned also affect how learning takes place."[23] Another problem is deciding what older curricula components will have to be sacrificed from the busy school schedule to make room for the new. Merely introducing one or two courses specifically intended to teach transfer and transferable skills won't be very effective, nor will having only a few teachers incorporate them as objectives in their regular academic or vocational courses. "Their effective development can only be accomplished if they are pervasive and deliberate objectives for an entire school program."[24]

Since the information or technology for developing such a school program has not yet been established, an alternative may be an adaptive methodology of teaching for performance in the world of work. The Transferable Skills project is working to advance this goal, and a current paper, *Teaching for Transfer: A Perspective*, by Selz and Ashley, discusses the previously-mentioned suggestions for practical application that teachers and trainers could adapt to their courses in the interim.

2. *Employers.* Businesses of all sizes face the continuous challenge of finding and developing talented individuals to match industry's changing staffing needs. The functions of employers in the realm of occupational adaptability seem to occur mainly in three arenas: hiring practices, on-the-job training and retraining, and cooperation with educational and other institutions concerned with employability.

Hiring practices tend to be archaic and short-sighted. The

inept "winnowing" process performed by most personnel departments and other persons charged with hiring responsibilities probably has more to do with the current rates of "misemployment" and employee turnover than any other employer practice. Accreditation of skills acquired and refined outside of a school or job context is a particular problem, because those skills represent a potential—but generally unidentified—gold mine of utility to employers. Also, hiring persons with good transfer skills and pertinent transferable skills should reduce the amount of formal or informal in-house training needed. Encouraging awareness and receptivity to occupational adaptability in the persons responsible for hiring, transferring, and promoting employees may be a great advantage for a business.

Assuming that many persons either coming into a firm or being transferred or promoted within it will not necessarily be as adaptable as desired, teaching for transfer and transferable skills may be an important objective for training and retraining programs. By emphasizing adaptability rather than specialization in training, it may be possible to bring some of the priorities of both business and organized labor closer together. In addition, human development programs that would raise employee consciousness about occupational adaptability, and the applicability of skills acquired outside of school or work, could have profitable results in encouraging employee initiative on and across jobs, as well as reduce anxieties about lateral transfers or expanding job responsibilities within a firm.

It has been suggested that adaptability is not a costless objective. Trainees who are taught highly transferable skills may take those skills and go to another company for more benefits. Inter-firm "piracy" could be countered by inter-firm cooperation, through which an entire industry would pool its training facilities and thus maximize the pool of trainees without sacrificing occupational adaptability as a training objective. Some firms are avoiding the entire piracy issue by going a different internal organizational route, such as the "paternalistic" industries of Japan. In such organizations, the need to develop and encourage occupational adaptability in employees must be a priority.

The use of transferable skills lists for trainee positions could be a help to businesses in the midst of forecasting their own future growth and staffing needs. It takes minimum effort for an employment manager to analyze entry jobs and career paths when considering transferable skills, and it greatly reduces the complexity of identifying truly eligible persons to fill those positions.

With occupational mobility a reality and occupational adaptability becoming a societal necessity, the cooperation of business in advancing adaptability will be increasingly vital. To deal with the problems, business will need to develop closer ties with government, organized labor, and, especially in regard to developing occupational adaptability, with education. Unfortunately, "Despite mutual interests, the fields of education and employment have remained aloof to one another."[25]

One way in which business can bridge this gap is to "help schools identify occupationally transferable skills, knowledge, and personal characteristics that have relatively broad applications and use."[26] Another approach is for a business to arrange tours for local school counselors and interested students, in order to offer a view of the occupations in the particular industry. Many firms do this, but employers can

> make their jobs meaningful to their visitors by describing jobs in terms of basic skills used in the various operations....It is the use of these transferable skills that counselors and employers, as well as students, should be trying to isolate and understand.[27]

Cooperative education is yet another approach to matching the needs of education and business, in which classroom instruction is related with practical career-related situations. An example is New York's Fiorello H. LaGuardia Community College, the state's "first postsecondary institution to offer a comprehensive program of cooperative education."[28] The program involves an on-the-job internship at three different jobs, as well as instruction in "job-coping skills, resume writing, and other practical ways of getting and holding a job."[29] Such a program could offer a relevant arena for both teaching about and physically demonstrating transferability in pertinent job clusters, and in helping people make real transfers from learning to performance.

3. *Career counselors.* Those involved in helping workers decide what work they want and can do, and matching workers to available jobs, can make immediate use of the concepts of adaptability and transferable skills. Not only can appropriate presentation of such skills to a potential employer give a job-seeker an "edge," they can greatly broaden the possible jobs to which a worker can apply, thereby increasing his or her "marketability."

Because "the person most affected by rapid changes in the workplace is the older person,"[30] the challenge to career counselors in helping older workers make career transitions—especially major transitions necessitated by the phasing-out of jobs—is enormous. By guiding such people to recognize, assess, and adapt the transferable skills they have already developed in life or on the job, counselors may be able to help workers bypass much unnecessary retraining, stress, and expenditure of effort. This applies equally to counselors working or consulting with industries to help recycle workers through transfers or expanding or changing job responsibilities. A counselor aware of the value of transferability may save a business time and money by ascertaining precisely how much and what kind of retraining adaptable workers actually need, rather than automatically recycling all workers through entry-level training programs.

4. *Legislators.* Legislation on the local, state, or federal level presents an avenue to foster the adoption of occupational adaptability in public schools. Much has been done along this line at the state level for Minimum Competencies. Some suggestions to facilitate this avenue, if it is deemed an appropriate one (it may not be, if for no other reason than that cited earlier: that adaptability may not be a positive value in all communities), include:

- Prepare a *clear plan* for how occupational adaptability can be developed in formal and informal education. One of the most effective means to cut through public and congressional disagreement and indecision is to *know what you want.*
- Identify your probable opponents and potential supporters. Some influential supporters may include not only educators and rapidly expanding businesses, but special interest groups such as minorities, women's rights groups, and government agencies in which human development programs for employees are an interest or practice.
- Keep all statements crystal clear. It's important to use the "right" kinds of words so that they may be picked up and implanted in the empowering legislation (e.g., "functional basic skills," "talents," etc.).

5. *Researchers.* The issues related to occupational adaptability cover a broad spectrum, from predicting trends in the labor market to assessing adaptability in individuals. As mentioned earlier, the Transferable Skills project has taken a fishnet approach to collecting and synthesizing what is known. Much remains to be done. Pat theories about occupational adaptability are not likely to be developed, especially not overnight; the variables are complex, and their relationships are not necessarily stable. Taking what *is* known—or knowable— and developing strategies, techniques, and instruments for practical implementation must be a priority, however, even if compromises with theoretical niceties are necessary. Patterns of occupational mobility appear to be stable, at this time, but the acceleration of change in Western society continues, and adaptability is needed *now.*

Some directions for R&D that have evolved from the work of the Transferable Skills project include:

First, basic information is needed to develop alternative ways to assess achievement and the ability to transfer or apply skills and knowledge in various settings. Second, basic information is needed about occupational change and mobility. Especially important is the need for basic information about the relationships of individual skills and abilities to job requirements and individual occupational change. New and innovative ways are needed to use available longitudinal data about workers and job mobility to better understand the relative importance and influence of individual attributes in job changing and occupational adaptability.[31]

Miguel, in his paper *Developing Skills for Occupational Transferability*, lists a number of other needs:

Strategies are needed for redesigning academic and vocational education curricula to provide for the development of occupational transferability.

Innovative instructional techniques designed expressly for developing occupational transferability are needed.

Students need monitoring and planning devices to help them keep track of the skills they are developing and relate those skills to a variety of occupational possibilities.

Counseling strategies are needed to meet the individual's life-long need for interpretation of skill transfer as it relates to new employment ventures.

Evaluation strategies are needed to assess the effects of learned skills on successful job moves.

Assessement instruments are needed to help employers determine the transferability of job candidates' skills.

Occupational information documents need to highlight the transferable skills and characteristics that are needed in each occupation.

An "awareness campaign" is needed to join employers, educators, and the general public in a common understanding of the transferability of skills among occupations.[32]

The "awareness campaign" may be the one immediately important and practical task to be undertaken. Bolles, Crystal, and Lathrop, through their books on job changing and life-long planning, have made a credible start. The Transferable Skills project, through its publications and presentations such as this, is trying to reach concerned audiences. The implications of occupational adaptability for enabling workers and businesses to meet each other's needs effectively are such that the campaign should not be left to the usual designated channels. It is an idea that each of us can help to develop and implement.

SUMMARY

"Change is the process by which the future invades our lives..."[33] One of the most crucial areas of our lives where change is being felt is in the world of work, which is in substantial flux. Unemployment and misemployment are the major symptoms of a failure to match the needs of workers and businesses to each other. These problems may worsen in the future, as industries undergo enormous change in their personnel needs.

The development of occupational adaptability can facilitate individuals' capacity to deal with such changes. Transfer skills and transferable skills are vital components of occupational adaptability, and an important arena in which to develop them is in education. Teaching for transfer may involve a revamping of educational programs to include and emphasize transferable skills, to develop transfer skills, and to make students aware of and able to assess their own occupational adaptability. Acquiring and understanding occupational adaptability should empower the individual to deal with change—either by adapting successfully to the altering environment, or altering the environment to meet the individual's own goals and needs.

NOTES

1. Alvin Toffler, *Future Shock*. (New York: Bantam Books, 1970), p. 1.
2. G. L. Martin, "A View of Work Toward the Year 2000." *Personnel Journal*, 1977, Vol 56, nr. 10, pp. 502–526.
3. L. R. Brown, "The Limits to Growth of Third World Cities." *The Futurist*. 1976, vol 10, nr. 6, pp. 308–309.
4. D. Little, "Post-Industrial Society and What It May Mean." *The Futurist*, 1973, vol 7, nr. 5, p. 259.
5. Martin, p. 504.
6. *Ibid*, p. 503.
7. P. Renwick, E. Lawler, etc., "What You Really Want from Your Job." *Psychology Today*, 1978, vol 11, nr. 12, p. 65.
8. W. Harman, "Chronic Unemployment: An Emerging Problem of Postindustrial Society." *The Futurist*, 1978, vol 12, nr. 4, p. 213.
9. Martin, p. 503.
10. Toffler, p. 403.
11. J. O'Toole, *Work, Learning, and the American Future*, (San Francisco: Jossey-Bass, 1977.) passim.
12. Toffler, p. 414.
13. F. Pratzner, *Occupational Adaptability and Transferable Skills*. (Columbus: Ohio State University, Nat. Center for Research in Vocational Education, 1978), p. 1.
14. R. Stomp, *Occupational Mobility and Career Planning: What is Needed?* Paper presented at the Second Career Educational National Forum, Washington, DC., 1976.
15. D. Sjogren, *Occupational Transferable Skills and Characteristics: A Review of Literature and Research*. (Columbus: Ohio State

University, Nat. Center for Research in Vocational Education, 1977), p. 22.

16. See R. Miguel, *Developing Skills for Occupational Transferability: Insights Gained from Current Practice* (Columbus: Ohio State University, Nat. Center for Research in Vocational Education, 1977).

17. D. F. Walker, *The Structure of Goals, Knowledge and Curricula in Schooling* (Stanford: Stanford University, School of Education, 1977), p. 26.

18. Miguel, p. 24.

19. Pratzner, p. 1.

20. Toffler, p. 411.

21. Miguel, p. 25.

22. R. N. Bolles, *The Three Boxes of Life and How to Get Out of Them* (Berkeley: Ten Speed Press, 1978) p. 24.

23. Pratzner, p. 31.

24. *Ibid.*, p. 2.

25. H. G. Pearson, "Person Skills vs Job Techniques." *Personnel Journel*, 1978, vo. 57, nr. 5. p. 247.

26. Pratzner, p. 2.

27. Pearson, p. 248.

28. W. L. Abbott, "Beating Unemployment Through Education." *The Futurist*, 1978, vol 12, nr. 4, p. 217.

29. *Ibid.*

30. *Ibid*, p. 215.

31. Pratzner, p. 3.

32. Miguel, pp. 27–29.

33. Toffler, p. 1.

TWO FUTURES FOR EDUCATION/WORK RELATIONS: TECHNOCRATIC VS. SOCIO-TECHNICAL DESIGN

Arthur G. Wirth

Part I
THE VALUE SPLIT: HISTORICAL BACKGROUND

"An emphasis has been on economic growth and increased output but not on what kind of men are being molded by the work process."[1]

"A democratic political-economy must begin and end with the person-in-society, seeing him as both end and means, and combining his reason and his actions in empowered participation."[2]

It is useful to perceive schools as work places. Historically, they have provided the transition between the family and paid work. Indeed, it is not surprising to find today that the character of life in schools is affected significantly by the values and organizational features of the world of work. This trend is further reinforced by society's expectation that schools will help people to do well in the economic system.

In the twentieth century the rationale and techniques of scientific management transformed the nature of work in America. Likewise, these techniques also spilled over into the schools, as Raymond Callahan pointed out in *Education and the Cult of Efficiency*.[3]

Presently the schools are being powerfully affected by the technocratic ideology and techniques of sytems management. But a new option is entering the scene in the work world— socio-technical design, or industrial democracy. Its philosophical features question the mainline economic tradition. There is a strong possibility that the future of education in the coming decades will be affected by a growing clash between these two belief systems in both the economy and in education. The industrial democracy challenge is developing most rapidly in Scandinavia. Scandinavian writings and experiences will, therefore, be used extensively throughout this paper to clarify the nature of this concept and its philosophy.

The tension between the two value orientations, while recent in some particulars, is rooted in a basic division of values embedded deeply in American culture. Daniel Bell has identified the issue perceptively when he said that there is a widening tension between an economic, technical, order oriented to functional rationality and efficiency (organized on the simple principle of economizing, of least costs, and optimization of production and profits), and counter trends concerned with "wholeness of persons" and the ethos of self-realization.

Early in the twentieth century, the underlying policy issues in American education were foreshadowed in the debate over vocationalism between John Dewey and the "social efficiency" philosophers. The social efficiency philosophers were in favor of school policies that would support the values and job needs of the industrial corporate system. Dewey challenged these value priorities and called for related institutional re-designs in both work and education.[4] Some would say the debate continues, with only minor modifications.

First some comments on the social efficiency approach to vocationalism. Among the early proponents for vocational education in the 1890s were representatives of the business community. These American businessmen, as revealed in their speeches at N.A.M. conventions, believed that the Social Darwinist theory of William Graham Sumner expressed the source of human progress. This ideology assumed that society consisted of isolated individuals of varying abilities and capacities. When left to pursue their self advantage in rugged competition they would bring forth the promise of increasing material plenty for all.

The manufacturers sought out sympathetic educators who became proficient articulators of a social efficiency philosophy. Among these were David Snedden who left a professorship at Teachers College to become Commissioner of Education in 1909 under Governor Douglas in Massachusetts. He appointed his colleague, Charles Prosser, later author of the Smith Hughes Act, to create and administer a new vocational program.

The rationales they developed to support technocratic training models were marked by a competitive laissez-faire philosophy, a methodology of specific training based on principles of stimulus-response psychology, and a curriculum designed according to the job needs of industry.

Snedden confidently viewed the growth of the burgeoning corporate-urban-industrial phenomenon as the foremost means for human progress. He called those who bemoaned the mechanization and depersonalization of work "simple-lifers" or "romantic impracticalists" who yearned for times that were gone forever. He surmised that modern men might be subjected to fragmented, routine job tasks; but production specialization and differentiation enabled them to live longer, more comfortably, and with the leisure to consume the arts. Moreover the application of mass production methods to *school life* could help to forward still new advances. As he put it, "Quantity production methods applied in education speedily give us school grades, uniform textbooks, promotional examinations ... strictly scheduled programs, mechanical discipline and hundreds of other mechanisms most of which are unavoidably necessary if our ideals of universal education are to be realized."[5]

As Snedden saw it scientific testing instruments combined with vocational guidance would make it possible for schools to do what Charles Eliot had suggested in 1907—differentiate children into programs according to their "probable destinies" based on heredity, economic, and social factors.

The model which emerged from this rationale was a Social Darwinist "job efficiency" approach. The nature of the jobs to be planned for kids in schools was roughly to parallel the design of jobs in the work world. Application of the rationalization of labor and quantitative measurement of outcomes could increase efficiency in both realms.

John Dewey, the philosopher of democracy, also was seriously involved with the policy issues connected with vocationalism. But he was bringing a very different frame of reference to the topic. In *Individualism Old and New* Dewey held that the basic problem for industrialized countries was a qualitative one. "Can a material, industrial civilization be converted into a distinctive agency for liberating the minds and refining the emotions of all who take part in it?"[6]

Dewey was blunt about what he held to be the "fundamental defect of our civilization." He noted that Americans now had available more power over nature and more intellectual resources than were available to classical Athenians or to the people of the Renaissance. Why, he asked, has this collective enrichment not operated more to elevate the quality of our lives? The "corrosive" materialism of our times, he said, "springs from the notion sedulously cultivated by the class in power, that the creative capacities of individuals can be evoked and developed only in a struggle for material possessions and material power."[7]

"... (Economic) associations are fixed in ways which exclude most of the workers in them from taking part in their management. The subordination of the enterprises to pecuniary profit reacts to make the workers 'hands' only; their hearts and brains are not engaged."[8]

As long as the priority is focused primarily on pecuniary gain rather than social utility, he said, the intellectual and moral development of both workers and management will be one-sided and warped.

The alternative, Dewey said, is to know how the power of science, industry and technology can be directed toward "making a different sort of world and society."—one designed to assure "an ordered expression of individual capacity and for the satisfaction of the needs of man ..."[9]

Dewey's aspiration was to redesign industrial and educational institutions so that they would be supportive of democratic values. He created his own laboratory school at the University of Chicago as an inquiry-centered, collaborative learning community for teachers, students and scholar consultants to illustrate his preferred values.

From this interchange one can see that the issues were joined early. As the twentieth century unfolded there have been pulls on the schools from both value traditions. The dominant theme emerging from this confrontation, in reality, has been the unfolding of the bureaucratic, competitive, efficiency model, moderated by peripheral reform features. By the mid-seventies the dominant pressure on schools clearly was coming from the technocratic ideology, manifesting itself in proposals designed to assure measurable educational productivity and bureaucratic control.

C. A. Bowers pointed out recently that the current concern for efficiency continues, manifesting itself powerfully in a sophisticated technocratic ideology, rooted in the language and world view of systems analysis. Our schools, likewise, embrace the assumptions of the conservative managerial center of society. One may recognize it in behavior modification, aspects of career education, and competency based education.[10] This educational tradition takes for granted the values of the corporate status quo. It sees itself as concerned with a neutral goal of improving efficiency (defined as increased measurable output). It tends to assume that only observable behavior is real, that anything real must be measurable, that significant learning consists of discrete components, and that the good self is operationally defined by scoring well on expert-designed tests. As Bowers points out, this rationale makes no reference to the individual who experiences existence as problematic and it is hard to find it the liberal concern for education as a rational emancipatory force.

In summary, by the late seventies one might conclude that the systems approach essentially has won acceptance. The time of overt protest is past. The majority seem to have opted in favor of what Adam Curle called the values of "competitive materialism."[11] But is there a consensus about such assurance? There is certainly serious concern both within corporate industry and the nation's schools about symptoms of alienation and lack of commitment: apathy, absenteeism, shoddy work, alcoholism, drug abuse, and mental illness. There is also the disturbing tendency of American consumers to have more confidence in the quality and price of foreign made products. Deep-seated doubts about "efficiency" continue to be expressed in many ways. Max Lerner, for example, noted how frequently civilizations have been weakened by a pathological insistence upon pushing to extremes their master institutions.[12] He thinks defensiveness about the business system may be vitiating qualities of democratic leadership "attuned at once to the life of nature and the life of the spirit."

Concern about problems related to the malaise of alienation have not been confined to the United States. In Scandinavia, for example, where the problems became acute in the sixties, an alternative philosophy and techniques for the design of work (known as socio-technical or industrial democracy design) were instituted and are now being systematically implemented.

It is important for educators to become familiar with this development. It involved exploration of bold alternatives to the rational, bureaucratic tradition. There were conscious efforts to seek a re-design for work which accommodated the needs for wholeness without sacrificing productive efficiency.

The second part of this paper analyzes the Scandinavian experiment. Their theoretical and adaptive efforts are having increasing impact on pioneers of work reform in America. If the trend continues, the meaning for education will also require analysis.

Part II
AN ALTERNATIVE KNOWN AS SOCIO-TECHNICAL OR INDUSTRIAL DEMOCRACY DESIGN

In *People At Work*,[13] Pehr Gyllenhammar, President of Volvo, reflects on changes that have taken place in his company which he believes lay the groundwork for far-reaching re-design of work. Growing alienation and unrest in 1969 spurred major organizational changes. Gyllenhammar points out that Volvo began automobile construction in 1927. The managers shared the assumption of the time that Taylorist efficiency principles were the means to successful competition. Management was tightly centralized—controlled by the President, a three man executive committee, and a large hierarchically organized administrative staff. Its production system was technically oriented and planned in detail, using the system of Methods Time Management imported from the United States.

By the end of the sixties, however, this orderly system was coming unglued. The new element was a change in the nature and attitudes of young men and women entering the work force.

In Gyllenhammar's words,

> "Like other good things, economy of scale turned out to have
> subtle limits. We begin to find today the symptoms of a new
> type of industrial illness. We invent machines to eliminate some
> of the physical stress of work, and then find psychological stress
> causing even more health and behavior problems. People don't
> want to be subservient to machines and systems. They react to
> inhuman working conditions in very human ways: by job-hop-
> ping, absenteeism, apathetic attitudes, antagonism, and even
> malicious mischief. . . . The younger the worker is, the stronger
> his or her reactions are likely to be. People entering the work-
> force today have received more education than ever before in
> history. We have educated them to regard themselves as mature
> adults, capable of making their own choices. Then we offer them
> virtually no choice in our overorganized industrial units. For
> eight hours a day they are regarded as children, ciphers, or
> potential problems and managed or controlled accordingly."[14]

With this situational change, Volvo leaders had to make a
crucial decision. One course would be to retain the old rules
and hire less-educated Finnish and Turkish workers. This
would acknowledge that industry could not utilize the most
highly educated Swedish youth in the country's history—and
it probably would invite social unrest. A second possibility
would be to engage in a bold break from the hierarchical industrial tradition. Volvo made the choice to join the accelerated Scandinavian move toward industrial democracy. The
opening sentence in *People At Work* sets the tone of the alternative: "People, not machines, are the real basis for the spec-
tacular growth of industry during the twentieth century."[15]

Behind this statement is the recognition that in advanced
stages of technology, education is the invisible asset for new
approaches to economic and social development. By the early
eighties 90 per cent of Sweden's young people are projected to
complete high school and 70 per cent are expected to continue
into higher education. In Gyllenhammar's words, "Among
these increasingly well-educated people Volvo will have to find
its future work force."[16] Democratic societies traditionally invest heavily in education to produce people who regard themselves as mature adults, capable of taking initiative and making intelligent choices. To neglect these new expectations and
capacities is to invite dissatisfaction and alienation. To accept
them as assets to be nurtured, forces one into paths beyond
the framework of traditional economic thinking. The basic
switch in attitudes is from viewing employees as "hired
hands" to seeing and treating them as adult persons.

Puzzling new questions have to be faced if old habits of

management are questioned: What kind of thinking takes place if one views workers as persons who want a chance to live and learn as mature adults in the work place? Is the production process a "given" to which humans must adjust, or can technology be redesigned to place it under the control of workers' intelligence and initiative? What qualities of leadership are needed to balance the claims of workers, stockholders, customers and general public?

The answer to these questions is dependent on one's conception of the basic goal of economic enterprise. The President of Volvo frames his answer as follows: "the purpose of business is to help achieve and maintain the public good" and the logical extension is the obligation "to administer the resources with which the company is entrusted and use them to create economic growth, taking into consideration all the interest groups involved with the company. This objective carries with it the demand to provide meaningful employment."[17] The Scandanavian goal, therefore, is to view every worker as entitled to a dignified work place with opportunity for personal development and a chance to influence the work commensurate with his or her abilities and to do it so that the enterprises "stay in the black."

In order to further portray the means to realize these objectives we may look briefly at developments in another of the pioneering plants—the Kalmar auto assembly plant. By the late sixties, Kalmar was in trouble. Wildcat strikes were erupting, employee turnover was 52 per cent per year and absenteeism was rising. Volvo leaders finally decided that the old technical solutions themselves were part of the problem.

Instead of using time and motion studies and more automation, the decision was made to create a work process which would increase worker autonomy, initiative and collegial collaboration. Operationally it meant relinquishing the long, straight lines of traditional assembly. The aim of new construction was to organize into small workshops, healthful and aesthetic, as part of the larger plant. A key change was to revise technology to give people the flexibility to reorganize themselves at work. Instead of attaching workers to a moving line, materials were to be brought to work stations where autonomous groups of 15-20 persons could accomplish their own organization. The Kalmar plant introduced moveable carriers (low self-propelling platforms, subject to a variety of controls by workers, on which assembly took place). Work teams could design their own work, rest rhythms, job rotation, collaborative plans for trouble shooting, etc. Responsibility for quality control was assigned to the units by asking each to conduct its own inspections.

From this description one gets a sense of the meaning of socio-technical design. At Kalmar the aim was to overcome low morale by involving people in collaborative human groups. They could not, however, realistically move toward such goals if they continued to use traditionally engineered technology. Gyllenhammar concluded, "Technology can strangle people. On the other hand if it is designed for people, technology can also be a liberator. . . . It is possible to devise new solutions to combine rational technological systems with greater freedom for human choice." [18]

The Scandinavians assume that their decision to develop a society of highly educated persons will increasingly lead to a growing demand for "good work." It rejects the contention that work requires "hired hands," managed by authoritarian leadership with a status gulf separating them.

Clarification of the possibilities of a different future for the workplace along these lines requires clear understanding of the theory. Pioneering in this area has been carried forward over the past several decades in the Industrial Democracy Project and the Work Research Institutes in Oslo, Norway, with conceptualizations by philosopher-practitioners like Einar Thorsrud, Fred Emery, and P. G. Herbst. [19]

In Norway in the early sixties the introduction of scientific management after World War II had strengthened industry's influence. There was an unusual agreement, however, among both employer and union organizations that is was showing its limitations in restricting cherished Norwegian qualities such as individual freedom, creativity and social life in the work place. There was sufficient concern to warrant a joint committee to study problems of industrial democracy in the 1961-2 the Trade Unions Council and the National Confederation of Employers. From that committee emerged joint action-research programs involving re-designs of work in industries, shipping, and more recently, education. After years of experience the investigators decided that the heart of the problem was in the hierarchically organized bureaucracy itself. This resulted in the creation of alternatives to hierarchies.

While classic bureaucratic models historically emerged to fill real needs, they increasingly became dysfunctional in societies with democratic traditions and with secondary, higher, and continuing education available to the citizenry at large. [20] An important question emerges: are workable alternatives to bureaucracies available when broader concepts of efficiency demand a shift of priorities to concerns for the quality of life? The leaders of the Industrial Democracy Project hold that the need to raise this question is rooted in more than idealistic humanitarianism. The need to redesign bureaucracies derives from fundamental changes in man's relationship to his environment. The bureaucratic model worked when man's fundamental relation to his world was the physical environment and the technology he developed to act on it. The environment could be conceptualized as an aggregate or cluster of elements which could be manipulated for human gain. Classical science built its theories of the universal and deterministic laws on just such an aggregate model. Classical economic and management theory incorporated humans as constituent elements of the aggregate.

The socio-technical theorists maintain that we are entering a new stage marked by the emergence of a turbulent environment.

"A turbulent environment is one in which directive correlations established with the environment, on which the survival of an organism depends, unexpectedly break down. Actions that are initiated become attenuated or build up uncontrollably, and goal-directed strategies can lead to the opposite of the intended result."[22]

The source of the turbulence lies in the shift from the physical environment and technology functioning as the medium for the relation of man to man, to an emerging stage where the predominant relation *is man to man.* "The turbulent environment is man himself,"[23] and efforts to solve turbulent problems with procedures based on principles of the mechanistic, aggregate model increasingly break down.

New types of technology are now emerging designed as integrated systems that can be operated by small staff teams. The rate of change in technological design increases so that "it now becomes necessary to build learning capacities into the organization of industrial work teams. This can be achieved by creating relatively autonomous matrix organizations in which neither task roles nor work relationships are fixed."[24] Within this framework, work teams of persons engaged in continuous learning, become capable of doing research both to find ways to improve production and to develop strategies for coping with changes in tasks. Linkages are established with universities and other research units.

The machine model is progressively replaced by

"A society in which there will be relatively little difference in the educational level and status of those who work in industrial, educational, research, and service organizations. Persons will differ more as regards their focus of orientation than as regards the nature of their work. The leading elements in the transitional stage of development are the rapid increase and diffusion of complex technologies which can be operated by a small number of persons, and the rapid increase and diffusion of higher education. In terms of their operational requirements these will up to a point be mutually supportive. As development continues, the traditional hierarchical type of organization based on the separation of doing, planning and deciding will be replaced by primary work groups in which these functions are integrated. The members of these groups will to an increasing degree be able to participate in policy decisions and be capable of using specialists as consultants."[25]

Socio-technical designers recognize also that key problems concern not only how to produce, but what to produce. Adequate thinking about institutional planning and functioning requires a conscious incorporation of ethical goals and choices. In the technical-bureaucratic state, thinking was more limited to how to get material and monetary results. As people become more aware that they have control over the means and methods they apply, they are less able to shirk the responsibility of assessing the consequences of their choices. Gyllenhammar reports, for example, on the consequences of deciding to choose alternatives to hierarchical bureaucratic control. He believes that the most effective changes made were those in which the workers themselves had the largest hand. He adds,

"It is almost alarming to realize how much know how and capability had been locked up in the work force, unavailable to managers who simply didn't realize what an important resource it was. Our experience at Volvo has changed my views of management somewhat. Unlocking working potential has become as important as any display of brilliance in technical terms."[26]

It is an existential choice whether to exercise or ignore the option.

Brief reference to another case may illustrate the on-going practical applications of the socio-technical design. Einar Thorsrud has reported on an experience in creating non-hierarchical autonomous matrix organizations in the Norwegian Merchant Marine. A case in point is the ship named Balao. In the sixties more highly educated Norwegian youth were refusing to enlist in the military-type work organization and rigid status system of the old merchant marine. Personnel turnover and traditional rating systems interfered with the need for stable, highly trained crews capable of flexible, ongoing learning—in ships (such as the Baleo)—increasingly equipped with sophisticated, automated technology. Social technical designers decided to shift the trend more toward "a small crew all of whose members have a professional or technical work role—that is basically an all-officer crew."[27] Alternatives both to the single hierarchical structure of tasks and roles, and to the old superior-subordinate relationship were developed in a decade of experimentation. Organizational options were designed for different purposes. In emergency situations, for example, relations are of the traditional military type; for ordinary operation and maintenance, skilled work teams function without any formal officer in charge; other persons assume leadership roles for planning educational and leisure programs on board ship and ashore. The trend is to train personnel in multiple roles, so that people in superior roles can switch to subordinate roles and vice versa to form structures appropriate for the tasks at hand. People retain primary professional identities but the former isolation of officers from crew is reduced.

In reflecting on features of socio-technical work changes, Thorsrud and colleagues have summarized some key ideas workers and management need if their goal is to create "good work." They need to create:

1. Allowance for decision-making. The sense that they are their own bosses and that except in exceptional circumstances they do not have someone breathing down their necks. . . .
2. Chances for lifelong learning and on-the-job training. We accept that such learning is possible only when men are able to set goals that are reasonable challenges for them and get a feedback of results in time for them to correct their behavior.
3. An optimal level of variety, i.e. they can vary the work so as to avoid boredom and fatigue and so as to gain the best advantages from settling into a satisfying rhythm of work.
4. Conditions where they can and do get help and respect from their workmates. . . .
5. A sense of one's own work meaningfully contributing to social welfare. . . .
6. A desirable future. Quite simply, not a dead end job; hopefully one that will continue to allow personal growth.[28]

A crucial point in developing leadership to produce "good work" is to sharpen awareness of the difference between this goal and traditional job enrichment, which may include new methods like flexible time scheduling, T-grouping or sensitivity training, or TM training for workers. What is the essential obligation of economic activity in a democratic society? If it simply is to increase GNP then managers view all items in the system in terms of their efficiency toward that end. Job enrichment is a means of manipulating the human variable (psychic dimension included) to increase productivity.

A new perspective is introduced when the society agrees that the purpose of economic activity is "to help achieve and maintain the public good." The socio-technical work theory assumes that its approach will be effective with material productivity, but it does not accept the proposition that any technical or psychological change that increases productivity is evidence of "good work."

This point of view, which coincides with the philosophy of socio-technical design, is based on the premise stated by Kalman H. Silvert: "a democratic political-economy must begin and end with the person-in-society, seeing him as both end and means, and combining his reason and his actions in empowered participation."[29] Taken seriously, this requires as Willard Wirtz states,

> "...a new economics that takes (the) human potential as its starting point... (This) new economics would start from a commitment to make the fullest practical use of the most highly developed form of whatever talents are inside people instead of starting from a consideration of the most profitable use or misuse of the elements inside the thin and fragile crust of the planet. Such a policy would measure all major enterprises in terms of their comparative drain on dwindling natural resources and their comparative use of the highly developed— meaning educated—human resource."

We might then, as Wirtz suggests, start evaluating our economic activity in terms of its contribution to Net National Strength (NNS) rather than to Gross National Product (GNP).[30]

IMPLICATIONS FOR EDUCATION

Schools are, in fact, work places for students and teachers. The question is how can they be made into "good work" places in E. F. Schumacher's sense. The quality of school life will continue to be affected significantly by values and features of life in the work world. The dominant technocratic ideology has had powerful effects on American schools, but conditions may be arising so that industrial democracy theory may gain influence. Educators should be aware of this development. Their own experience teaches them that they will continue to be affected by changes in job-related thinking, and if management develops more of a social design in industry, it will have implications in education.

This author assumes that technocratic, competitive practices will be challenged (although the material benefits have been great). There is truth, however, in Herbst's description of a turbulence in our time—an underlying uneasiness, discontent and skepticism about the adequacy of seeking solutions solely by technical, utilitarian means. Turbulence can be frightening and there are no sure predictions what reactions will be. When the turbulence manifests itself in public schools, for example, there is a powerful tendency to step up the machinery of bureaucratic control. If the behavior of America's youth is disturbing—marked by absenteeism, apathy, drug and alcohol abuse, vandalism and disrespect, administrators can try behavior modification, restore corporal punishment, increase school security guards (at a price of $240,000,000 in 1974), and preach the virtues of the work ethic.

It would be misleading to say that neat, blue-print extrapolations can be made from socio-technical design theory for education. The movement within work design is broad, and eschews a single "right way." It is deliberately experimental and evolutionary in spirit and practice. Nevertheless it is possible to predict some philosophical inclinations that would be relevant for education if the design gains popularity.

It is relevant to note that Norwegian theorists were influenced by the tradition of Kurt Lewin—socio-technical theory is projected as a democratic alternative to both authoritarianism and romantic freedom. If people view schools from this perspective it may be useful to consider educational designs which explore the creation of small learning communities within larger systems. Collaborative learning involving joint planning, projecting and testing plans of action might be relevant. This would seem to call for a second look at alternative education efforts which flared briefly in the turbulence of the early seventies. They represented reactions against impersonal school bureaucracies and moved toward humane learning communities either within or apart from mass school systems.

A socio-technical perspective of schools as work places might help to reflect why alternative schools failed to fulfill their promise. The alternative schools strongly reacted against purely technocratic efforts to engineer educational results. The ones which foundered, however, tended to slide into the kind of romantic, laissez-faire freedom that Lewinian theory warned against. Our is a technological era in which survival depends on mastery of technical-conceptual skills. Schools as good "work places" require a caring concern for rigorous intellectual effort, a supportive community, and a place to learn job-related skills. The industries which try to create good work in the socio-technical sense cannot settle for better worker-management relations alone. They have to produce quality products. A core hypothesis of socio-technical philosophy is the conviction that people need a chance to be in touch with the full range of their powers and need the opportunity to put them to work. They can be asked to make the hard efforts to develop those powers if they are provided settings to be engaged as persons.

There is no slick, final formula for education. Perhaps a growing wisdom based on reflections on the traumas of our twentieth century experience will help us see that our best bet is a difficult, unending search for how to bring polar human needs for individuality and community, freedom and discipline into satisfying balances. The temptation to cure the shortcomings of one by turning to the excesses of the other bring only new rounds of self-defeat. The philosophy of social-technical design might provide insights for reconceptualizing the quality of life in both work places and school settings. To do so would require that the society change its emphasis from win-lose to win-win mindsets where all persons are given opportunities to "combine their reason and actions in empowered participation."

NOTES

1. Daniel Bell, "Work, Alienation and Social Control," *Dissent*, Spring 1974, 211.
2. Kalman H. Silvert, *The Reason For Democracy*. (New York: The Viking Press, 1977, 177).
3. Raymond Callahan, *Education and the Cult of Efficiency*. (Chicago: University of Chicago Press, 1962.)
4. Arthur Wirth, *Education In the Technological Society*. (New York: Intext, 1972).
5. David Snedden, *Toward Better Education*. (New York: Bureau of Publications, Teachers College, 1931, 330–331.)
6. John Dewey, *Individualism Old and New*. (New York: Capricorn Books, Copyright, 1935, 124.)
7. John Dewey, *Liberalism and Social Action*. (New York: Capricorn Books, 1935, 89.)
8. John Dewey, *Individualism Old and New*, 131–.2
9. John Dewey, *Liberalism and Social Action*, 88.
10. C. A. Bowers, "Emergent Ideological Characteristics of Educational Policy," *Teachers College Record*, September 1977, Vol. 79, No. 1.
11. Adam Curle, *Education For Liberation*. (New York: John Wiley and Sons, 1973.)
12. Max Lerner, *America As A Civilization*. (New York: Simon and Schuster, 1957, 947.)
13. Pehr G. Gyllenhammar, *People At Work*. (Reading, Mass.: Addison-Wesley Publishing Company, 1977.)
14. *Ibid*, p. 4.
15. *Ibid*, 2.
16. *Ibid*, 21.
17. *Ibid*, 29.
18. *Ibid*, 68 and 159.
19. See for example, E. F. Emery and Einar Thorsrud, *Form and Content In Industrial Democracy: Some Experiences From Norway and Other European Countries*. London: Tavistock Publishing, Ltd., 1969, 9.
20. P. B. Herbst, *Alternatives to Hierarchies*. Leiden: Martinus Nyhoff Social Science Division, 1976, 17.
21. P. G. Herbst, *Socio-Technical Design*. London: Tavistock Publications Ltd., 1974, 205.
22. *Ibid*, 204.

23. *Ibid*, 205.
24. *Ibid*, 207.
25. *Ibid*, 208.
26. Gyllenhammer, *op. cit.*, 123-4.
27. Herbst, *op. cit.*, 48.
28. Fred Emery and Einar Thorsrud, *Democracy At Work*. Leiden: Martinus Nyhoff, 1976, 159.
29. Kalman H. Silvert, *The Reason For Democracy*, 117.
30. Willard Wirtz, "Education for What," in Dyckman W. Vermilye, ed., *Relating Work and Education*. San Francisco: Jossey-Bass, 1977.

SOME THOUGHTS ON THE FUTURE OF SPECIAL EDUCATION

James P. Gelatt

There is a basic question to be asked in considering the future of special education—the education of handicapped children: "Are things getting better or are they getting worse?"

A second question follows the first: "What can be done—either to maintain a promising outlook, or to improve on a disappointing one?" In other words, "How can we best *invent* a promising future for handicapped children?" This paper has several purposes:

First, to review some of the literature regarding educational futures of handicapped children;

Second, to suggest that there are some hard questions which must be addressed, in order to plan effectively for the future of this population;

Third, to describe some of the obstacles and challenges involved, and suggest an approach to dealing with them.

A few words of caution: Thomas Dye, in a book on policy analysis,[1] noted that societal problems are indeed complex, and as such may be beyond the ability of social scientists seeking to make accurate predictions about the impact of proposed policies. Educational futures is a relatively new field, and futures research regarding the handicapped is minimal. That may be an advantage—in that we can start now, to develop a coherent approach, grounded in logic, which seeks to improve the future of children whose lives have been circumscribed by disability.

WHO ARE THE HANDICAPPED?

There are some eight million children in this country identified as handicapped, and many more not yet identified. They are handicapped either mentally or physically, and in some cases both. Each year about 200,000 children are born with congenital malformations;[2] others become handicapped through disease or accident.

Emotional handicaps account for some 1.4 million children,[3] and as many as *half* of the persons now in institutions for the mentally retarded—some 100,000 people—are children.[4]

SOME RECENT TRENDS

One means of determining where the future lies, is to examine where we have been. Certain trends are evident, as they relate to the education of handicapped children.

The best known of these would likely be the passage of Public Law 94-142, the Education of All Handicapped Children Act. Passed in 1975, the law mandates that each handicapped child receive a free, appropriate, public education. The law hangs on words two and three of that mandate: "appropriate," which has been typically defined as in "the least restrictive environment"; and "public," which has led to the massive effort underway to "mainstream" handicapped children.

The challenges of implementing Public Law 94-142 are obvious to anyone involved in education, and will not be dwelt on here.

A second major thrust has been in what is called "deinstitutionalization"—simply, taking handicapped children, and especially the retarded, out of the warehouses that were called institutions, and placing them in smaller, community-based settings. This is part of the process of "normalizing" handicapped children.

How far the process of deinstitutionalization will extend, and what effect it will have on education, cannot yet be determined. The answers may hinge on the final outcome of what is called the Pennhurst decision. On December 23, 1977, the District court in Pennsylvania handed down its decision regarding the suit, brought on behalf of an institutionalized retarded girl, against Pennhurst institution in Pennsylvania. The court ruled that the very existence of the institution violated federal and state law; and said further that every resident presently in Pennhurst could and should be living in community facilities.[5]

Education for a profoundly handicapped child is measured in small gains: an ability to control bowel and bladder functions; reduction in aggressive behavior; some awareness of self and surroundings. Residents at Pennhurst who were tested on the Vineland Scale of Social Maturity were found to have declined in social skills since they were institutionalized.

Real educational programs were at a minimum; the average time actually spent per resident on habilitation—helping the child to cope in society, which is indeed a function of education—was fifteen minutes a day.[6]

The third thrust which can be observed is really the motivation behind the other two. *Newsweek* has called the handi-

capped "the next minority." Those who can are becoming
vocal consumers, taking on the tactics of previous civil rights
groups in order to gain equal rights. They are aided by advocates, both parents and professionals, who seek to speak up
for the rights of handicapped children who cannot speak for
themselves.

SOME PROJECTIONS

Much of the futures work in special education has been
conducted at the federal level, by agencies representing handicapped children. The following projections on the future of
special education are based on an amalgam of studies, including the following:

The 1976 *Annual Report of the National Advisory Committee
on the Handicapped,*[7] the Futures Project of the President's
Committee on Mental Retardation,[8] and a Delphi study conducted by the National Association of State Directors of Special Education (NASDSE).[9] These were supplemented by a
report from the Council on Exceptional Children,[10] and some
general material from *Toward the Year 2000,* edited by Daniel
Bell.[11]

Some General Trends. Many of the futurists consulted felt
that ours would be an increasingly urbanized, sprawling country, linked by better transporation and communication. This
is important for any educator, but particularly for those concerned with transporting handicapped children to and from
learning environments.

Advances in technology are considered undeniable, although there is some question of their ethical use, especially
in medicine, and the field of bioethics. Several futurists, perhaps reflecting their own hopes, envision the growth of community-based activities, which would in turn lead to an increase in community feeling. If this projection is viable, the
requirement for mainstreaming would be less of a burden than
it is now.

Demographically, by the year 2000, each family will have 2.1
children; the median age will be between 28-36. Smaller families might lower the incident of birth defects—fewer, better
controlled pregnancies, and better care at home might be
"built-in" warrants.

How the economy affects the handicapped is not clear. There
is some evidence that handicapped workers are among the
first to be laid off, and that there is a general discrimination
against the handicapped worker. However, many futurists feel
that if growth were to be slower, and better controlled, there
would be less of a need for job lay-offs through "dynamic
contraction."[12]

Who will be the Handicapped of the Future? There will be an increased effort toward serving handicapped children at a younger age. There will also be emphasis toward more adult and continuing education for handicapped adults, who, like their able-bodied counterparts, will need to perpetually renovate their knowledge and skills in order to compete in the labor market.

Defining who is handicapped will continue to undergo change, as opposition to "labeling" leads to more functional classifications.

Research and Prevention. One of the areas in which there seems to be consensus is in research. Most of the experts polled felt that the next 10 to 25 years would see breakthroughs in medicine, genetics and pharmacology. Early detection, say of Down's Syndrome, which could lead to prevention, was offered as a real possibility. Geneticists are close to eliminating those disorders which are due to abnormalities in a single gene or chromosome. Other breakthroughs in pharmacology are occurring virtually daily.

Research brings with it some obvious dangers of misuse. One potential area for such use is in the control of behavior through drugs. This is not to say that predictions have been made that such misuse would occur; rather that the potential will increase. On the positive side, however, there seems to be little consensus that controlling birth defects would require controlled mating. This may be a growing issue, as retarded persons are more and more placed in community settings, classrooms, and places of work.

It seems generally agreed that advances in terms of prevention of disability can be expected. These may include an increased capability to detect abnormal conditions in early pregnancy, and with it an improved capability for genetic counseling, computerized clinics for early screening, and generally advances in cell production.

Technology. In a related area, there seems to be a strong feeling that technology will continue to become more sophisticated, and more useful (if it is affordable). Two potential benefits for education might be: sensory inputs, which could augment the learning process, and new modes of processing information (just what these modes and inputs would be is not delineated); and new prosthetic devices—devices which could aid in eliminating barriers of communication or mobility.

The degree to which technology will benefit the handicapped person is difficult to assess. Advances in prosthetics could be of real help, but there is some indication that mildly retarded persons function better in a less complex society.[13] The more physically or mentally handicapped the child, the more the child might find himself to be lost in a technological maze.

Networks. One of the more exciting dimensions for the future of education is in the development of what Ivan Illich and Robert Theobald call "networks." Several of the futures studies on handicapped persons saw this as an area of real opportunity. Among the possibilities: the growth of national and regional libraries, linked by computer. Handicapped persons, and in particular those with sensory limitations, suffer from a lack of information. This could be a boon to them, if the information is available on teletype (TTY) for the deaf, and braille or cassette for the blind.

The President's Committee on Mental Retardation projected a nationwide network of services—linked by what the Committee called an Institutional Brokerage Company—an nonprofit organization, perhaps, that functioned as a neutral focus to bring user and supplier together. The national broker would be linked in turn to local community services, and both would survive on a fee-for-service basis. Among the duties of the brokers would be to develop technical backups for information systems, as needed, develop transportation capabilities for disabled persons, and work in the community to develop cooperative ventures.

The NASDSE survey viewed such networking as a highly valued event—predicting that a nationwide information retrieval system was likely by the year 1985; that by 1995 the handicapped would have virtually total access to public communication; that State Education Agencies (SEAs) would themselves form information exchanges, using telecommunications, by 1990; and that by 1985, some 75 percent of all states would have a "locator system" to identify and find parents who were high risk of having handicapped children. The cost of such systems, however, might be a determinant.

Talk of networking often leads to talk of the "voucher system." It is interesting that those surveyed by NASDSE—all of them tied into special education in some way—saw the use of vouchers as a neutrally valued idea. Perhaps if the handicapped student were to receive a large number of vouchers, this would have been received more positively.

In the Classroom. Anyone involved in education could have predicted that mainstreaming would present some problems to the classroom teacher. A recent NEA study found that classroom teachers were not sure mainstreaming could work effectively without disrupting the learning of others. One area that will be affected is in preparation of teachers to deal with this new challenge, and virtually all of the studies cited previously indicated that increased preservice and in-service training would be needed. Such training should, in the view of the President's Committee, be interdisciplinary—crossing disciplines and teaching disciplines the importance of working together.

From the NASDSE study, the following were considered as highly probable. By 1980, some 70 percent of teacher training programs will require at least six hours of study in the exceptional child. Such training will increasingly be provided not on the college campus, but within the school system.

Instruction and evaluation may be changing as well. It was the consensus among special educators that a "zero reject" philosophy would be nationwide by 1990, and that a majority of teachers would use an individualized educational approach by the year 1987.

Due Process and Litigation. The 1970s may be remembered as the "age of the lawyer." Equal educational opportunity has been mandated by law, and the futurists surveyed seemed to feel it will come about. But the leverage will come from the courts. Litigation will likely increase against schools, less and less in order to gain access to schooling, and more to demand a quality education for the handicapped. As accountability in the classroom rises, so too may liability suits.[14] There seems to be indication of this now, among parents of normal children who are graduating and cannot read.

Unlikely Events. It's interesting to note some of the events that were determined unlikely by experts: that the Bureau of Education for the Handicapped (BEH) will be decentralized; that large centers will replace neighborhood schools; that the educably retarded child will no longer be considered "handicapped." While it appears that mainstreaming is here to stay, it seems also true that in the year 2000, state residential centers, which educate some handicapped children, will remain.

Some Difficult Questions. The difficulties involved in mainstreaming handicapped children are becoming increasingly known, but we will not know how well they can be resolved until two things happen: (1) mainstreaming is tried, using teachers who have been given training—including attitudinally; (2) both educators and those advocating for the handicapped accept a realistic assessment of what can be accomplished.

There are other questions, however, and in order to understand them, it is necessary to recognize from where many of our handicapped children of tomorrow will be coming. Roughly one quarter of our nation's children live in families with an income judged insufficient to provide adequate nutrition. Between one-half to two-thirds of pregnant women in such surroundings are themselves malnourished.[15] The danger of low birth weight—a high risk indicator of disability—is more common among teenage mothers, especially those under age 15. In 1973, some 600,000 teenage girls gave birth.

Galtung states, "The future of education in general, and of schools in particular, cannot be understood in isolation."[16] This is particularly true for the handicapped child whose disability is a result not of birth accident, but of sociocultural forces. And while the President's Committee's futurists were basically optimistic, they were much more uncertain about the likelihood of changing the "culture of poverty." What would be required—an all-out effort—was seen as remote.

There is a further irony. There is some indication that mental retardation is a result not of poverty, but of status in society. If this is true, an improved economy will not lessen the harmful consequences that fall to the young, uneducated and poorly nourished girl from a minority, who is a mother while still a child.

The issue raises some difficult questions. Will Americans be continually willing to invest large sums of money in programs directed at diminishing the number of ill fed and unemployed—or is California's Proposition #13 a warning that our patience is waning?

And if Americans are willing to support programs of relief, will it be with certain contingencies? Can citizens ask that in order to receive free medical care, the teenage mother be required to undergo behavioral modification, attend birth control classes, or to provide a proper diet to the baby she now carries?

What Americans are saying, if they link funding with such demands, is that they have certain expectations, and the dollars are contingent upon them. This stance, while practical and perhaps justified—if not necessary—contains some real dangers in regard to educating handicapped children.

Education is linked, in the American ethos, with equality. Equal education is a measure of equality, and equal education is a means of raising persons to a level of equality. Harold Shane, in *The Educational Significance of the Future*, warns that "education in the next decade may need to emphasize concepts of greater equity," as opposed to equality. We can no longer, he continues, "sell the Horatio Alger myth."[17]

This is a hard fact, but one that will make educating handicapped children more realistically based. Educators can provide the deaf child with an integrated education, but they may have to always treat him *unequally*: that is, to see that he has an interpreter, even as a working adult. One can accept the child with a physical disability into the classroom, but must also modify the physical environment to do so.

The danger of the Horatio Alger myth, as Shane implies, is that it raises unfair expectations, both on the part of the learner (and his or her family) and the educational system.

Dr. Robert Cooke is one of the architects of legislation on behalf of the retarded. Programs for the mentally retarded and developmentally disabled, Cooke maintains, will depend more on ethical principles on which society acts, than on technical developments in the biomedical or behavioral sciences. Similarly, the extent to which we are willing to provide service to such persons, is dependent on the extent to which we feel ethically obliged to do so.[18]

The term "exceptional children" has traditionally included the extremes of the intellectual spectrum—with the most severely retarded, with IQs virtually below point of measurement at one end, and the gifted child at the other. It is fairly easy to build a case for why one should invest in special programs for the gifted, as has been the case in Iran. That country set about locating its gifted youth, and then providing a concentrated, accelerated program for them. But the rewards for doing so are obvious.

The National Advisory Committee on the Handicapped has said that handicapped persons should be judged not on their limitations, but for their qualities as human beings. There are two dangers implicit in that statement: first, that handicapped persons should be judged at all; and second, that we should be forced to set up criteria to determine qualities that make them human, and therefore valuable.

Education of some handicapped children can be looked at as an investment, and in one sense, then, it could be argued that such programs serve a utilitarian function: educate the child, and that child will become a productive member of society. That is to some degree true, with *some* children, with *some* disabilities. But what of those children who will never be "productive" in normally accepted terms? What of children who will always need special assistance to be productive?

It could be argued that educating handicapped children is only just—that is indeed the basis of Public Law #142. But what that ignores, is that education must favor the handicapped child, in order to provide an equal education. This, is seems, was the crux of Bakke case. How do you combine the need to provide special circumstances for some, with the goal of equal education for all?

One of the more gloomy forecasts of the President's Committee's Futures Project was this: there is "some likelihood that time will run out on people's willingness to support mentally retarded people and programs dealing with mental retardation."[19] If indeed we are entering an age of dynamic contraction, if resources—including government spending—are finite and we are nearing that finitude then planning for the educational future of handicapped children should be based on some hard realities.

Harold Shane, in his recommendations to the Commissioner of Education, said: "Avoid overemphasis on the atypical . . . child and youth and with problem situations to the neglect of the larger pupil population."[20] If we base our programs to educate handicapped children on utilitarian principles—if we link outcome with income—we will in fact run the risk of realizing the fear expressed by the Futures Project. One of the advocates in the Pennhurst case carried this reasoning to an extreme, when he noted; "It is expensive to run institutions, it is cheaper to have people in the community, but it is cheaper yet to forget about them."[21]

Forgetting about the handicapped is unlikely. But confrontations between the demands of the handicapped, and both the resources and attitudes of the general public, seem inevitable unless some steps are taken. Development of an Individualized Education Plan (IEP) is not in itself a poor educational practice, and there is some indication that it can work.[22] What may make it an issue is that it singles out the handicapped child for special treatment. Would it not be better educational practice to look at all children individually, and to prescribe programs which fit their individual needs? That rather dream-like goal is well delineated in George Leonard's *Education and Ecstasy*. Whether or not it can come about is another question.

Perhaps what is more practical is to strive toward having schools of education train educators in human values which encourage cooperation rather than competition, and recognize the beauty of individual differences.[23]

"The essence of planning," as Peter Drucker points out, "is to make present decisions with knowledge of their futurity." That is, at best, difficult to accomplish. What we might be able to do is to plan with certain human goals in mind—goals that in themselves do not change with changes in circumstances.

Confrontation is inevitable unless parents and advocates are also part of the educational process-knowledgeable about the child's rights, but aware of the limitations. This is no different than what we should be doing with all parents—bringing them into the educational setting, so that education is not defined by school walls alone; but also helping them to set some realistic expectations about their child's future.

The argument, it would seem, should be less about the rights of handicapped children to a good education, than about our responsibility to all children, and in particular, to those least able to make demands upon us. "The question is not whether they are human persons, but rather what kind of care should we give them in order for *us* to be human."[24]

NOTES

1. Thomas R. Dye, *Policy Analysis: What Governments Do, Why They Do It, and What Difference It Makes*, Alabama: University of Alabama Press, 1976.
2. The National Foundation/March of Dimes, *Facts: 1977*, White Plains, N.Y., 1976.
3. Henry C. Kempe and Doris Howell, *The Future of Pediatric Education: A Report by the Task Force on Pediatric Education*, St. Louis, Mo.: The American Pediatric Society, n.d., p. 8.

4. HEW *Source Book*, 1972, quoted in Kempe and Howell, *The Future of Pediatric Education*, p. 8.
5. David Ferleger, "The Future of Institutions for Retarded Citizens: the Promise of the Pennhurst Case," *Mental Retardation and the Law: A Report on the Status of Current Court Cases*, Washington, D.C.: The President's Committee on Mental Retardation, July, 1978, pp. 28-42.
6. Ferleger, p. 33.
7. The National Advisory Committee on the Handicapped, *The Unfinished Revolution: Education for the Handicapped; 1976 Annual Report*, Washington, D.C.: United States Government Printing Office, 1976.
8. The President's Committee on Mental Retardation, "The Face of the Future," *Report to the President: Mental Retardation, Century of Decision*, Washington, D.C., 1976.
9. William V. Schipper and Leonard A. Kenowitz, *Special Education Futures: A Forecast of Events Affecting the Education of Exceptional Children, 1975-2000*, Washington, D.C.: National Association of State Directors of Special Education, 1975.
10. Maynard C. Reynolds, ed., *Futures of Education for Exceptional Students: Emerging Structures*, Reston, Va.: The Council for Exceptional Children, 1978.
11. Daniel Bell, ed., *Toward the Year 2000: Work in Progress*, Boston: Beacon Press, 1969.
12. Roy A. Weaver, "Whither Goest Future-[es]-[ism]-[istics]-[ ]* in Education," *Educational Research Quarterly*, Winter, 1977, Vol. 1 (44), p. 10.
13. Nancy M. Robinson, "Mild Mental Retardation: Does It Exist in the People's Republic of China?" *Mental Retardation*, August, 1978, Vol. 16 (4), pp. 295-299.
14. John W. Melcher, "Law, Litigation and Handicapped Children," *Exceptional Children*, November, 1976, Vol. 43 (3), pp. 126-130.
15. Eli H. Newberger, Carolyn Newberger and Julius B. Richmond, "Child Health in America: Toward a Rational Public Policy," *The Milbank Memorial Quarterly*, Summer, 1976, pp. 249-298.
16. J. Galtung, "Schooling and Future Society," *School Review*, Vol. 83 (4), 1975, p. 533.
17. Harold G. Shane, *The Educational Significance of the Future*. Bloomington, Indiana: Phi Delta Kappa Educational Foundation, 1973, p. 85.
18. Robert Cooke, "Societal Obligations for Care," *Developmental Disabilities: Future Directions and the Challenge of Applying What We Know* (conference), June, 1978, John F. Kennedy Institute, Baltimore, Md.
19. President's Committee on Mental Retardation, p. 55.
20. Shane, p. 104.
21. Ferlger, p. 41.
22. Roland K. Yoshida, Kathleen S. Fenton, and Martin J. Kaufman, "Evaluation of Education for the Handicapped," *Phi Delta Kappa*, Sept., 1977, pp. 59-60.
23. Shane, p. 65.
24. Stanley Hauerwas, "Must a Patient Be a 'Person' to Be a Patient?" *Connecticut Medicine*, Vol. 39, 1975.

WHAT TEN YEARS OF TEACHING ABOUT THE FUTURE HAVE TAUGHT ME

W. Basil McDermott

THE OPTIMISM-PESSIMISM CONTROVERSY: TRANSCENDENCE

There is a hero to this story. He once found a durable perspective on human experience and was hence liberated from the distractions of both hope and despair. His outlook was timeless and therefore equally relevant to past, present, and future considerations of life-choices. I shall center my discussion around this point of view as I explain what ten years of teaching about the future have taught me.

An old man lived with his son in an ancient disused fort on a hill. One day, his horse, on which he depended, strayed and was lost. His neighbours came and sympathized with him on his bad luck. "How do you know this is bad luck?"he asked. Some days later his horse appeared, together with some wild horses, which the man and his son trained. The neighbours this time congratulated him on his good luck. "How do you know this is good luck?" asked the man. And as it happened, his son, while riding one of the horses, was thrown and became permanently lame. His neighbours condoled with him, and again spoke about his ill-luck. "How do you know this is ill-luck?" he asked. Not long after, war broke out, and the son, because of his lameness, could not go.[1]

According to the old man on the hill, humanity needs a philosophy that can transform the meaning of the transitory nature of both success and failure, war and peace, sickness and health. One needs a point of view that does not over-identify with the vagaries of life. The world needs such an outlook because it is not inherent within knowledge to control all the events which will shape future prospects.

The story of the old man teaches different lessons, on multiple levels, in harmony with previous preparation and understanding. The inner meaning concerns the fate of rash and premature judgments. There is an instability to the world of final judgments and especially so whenever they embrace opposite conclusions so readily. Nevertheless, in sympathy with archaeologists, detectives, and historians, we all can potentially revise our estimations of the significance of past events in light of what we consider to be new evidence. The problem is that what a person concludes about almost anything in life depends on *when* he peeks at an event, *how long* he gazes, the looking glasses he uses, and what he hopes, fears, or expects to see. This relativity and flexibility of our conclusions about what is important in a given event has a direct bearing on our evaluation of how serious the future is likely to be. When the old philosopher repeatedly asked his neighbours to ponder how they knew whether the latest "happening" was good or bad, he revealed how their beliefs determined what they were able to see in the immediate event. Implicit in his detachment from optimism or pessimism is the suggestion that such a way of thinking about life is wiser than its competitors.

What impresses one person may depress, alarm, or antagonize another. And there is an element in the old sage's attitude that is open to the charge of fatalism and resignation. Does this outlook on life imply that societies live in the best of all possible worlds? Does he mean to say that people must simply accept whatever happens in life without question? Is there no way to make sound judgments on events? Or more pointedly, with a specific example: What would the old man on the hill have to say about the Nazi genocide program?[2] Ten years of teaching about the future have taught me that there are no answers to any of these questions that are equally convincing to all people. I pose such questions to illustrate an awareness that such a perspective on life is clearly offensive to our action oriented stance towards the future. Futurists do not take kindly to even the mildest suggestion that life is mostly something that happens to us, that human beings are more shaped by experiences than shapers. It is, furthermore, interesting to note that even in the days of Lao-Tsu, there were evidently people who were similarly appalled by his "subversive" views. He was, moreover, quite aware that his outlook could be interpreted in different ways and even offered a limited amount of clarification.

Be utterly humble
And you shall hold to the foundation of peace.
Be at one with all these living things which, having arisen
    and flourished,
Return to the quiet whence they came,
Like a healthy growth of vegetation
Falling back upon the root.

Acceptance of this return to the root has been called 'quie-
tism',
Acceptance of quietism has been condemned as 'fatalism'.
But fatalism is acceptance of destiny.
And to accept destiny is to face life with open eyes,
Whereas not to accept destiny is to face death blindfolded.[3]

We moderns are terribly uncomfortable with the notions of
destiny and fate. We see ourselves as possessors of sufficient
knowledge to control the future in ways unimagined by our
ancestors. The future we envision is based on the beliefs we
have about the nature of our knowledge. We assure ourselves
that new knowledge is growing much more rapidly than our
social problems. Attempts to doubt this conventional wisdom
engender severe confict within the doubter as well as invite
condemnation by activists of all ideological persuasion. A contemporary illustration of this process is found in Robert Heilbroner's *An Inquiry into the Human Prospect*. A year after
original publication, he added a brief section entitled, "Second
Thoughts on the Human Prospect." He wrote:

> "If the reviews and criticisms I have received during the past
> year have taught me anything, it is that a critical detachment
> from the historic future is the most difficult attitude to express
> or to defend."[4]

Aware that his analysis of the long term prospects for the
human race will strike most people as exceedingly dismal and
pessimistic, he candidly expresses his personal anguish at
adopting such a stance and wonders aloud:

> "Is this a responsible attitude to take? Is there not a more
> activist philosophy that would still be appropriate to the diag-
> nosis of the text?"
> "I must confess that I have worried over this aspect of *The
> Human Prospect* more than over any of its premises or conclu-
> sions. I have been concerned lest my attitude lead to a self-
> fulfilling prophecy of defeat, to a cowardly passivity, to an un-
> bearable conflict of hopes and fears."[5]

Yet he finds himself unable to forsake the conclusions he has
embraced. He cannot return to the activist camp of his intellectual youth. Instead, I can see the courageous Heilbroner
steadily trudging up the hill to live with the old man and his
son in the fortress. At their first meal together, Heilbroner
confides that it took him a long time to formulate the conclusion he penned at the end of his book:

> "To accept the limitation of our abilities, both as individuals
> and as a collectivity, seems to be the most difficult idea that
> Promethean man must learn."[6]

The old man nodded and said, "How do you know that the events which have led you to this conclusion are good or bad?"

With the old man's perspective firmly in mind, this author shall continue. There have been occasions during the past decade when students have asked me when I was going to tell them what I really thought about the various problems and prospects presented during the semester. As I have been teaching a course entitled "The Study of the Future" since the Autumn of 1968, there is some sympathy for the belief that perhaps I had some inside tips on the future. I should confess, however, that these questions frequently struck me as containing a dark hint that I was deliberately concealing my own ideas. At such moments, I repressed a devilish desire to admit such suspicions were entirely correct. My real intent was to postpone the ultimate meaning of the future, which I would reveal in a special lecture, not on the course outline, entitled, "The TRUTH about the Future." More candidly, however, I have always been somewhat puzzled that they seemed unable to believe that I had been telling them what I thought throughout the course. Perhaps some were looking for certainty; a few were seeking a cause; others were collecting credits in their grand march toward graduation; some were merely curious about the type of approach and topics such a course might include; and a few sought greater understanding of what seemed to be happening in our world. But none could easily think about the future independently from his own personal history. Nor can I, for that matter. Indeed, the degree to which our personal experiences contaminate more than clarify our ability to think astutely about the future should disturb us more than it often does. At any rate, one early lesson I learned is that believing is seeing much more often than the converse.[7] Both our willingness and ability to envision the future depend in large part on our belief systems. This, of course, has direct consequences for how we live, since "it is what we think the world is like, not what it is really like, that determines our behaviour."[8] These processes of perception are normally in greater disarray than we suspect. Our thinking about many aspects of life is much more chaotic, confused, incomplete, and even irrational than we are often willing to concede. It is of no small importance to question the confidence we should have in our own opinions about the future as we become more aware of their shady background and unstable future. Perhaps our basic capacity to conceptualize the future properly is much more doubtful than we have been led to believe. At any rate, if there are greater limits on our abilities than we currently recognize, then these constraints and liabilities will have profound consequences in the future. I shall discuss the evolution of my thoughts on these matters by concentrating on the nature of knowledge control, and consciousness.

ON THE GROWTH OF KNOWLEDGE AND IGNORANCE

We think about knowledge improperly. We do not understand the relative nature of ignorance and knowledge. This misleads our thinking about the type of knowledge we assume we need, the minimal amounts necessary, and the problems of application. By all of this, I mean we have mistaken notions about how much we know, how well we know it, and what can or should be done to apply what we know. Suppose we ask ourselves, "Just how serious is the future anyway?" A careful answer to this question inevitably revolves around the state of our knowledge as well as our goals. The extent to which we think the future is serious depends on what we want to do with our lives. The degree to which we will be able to do what we desire depends in large part, however, on the sufficiency of our knowledge to enable such desires to be accomplished. More pointedly, there can be a vast gap between commitment and competency. Sometimes, we speak about the seriousness of the future as if the major problem is that we do not seem to care enough about the state of suffering humanity. The assumption seems to be that we could actually master the problems of our age if we would only be willing to make the necessary sacrifices. This assumption, I believe, disastrously ignores the difficulty of assessing the sufficiency of our current knowledge to accomplish such ends.

Nevertheless, the dominant outlook among those who are worried about the future is to argue that the dangers of apathy, selfishness, and even malevolence far outstrip the concern we should give to the significance of our ignorance.[9] I was once more sympathetic to this outlook, but ten years of "future-watching" have led me to focus greater attention on the seriousness of our ignorance than on our presumed wickedness or callousness. Thus, there has been a subtle shift in my thoughts concerning what it means to be serious about the future as well as about how serious the future is likely to be.

I commenced my journey through the academic wilderness of futurology with an unexamined faith in the sufficiency of our existing knowledge to reduce human misery if only we would apply it. Furthermore, what we could not solve today, we would be able to tackle adequately tomorrow. If anything was certain in our uncertain world, it was surely that knowledge itself had a bright future ahead. Indeed, the fanciful question about whether ignorance was ever more blistering than blissful never struck me as especially serious because I assumed that the frontiers of human ignorance were being rapidly explored and settled. If there were limits on the expansion and growth of knowledge, then I assumed that these were so distant from the present that they were not worth pondering.

At this point, perhaps, I should add that my background as a political scientist unavoidably influenced how I viewed the alleged major sources of human misery. By and large, those who study political life find themselves obsessed with power, conflict, and self-interest. Some are fascinated by what has happened; others are appalled. But under the guise of being 'realistic', attention is subtly focused on a particular view of history and human relationships. Karl Popper complained about this peculiar way of viewing the human past:

> "There is no history of mankind, there is only an indefinite number of histories of all kinds of aspects of human life. And one of these is the history of political power. This is elevated into the history of the world. But this, I hold, is an offense against every decent conception of mankind. For *the history of power politics is nothing but the history of international crime and mass murder* (including, it is true, some of the attempts to suppress them). This history is taught in schools, and some of the greatest criminals are extolled as its heroes."[10]

These stinging phrases include two indictments that are relevant to my inquiry about the adequacy of our knowledge to control the future wisely. First, there is the charge of willful scholarly distortion of the human record. Second, there is outrage that the perpetrators of human cruelty have so often been awarded medals for their evil. On the first point, it is likely that most academics would vigourously deny his accusation. Moreover, some would argue to the contrary that their investigations are, in fact, leading the human race to a much more accurate understanding of reality. I will turn to this in a moment, as it does not excite passion as much as discussions about human injustice often do.

Let me say at the outset, that I have found discussions about the nature of cruelty, injustice, and evil to be immensely frustrating and difficult. We all have much more definite and rigid conceptions of what is right and wrong in the world than we sometimes realize. When someone seems to disagree with us on these matters, we often find ourselves reacting in a very negative and argumentative manner. My experience has led me to believe that we do not eagerly seek to understand why another person holds a different way of viewing the world; rather we seek to confront, to condemn, and to change. With these cautionary words in mind, I proceed.

A denunciation of political oppression often contains a call to action. In the presence of human pain, suffering, and undeserved hardship, a special type of response is demanded, and it certainly is not "value-free social science." The trouble is that people quarrel quite vigourously over what constitutes avoidable (as distinct from unavoidable) evil. As far as the major sources of evil are concerned, however, I suspect our knowledge is deficient to produce relatively durable solutions. Although we may identify certain patterns of evil, it may well be beyond our power to do much about them. Furthermore, it is crucial to realize that a cessation of existing exploitative practices will not necessarily create the society we desire.[11] All collective solutions are inherently unstable and consistently produce unanticipated problems. There is, of course, strong dissent from this outlook. The social reformer resists these conclusions because he is convinced they imply a passive tolerance of evils we could alleviate if only we would apply the knowledge we already possess. The only way out of this dilemma, I believe, is to bring greater specificity to what a person wants to do, what resources he can bring to the task, and what consequences he anticipates from undertaking a given program of human betterment. I should add that my thoughts on these matters have not led me to embrace "the position of ultimate caution," namely, that nothing should ever be done for the first time for fear that it will turn out badly. Rather, we must be sensitive to the fact that whatever action we take to accomplish what we consider to be an improvement in society will inevitably produce a new set of concerns and issues, some of which will be viewed as equally obnoxious and evil as those previously "solved." Man lives under "the law of the conservation of misery" and neither his aspirations nor his knowledge permits him to escape for very long from its mournful operation.

The nightmares of human injustice (that haunt the consciousness of the social prophet committed to the reduction of evil and misery in this world through direct political action) take a much different form in the dreams of those modern scholars who are also interested in the protection of planet earth. These hopeful dreams represent a rebuttal of Popper's accusation of intellectual irrelevance and distortion. They also constitute an unexamined justification for academic specialization and basically support an elaborate myth about scholarly life. These are dreams about what I call "The Cathedral of Knowledge," that vast edifice of ultimate truth, beauty, and wisdom to which each scholar, in his or her own small way, contributes. The growth of the Cathedral is dependent on the construction of small intellectual bricks of knowledge that each person fashions during his academic career. It is as if all the conversations, lectures, articles, conferences, and books will inevitably be assembled according to a preordained blueprint. Though each scholar is ignorant of precisely how his research will fit into the ultimate design, he sleeps more comfortably with the belief that his efforts really do matter.

This is a surprising expression of faith in the development of knowledge to create heaven on earth. And I suspect it is an improper faith to have in the collective fate of the accumulated information of our age. We should not be too surprised if some future historian two hundred years hence unflatteringly characterizes much of modern scholarship as a virtuoso performance of intellectual effort signifying, on the part of the performer, an ability to say things of little value in obscure places in a more ambiguous manner than his competitors.[12] The truth is that the exponential growth of information inevitably creates areas of increasing ignorance since no one can master even an infinitesimal part of what is available.[13] All specialists find themselves in the impossible position of having to redouble their efforts to master less and less, lest they be considered obsolete and anachronistic. Even those who attempt to discriminate as carefully as possible about which ideas seem most important are still unable to find sufficient hours to master the unending flow of new information.

Man's quest for knowledge and potential understanding in one area of life is thus inevitably connected to a growth in ignorance and actual misunderstanding in other areas. Humanity wants to believe that knowledge is cumulative when, in fact, it is only so potentially, and in reserve. Much of what is known, moreover, is known only by the elect. A considerable portion of scientific discourse is shrouded in a language, mystique and complexity that is quite beyond comprehension of other members of the intellectual establishment, and more so for the general public. In more ways than we care to imagine, we are all like children roaming the stacks of a grand library whose available books are inaccessible due to our illiteracy. Unable to understand the contents we are apt to take pride in the sheer size, growth, and development of the library. But as we learn to read and to understand a small part of what is contained within these sacred texts, we are likely to run afoul of an additional illusion about the relative nature of knowledge and ignorance.

Attempts to evaluate the seriousness of our ignorance tend to flounder on improper historical comparisons concerning our knowledge supply. When we think about the growth of knowledge, we frequently compare how much more we know than past civilizations, especially in terms of our understanding of science and technology. This is an inadequate test. It is not how much more we know than the ancients but rather what we need to know today in order to control contemporary problems. In the place of general expressions of faith that the direction and momentum of our scientific knowledge system will inevitably enable us to cope with our multiple problems, we need more specific scrutiny of the precise type of knowledge we need and the conditions under which it might be applied. Such specificity will, I submit, reveal embarrassingly critical areas of ignorance that will undermine our noblest efforts at stable control.

ON THE CONTROL WE DO NOT POSSESS

It would be an unforgivable intellectual heresy to confess that one has lost his faith in the ultimate benefits the growth of knowledge will confer on the human race. Nevertheless, the persistence of historical patterns of human suffering seems more impressive and serious than generally understood. Mankind still does not know how to control the major sources of human misery on this planet. Indeed, mankind does not understand what is involved in the very concept of control itself, and we thus find ourselves commencing actions that we cannot complete. Furthermore, we are constantly being surprised that unanticipated consequences of a troublesome nature are a normal result of our attempts at control.[14] This author would go so far as to suggest that we are dealing with a poorly understood law of inevitable deviation of control away from its original purposes. More pointedly, where is that body of knowledge that will enable us to abolish war? Who can fathom the type of control system minimally necessary to bring human populations into harmony with the resources necessary for decent living? Who can possibly understand the intricacies of ecological stability which many sensitive and intelligent observers insist is mandatory? It is a curiosity of devastating significance that the world is resigned to so much human misery in actual practice, and yet finds it repugnant and intolerable whenever specific attention is drawn to it. This verbal expression of indignation satisfies us that we truly care about such problems. This emotional satisfaction, however, is often devoid of practical significance for the alleviation of the actual problem.

The amount of attention devoted to an issue can be a rather poor indication of its actual gravity. One can discover, for example, that the local newspaper can devote a front page headline to a stranded hiker lost overnight on a mountain. The death of 20,000 in an Iranian earthquake, however, may receive only three inches buried deep within the newspaper. It would appear that people desire tragedies in manageable doses. One grows accustomed to routine suffering and can fail to take seriously its toll.

A detailed examination of the social costs of alcohol would surely reveal that people do not know how to be serious about a problem that touches so many lives in different ways. Nor is there knowledge available that would enable us to control persistent hatreds based on race and religion. In a word, mankind simply does not possess the type of political, social, or economic knowledge to control reality in accordance with its illusions. This does not mean, of course, that societies should burn their books and close their laboratories. The general stance towards the relationship of knowledge to control is as admirable and correct as can be mustered at this time.

Understanding, then, is indisputably a precondition for the exercise of proper control. In agriculture and medicine, for example, an increase in specific understanding has led to greater controls over productivity and health. But even these advances do not escape the law of the conservation of misery. Relative immunity from premature death simply exposes an increasing world population to the constant onslaught of different worries and troubles. Moreover, the general truism about knowledge and control is not universally applicable. The understanding of the astronomer, for instance, does not prompt him to advocate a program of cosmic traffic control so that the planet earth might be spared unruly comets and asteroids. What if, however, the social world in which we live and move actually has more in common with the uncontrollable movement of the stars than previously suspected?

This author suggests that the cumulative result of the march of modern knowledge has been to produce an image of reality that is largely beyond comprehension and quite beyond control. This is not widely recognized and is, in fact, a most unexpected turn of events. Modern star gazers have attained the status of cosmic eavesdroppers and voyeurs cocking their technological ears and eyes into the universe across unimaginable distances. One result has been to produce an almost unbearable loneliness for the planet earth. The archaeologists have cruelly sprung several million years of prehistory for us to examine in our search to understand the transition from our presumably pre-human ancestors to that unknown date when man acquired intellectual capacities similar to our own. The behavioral sciences have shattered many illusions about human rationality. The molecular biologists have opened an era of genetic manipulation that promises to alter traditional boundaries between science fact and fiction. Finally, there is the astounding acceleration of the arms race with its incalculable misuse of human intelligence and resources, let alone the monumental suffering imposed through war. Thus, in my darkest moments, I would characterize my gloom as follows:

> Science you know
> Is a virtuous mistress.
> She gives us knowledge;
> Men give us mischief.
>
> For knowledge is neutral;
> It can be misused.
> For good or for evil;
> Whatever men choose.
>
> It's a two edged sword
> Say the academicians.
> Men who are wise
> In all propositions.

For good or for evil,
Each one must have trust,
In the side of the blade,
The Swordsman will thrust.

ON THE CONSCIOUSNESS WE HAVE NOT ACQUIRED

Our emergence from the darkness of ignorance that domi-
nates our lives depends on a constant reconsideration of what
is important in life.[15] Man emerged from this part of the galaxy
as an experiment in self-evolution. As it now stands, he continues to live in a state of incomplete consciousness and awareness. He does not understand himself properly nor can he
control his personal or collective destiny in a consistently humane or intelligent fashion. His great error is to ascribe to
himself illusory competencies which he does not yet possess in
his current state of partial development, but which are his
prerogative to earn through the proper type of effort and
understanding. Currently, however, man is most often torn
and driven by many contradictions and inconsistencies. Man
lacks the type of unity that is a precondition for effective
living. Thus, it is unsurprising that many of his efforts in life
are self-defeating. For man is the creature that constantly
diets and exercises in the pursuit of virtues in one area of life
only to undermine the process with excesses in other areas.

Over the past decade, this author has approached the study
of the future on two levels, the social and the personal. The
reader has been subjected to a few reservations expressed by
the author about the adequacy of our social knowledge to
control our collective global problems. As far as our knowledge
about personal development is concerned, however, our difficulties are of quite a different nature. Collectively speaking,
the well of usable knowledge is constantly running dry. But
personally speaking, we refuse to drink what is available.
There is sufficient knowledge in existence to enable individuals to live effectively in spite of the external hardships they
cannot avoid. The question remains, however, whether or not
mankind will ever use it.

A SECOND EDUCATION

In the deepest sense, no human can exercise sufficient control over the external aspects of life in a manner that will
guarantee happiness, security, or prosperity. At best, people
can learn to transform their own reactions to what happens
as a basis for the creation of a meaningful life. This learning,
however, consists of as second "education" and involves a considerable amount of "unlearning" (suspending some of one's
most cherished prejudices in order to study them uncritically).
Unless this occurs gradually, a person is likely to be over-

whelmed with the painful realization that he is not at all what he has been pretending to be. One normally escapes any consistent awareness of such contradictions by focusing attention on the flaws of other people. When it is said that fate is another word for personality, some take offense. But all that is meant is that one's future way of living is strongly determined by one's past. If there is not a fresh way of thinking and feeling that slowly alters how we interpret our experiences, then our lives often become mechanical and repetitive cycles, especially in emotional and psychological terms. Our first education places us squarely under "the law of the pendulum" in which our moods, expectations, hopes and fears are constantly swinging back and forth. This is a world of psychological opposites, of those constant movements from elation to despair. It is surprising to hear people speak about the need to control the problems of war, population, and environment when they cannot even control how the weather influences their moods and outlook.

This paper is not a blueprint for collective survival. Neither is it a continuation of the debate about whether social improvement is likely to be accomplished more through stressing individual change as distinct from institutional change. That debate has always been misleading, offering false choices. Rather, the author suggests that our collective problems are inherently uncontrollable in any durable or permanent fashion and that individuals must adjust to that prospect. How they adjust constitutes the meaning of their lives. This point of view is especially difficult to fathom for those considered to be "successful." Many manage their anxiety about the meaning of their lives mostly through compulsive work. Thus, accomplishment often leads to alienation; possibly the most "successful" are also the most lonely and miserable.

Man lives in an inner world of successive psychological states over which he often has little control and less understanding. His belief that tight control over external events will somehow bring him satisfaction will always be an illusion as long as he remains unbalanced. Only his second "education" can give him the harmony he needs in order to become what he should. And that is the essential purpose of life.

NOTES

1. This parable is attributed to Lao-tsu. It is quoted without a reference by C. S. Nott, *Teachings of Gurdjieff: The Journal of a Pupil* (New York: Samuel Weiser, Inc., 1962), p. 110.
2. It is disconcerting at first blush to consider that such a view may not be as perverse or fanciful as we are tempted to believe. For example, William Irwin Thompson, *Evil and World Order* (New York: Harper Colophon Books, 1976), p. 80, writes: "If evil can grow out of our efforts to do good, it also seems to be the case

that good can grow out of our efforts to do evil. The Roman military engineers built the roads that the Christian missionaries travelled to convert an empire. The British executed, by firing squad, the Irish rebels of 1916, and thus helped to free Ireland. The Nazis executed the six million, and thus helped to bring the state of Israel into existence. But much of this seems unconscious, for those who do evil certainly do not plan to have good result from it, and those who think they are working for progress do not wish to create Apocalypse."

3. *The Way of Life According to Lao-tzu*, translated by Witter Bynner (New York: Capricorn Books, 1962), pp. 33–34.
4. Robert L. Heilbroner, *An Inquiry into the Human Prospect* (New York: W. W. Norton & Company, 1975), pp. 150–151.
5. *Ibid.*, pp. 164–165.
6. *Ibid.*, p. 168.
7. Bernard Berelson & Gary A. Steiner, *Human Behaviour* (New York: Harcourt, Brace & World, 1964), pp. 663–664: "In his quest for satisfaction, man is not just a seeker of truth, but of deceptions, of himself as well as others. . . . When man can come to grips with his needs by actually changing the environment, he does so. But when he cannot achieve such 'realistic' satisfaction, he tends to take the other path: to modify what he sees to be the case, what he thinks he wants, what he thinks others want. Thus, he adjusts his social perception to fit not only the objective reality but also what suits his wishes and his needs; he tends to remember what fits his needs and expectations, or what he thinks others will want to hear; he not only works for what he wants but wants what he has to work for; . . .in the mass media he tends to hear and see not simply what is there but what he prefers to be told, and he will misinterpret rather than face up to an opposing set of facts or point of view; he avoids the conflicts of issues and ideals whenever he can by changing the people around him rather than his mind and when he cannot, private fantasies can lighten the load and carry him through."
8. Kenneth E. Boulding, "National Images and International Systems," *The Journal of Conflict Resolution*, III (June, 1959), p. 120.
9. Indeed, the case has been made that our ignorance about the difficulties of a given task is a benevolent principle that encourages us to undertake action which is actually within our capacity to complete but would not have commenced if we had been fully cognizant of all the problems involved. Albert O. Hirschman, "The Principle of the Hiding Hand," *The Public Interest*, #6 (Winter, 1967), p. 13. For a discussion of the problems of "symptoms" rather than "causes" one might examine Amitai Etzioni, "'Shortcuts' to Social Change?" *The Public Interest*, #12 (Summer, 1968), pp. 40–51. This is especially interesting from the standpoint of "the law of the conservation of misery" which I discuss later. Etzioni argues that "fundamental" change is beyond our capacity to control and hence we need a more practical approach to the limited things we might do to alleviate social problems.
10. Karl Popper, *The Open Society and Its Enemies* (New York: Harper & Row, 1962), Vol. II, p. 270.
11. Many people have anguished over this issue. Here is Barrington Moore, Jr., *Reflections on the Causes of Human Misery and Upon*

Certain Proposals to Eliminate Them (Boston: Beacon Press, 1972), p. 38: "Why is it that revolutionaries sooner or later adopt, and sometimes intensify, the cruelties of the regimes against which they fight? Why is it that revolutionaries begin with camaraderie and end with fratricide? Why do revolutions start by proclaiming the brotherhood of man, the end of lies, deceit, and secrecy, and culminate in tyranny whose victims are overwhelmingly the little people for whom the revolution was proclaimed as the advent of a happier life?" He concludes these reflections on the contradictory uses of violence with an idea that is shared by few: "Mankind can expect to oscillate between the cruelties of law and order and the cruelties of changing it for as long as it leaves the globe fit for human habitation." p. 39. Acceptance of this notion has contributed to my own views on the importance of learning how to transform our own personal potential for negativity and violence. I discuss these ideas briefly in the last part of the essay.

12. This is closely akin to "The Yellow Pennant Problem" found in Joseph Heller, *Catch-22* (New York: Simon & Schuster, 1961), p. 71: "Each of the parading squadrons was graded as it marched past the reviewing stand, where a bloated colonel with a big fat mustache sat with the other officers. The best squadron in each wing won a yellow pennant on a pole that was utterly worthless. The best squadron on the base won a red pennant on a longer pole that was worth even less, since the pole was heavier and was that much more of a nuisance to lug around all week until some other squadron won it the following Sunday. To Yossarian, the idea of pennants as prizes was absurd. No money went with them, no class privileges. Like Olympic medals and tennis trophies, all they signified was that the owner had done something of no benefit to anyone more capably than everyone else."

13. Fortunately, there are people who understand that this treadmill approach to the eternal consumption of information is both futile and unnecessary. For example, Kenneth Boulding. *The Meaning of the Twentieth Century* (New York: Harper & Row, 1964), p. 71, notes: "It is probably fundamental to all knowledge processes that we gain knowledge by the orderly loss of information." And Jay Forrester, *World Dynamics* (Cambridge, Mass.: Wright-Allen, 1971), p. 17, stresses the same need for specificity in knowing what to include and exclude: "In constructing a computer model of a social system, the selection and arrangement of information about the real system is crucial. Generally we are handicapped not so much by a shortage of information as by an excess of information from which to choose. Not only is there far more information available than it is appropriate to include, but also the information is unstructured. The unrelated fragments of information must be organized."

14. Barry Commoner, *Science and Survival* (New York: Viking Press, 1963), p. 23, cites his personal involvement in how we learned about the unanticipated consequences of DDT. He then added: "Such unexpected twists are often encountered when new synthetic substances are thrust into the complex community of life: *a wholly unanticipated development wipes out their original usefulness, or sometimes creates a problem worse than the original*

one." Although there is obviously an increasing sensitivity to this problem as far as the physical environment is concerned, there is far too little appreciation of this concept in the social world. Consider, for instance, the difficulty most people have in taking seriously the following conclusion one political scientist made: "It can rarely be known what concrete future effects public laws and acts will bring. . ." Murray Edelman, *The Symbolic Uses of Politics* (Urbana, Illinois: University of Illinois Press, 1964), p. 193.

15. I have long been impressed with what we may call "St. Paul's Quandary" as expressed in Romans 7:19: "For the good that I would I do not: but the evil which I would not, that I do." B. F. Skinner, *Beyond Freedom and Dignity* (New York: Alfred A. Knopf, 1971), has more to say about this problem than his detractors have been willing to concede. But as far as the development of human consciousness is concerned, I am afraid that at best Skinner is a closet Sufi. My ideas on these matters have been especially shaped by the following works: P. D. Ouspensky, *In Search of the Miraculous: Fragments of an Unknown Teaching* (London: Routledge & Kegan Paul, 1950); P. D. Ouspensky, *The Fourth Way* (New York: Vintage Books, 1971); and Maurice Nicoll, *Psychological Commentaries on the Teaching of G. I. Gurdjieff & P. D. Ouspensky* (London: Robinson & Watkins), five volumes.

EDITORS' POSTSCRIPT

In the true sense of shared vision and networking, the editors and contributors to SOURCEBOOK I invite comments, criticisms, and other types of feedback on this initial effort. General responses should be addressed to: Educational Futures, Box 26, University of Houston at Clear Lake City, 2700 Bay Area Boulevard, Houston, Texas 77058. Reactions or comments about specific papers should be sent directly to the author(s) (see About the Authors). Succeeding volumes and conferences of the Education Section will benefit by such interactions. Copies of this book and future conference volumes will be available through the WFS Book Service. The Education Section is planning yearly conferences to share ideas and efforts of educators throughout the world. The 1979 meeting is scheduled for Minneapolis, and the 1980 meeting will be at the University of Massachusetts at Amherst. All individuals are invited to attend these and other conferences of the World Future Society. For information about conference registration and WFS membership, write to: World Future Society, 4916 St. Elmo Avenue, Washington, D.C. 20014 (ask for Education Section membership information).

ABOUT THE EDITORS

Fred Kierstead, Jim Bowman and Chris Dede are Associate Professors in Education and Futures Studies at the University of Houston at Clear Lake City. Bowman and Kierstead are coordinators of the M.S. specialization in Futures Studies in Education at UHCLC, and are contributing editors to *Education Tomorrow*. Dede is President of the Education Section of the World Future Society, and is Co-Chairperson of the Committee for Futures Research at UHCLC. All are co-authors of *The Far Side of the Future: Social Problems and Educational Reconstruction*. The authors have published numerous works and have extensive consulting experience concerning the future of education.

CONTRIBUTORS TO THE CONFERENCE

KEYNOTE ADDRESSES

"The 'State of the Union' in Educational Theory"
Chris Dede, President, WFS

"Human Needs and Education"
John McHale, Director, Center for Integrative Studies
University of Houston

"The Nature of Education: A Fundamental Reconsideration"
Robert Theobald
Participation Publisher

"The Education of Educators"
Ervin Laszlo, Special Fellow
United Nations Institute for Training and Research

PAPER SESSIONS

"Bright Glow or Dark Shadows in Education's Crystal Ball?
Prospects for a Humanistic Curriculum"
Judith M. Barnet, President, Instructor, Consultant
Judith Barnet Associates, Cape Cod Community College

"Values for Learning"
Nancy Dixon, Supervisor of Testing Center
Brookhaven Community College

"Zeitgeist Communication and the Fast Forum (R) Technique"
Richard J. Spady, President
Forum Foundation

"2001: A Counseling Odyssey"
Donald G. Hays, Administrator
Pupil Services, Fullerton Union High School District

"Occupational Adaptability and Transferable Skills:
Preparing for Tomorrow's Careers"
William L. Ashley, Research Specialist
National Center for Research in Vocational Education

"Future-Oriented Counseling"
Delores Harms, Professor
University of Wisconsin

"Learning and the Art Sense"
Jacob Landau, Professor, Artist
Pratt Institute

"University Planning Based on Societal Trends and Values: A Participatory Process"
Marina Buhler-Miko, Acting Director
Resource Center for Planned Change
American Association of State Colleges and Universities

"A Possible Role for Artists in Future Education"
S. B. Dakin, Board Member, Pacific Futures, Inc.

"Exploring the Future(s) with Both Sides of the Brain"
O. W. Markley, Associate Professor
University of Houston at Clear Lake City

"What Ten Years of Teaching About the Future Have Taught Me"
W. Basil McDermott, Faculty of Interdisciplinary Studies
Simon Fraser University

"Teaching College Futurism: An Interdisciplinary Approach"
Stephen L. Albert, Environmental Psychologist

"American University 1998"
Leatha Miloy, Director, Educational Information Services
John Hoyle, Associate Professor
Texas A&M University

"The Creation and Continuance of Futures Studies for a University and Beyond: A Practical Example"
Berenice Bahr Bleedorn, Consultant
Metropolitan State University

"The 'No-Future' Psychology Among Potential School Dropouts"
William E. Bailey, Director
Pacific Futures, Inc.

"Planning for the End of Schooling"
H. Jerome Freiberg, Director, Teacher Corps, University of Houston

"An Educational Model for the Future"
Robert L. Fizzell, Assistant Professor
Western Illinois University

"The Education Organization of the Future: A Model"
John C. Croft, Professor
Ronald G. Frankiewicz, Associate Professor
University of Houston

"Future of Municipal Leisure Delivery Systems: A Delphi"
Richard Mansell, Instructor
University of Waterloo

"Toward a Philosophy of Service/Leisure"
Albert Hamel, Professor
California State University, Long Beach

"Vocationalism and the Future"
Lee Smalley, Professor
University of Wisconsin

"Vocational Education During the Approaching Disequilibrium"
Raymond H. Walke, Environmental Engineer
Greenhills Center and Experiment Station

"The Community College and Future Work"
William L. Abbott, Director
American Association of Community and Junior Colleges

"Work Values of Youth"
James F. Acord, Assistant Professor
Oklahoma State University

"Public Learning Network: Agent for Societal Transformation"
Francis J. Wuest, Program Director
Kansas City Regional Council for Higher Education

"The Future of Distance Learning Technologies"
V. Douglas Hines, Director, Open University
University of Maryland

"Caesar, Computers, Cybernetics, and Humanpersons for Beyond
Year 2000
John N. Falzetta, Professor
Glassboro State College

"The Uses of Teleconferencing in Post-Secondary Education"
Barbara McNeal, Research Assistant
Institute for the Future

"University Television in Northeastern California: A Partial Solution
for the Future?"
Charles F. Urbanowicz, Associate Dean
California State University, Chico

"Communication Systems for Formal and Non-Formal Learning"
Jock Gunter
Clearinghouse on Development Communication

"Values Education: Old Problems and New Possibilities"
Don Evans, Student
Washington University

"Education and Wholeness: From Lawyer to Educator and Beyond"
James M. Olson, Attorney

"The End of Publicly Supported Education *or* How I Learned to Stop
Worrying and Love the Company School"
Russell Doll, Professor of Education
University of Missouri

"Futuristic Forecasting—Calculated Curriculum Relevance"
Gerald N. King, Controller
Dallas Independent School District

"A New Model for Learning in a New Age"
Louise Marks, Doctoral Candidate
Union Graduate School

"A Prep School and the World of Future Shock"
Peter R. Holroyd, Chaplain/Chairman
The Taft School

"Planning for the Future in Education: An Analysis and Planning Model for Colleges and Universities"
William W. Chmurny, Dean, University of New Hampshire
John F. Dalphin, Dean, Indiana-University-Purdue University

"Needed: A New Graduate Education System for the Twenty-First Century"
W. Paul Fischer, Assoicate Professor
Pepperdine University

"The Making of the Film *Toward the Future*: Media as Educational Tool"
Roy Mason, Roy Mason Associates

"Alternative Futures and the Education of Teachers"
Norman Henchey, Associate Dean
McGill University

"Futures Education in a Core Curriculum (A Case Study)"
Jim Reynolds, Director
New Center for Learning, East Texas State University

"The Classroom Need Not Be a Battlefield"
Phillip A. Sinclair, Professor
University of Toledo

"Education—Communications in the Future: The Government's Role"
Robert L. Hilliard, FCC
Carolyn Sachs, House Subcommittee on Communications
Howard Myrick, Deputy Director of Research
Gordon Law, Assistant to the Secretary and Science Advisor, U.S. Department of Interior
Dorothy Deringer, National Science Foundation
John Richardson, National Telecommunications and Information Agency, U. S. Department of Commerce

"UMass Future Studies Program: Recent Work"
Allan Peakes, John McClellan, Cathy Horvitz, Robert Kahn
Doctoral Candidates, UMass School of Education

"The Coming Obsolescence: The Residential Liberal Arts College in the Year 2000"
Samuel L. Dunn, Director, Seattle Pacific University

"The Future of General Education in Higher Education"
Richard Hartnett, Associate Professor
West Virginia University

"The Future of Higher Education: A New Renaissance"
Timothy J. Bergen, Jr., Associate Professor,
University of South Carolina

"The Recognition of Futures Research by Large Corporations and by
Colleges of Business Administration"
Donald F. Mulvihill, Kent State University

"Business Journals and Futurism: Current Status and Suggested
Direction"
Eugene Laczniak, Marquette University
Robert Lusch, Univ. of Okla.

"Educational Programs in Administration and Management"
Donald Mankin,
University of Maryland University College

"Creative Thinking for Creative Teaching"
Joseph H. Herold, Controller
Educational Testing Service

"Critical Experience Amidst Bureaucratic Structure: Dialogue in
Educational Futures"
Jeff Crawford, Assistant Professor
Robin Herman, Assistant Professor
Central State University

"Humane Living Spells Happiness"
Sita Akka Paulickpulle, Secretary/Treasurer
Project Humane Concern, Inc.

"Teaching for the Future"
Linda Tinelli Sheive, Teacher
School Without Walls

"Futurizing the Classroom: A Validation Study of Futuristics"
Lee Hay, Teacher of English
Manchester High School

"Futuristics and Geographic Education"
Robert L. Janiskee, Assistant Professor
University of South Carolina

"Cross Lingual Information Systems for Mathematics (K-12th
Grade)"
Jim Kelly, Engineer

"Ethnographic Futures Research as a Promising Educational Tool"
Robert B. Textor, Professor of Education and Anthropology
Stanford University

"Compact Policy Assessment: Application to Planning for Educa-
tional Futures"
Barclay M. Hudson, Principal
Hudson and Associates

"Alternative Futures for Adult and Continuing Education in North Carolina: A Delphi Futures Planning Study"
Paul F. Fendt, Associate Director of Extension Credit & Certificate Programs,
University of North Carolina

"Futurizing State-Level Educational Policy: A Case Study Involving Forecasting of Social Trends and Participatory Planning"
K. Fred Daniel, Florida Department of Education
Arthur J. Lewis, Professor of Education, University of Florida
Pauline M. Masterton, Associate for Program Policy Analysis
Florida Department of Education

"A New Model for Interagency Cooperation in the Future"
Bernard S. Schwartz, Adjunct Professor
Roosevelt University

"Some Thoughts on the Future of Special Education"
James P. Gelatt, Director, Special Projects
John F. Kennedy Institute, John Hopkins University

"Future Directions for a Learning Society"
Rexford G. Moon, Jr., Managing Director
The College Board

"Comprehensive Academic Planning for Technical Education"
Warren H. Groff, Vice President for Academic Affairs
North Central Technical College

"Future Studies in Higher Education: A Report on One Experimental Program"
C. Murray Austin, Chairman, Future Studies Program Board
University of Northern Iowa

"Summary of A Seven-State Delphi Study on the Future of Continuing Education"
Jim Cobb, University of Northern Colorado

"Drastic Measures: Trying To Get Students to Think Beyond *BUSINESS AS USUAL*"
James E. Moore, Master
George Holman, Chairperson,
University of Texas at Dallas

"History and the Future, A Paradigm for Values Studies"
Todd A. Britsch, Professor
Brigham Young University

"Community Education and Community Values in the Restricted Environs of a Space Colony"
Kenneth Heuser, Associate Professor
Plymouth State College

"Projected Changes in Educational Ambience: Short Term and Long Term"
Gene Bammel, Professor
West Virginia University

"How the Universe Structures Learning"
August T. Jaccaci, Interrobang Ideas

"National and International Sport in the Year 2000"
John Lucas, Professor,
Pennsylvania State University

"Split Brain Research: Its Educational Implications"
Doris M. Acord, Instructor
Oklahoma State University

"Why Not Add Social Development to Cognition in Public Schools?"
John H. Boynton, Graduate Student
University of Houston

"The Problem of Creating Authority in Schools of the Future"
William Spady, Senior Research Sociologist
National Institute of Education

"A New Public School Compromise for the Twenty-First Century:
New Mechanisms for Formulating Educational Policy"
Austin D. Swanson, Professor/Chairman
Department of Educational Administration, State University of New
York

"The Educator as a Philosophizing and Futurizing Agent Within An
Educational System"
John M. Could, Director
Reynolds School District

"Choosing a Future: Human Values and Educational Goals"
Max Oelschlaeger, Chairman
North Texas State University

"Quantum Mechanics, Consciousness, and the Future of Education:
The Age of Science Rising to the Age of Enlightenment"
Robert W. Winquist, Assistant Professor
Maharishi International University

"Introducing Peace Studies into the Curricula of the Future"
James Collins, Manhattan College

"Implications of Health Care Futures for Medical Education"
Robert C. Brictson, Professor
Michigan State University

"Education for Basic Cultural-Change: A Proposal for Change of
Education in the Human Science Progressions"
James E. Herrick, Associate Professor
University of Washington

"Work, Leisure, and 'the Second Sex'"
Lei Lane Burrus-Bammel, Professor
West Virginia University

"Cultural Endgames: Alternative Life Styles for the Future"
Alan R. Cleeton, Professor of Humanities and Social Sciences,
Wentworth Institute of Technology

"Considering Future Alternatives on the Secondary Level Through Reading, Discussing, Imagining, and Creating"
Katherine M. Conover, Teacher
Jamesville Public Schools

"To Choose Our Future Creatively and Courageously"
Sister Ellen Marie Keane, Chairperson,
Marymount College

"Theoretical Knowledge as the Axial Principle and Education as the Axial Structure of Modern Society"
Richard C. Phillips, Professor
University of North Carolina

"Transfer of Technology for the Third World: To What End?"
Cynthia Shepard Perry, Director, Center for International Student Affairs
Texas Southern University

"An Introduction to the New Games"
Emil Karam, Assistant Superintendent of Special Programs
Houston Parks and Recreation Department

"Some Neglected Fundamentals in Teaching the Processes of Forecasting"
Bruce Peseau, Associate Dean
University of Alabama

"The Age of Numeracy"
Norman Lee, Adjunct Professor
Fairleigh Dickinson University

"Interim Strategies for Digital Video Graphics/Microcomputer-Assisted Instructions"
Wendell H. Hall, Associate Professor
Brigham Young University

"Future of Management: A Delphic Replication 1970-1978"
Harvey Nussbaum,
Wayne State University

"Future Business Applications of Delphic Research in Future Studies"
Robert C. Judd
Governors State University

"Planned Innovation"
Frank Bacon
Michigan State University

"Entrepreneurship and Enterprise Tomorrow: An Inductive Approach to Secondary School Business Education"
Timothy S. Mescon and George S. Vozikis
Department of Management
University of Georgia

"Adaptation of Futurist Methods for Classroom Use: Strategies For Future Study in the Secondary School"
Eugene Bledsoe, Resident Director
Georgia's Governor's Honors Program

"Project REAL: *R*elevant *E*ducation through *A*lternative *L*earning"
Jerry McCamly and Janis Rosene, Teachers
El Camino High School

"Using Futuristics as a Vehicle for Initiating Educational Change in Your School and/or Classroom"
John R. Eggers, Assistant Professor,
University of Northern Iowa

"Preparing for Tomorrow's World: An Alternative Curriculum Model for the Secondary Schools"
Louis Iozzi, Director, and Janey Cheu, Institute of Science
Rutgers State University

"Designing Educational Futures: An Application of Comparative Futurology to Education"
F. James Clatworthy, Associate Professor
Oakland University

"The Child's Sphere Year 2000: A Learning Environment for Young Children"
Peggy Peterson, Education Commission of the States

"New Strategies for Early Childhood Education"
Annie L. Butler, Professor of Education
Indiana University

"Futurology in the Boonies"
Cheryl Rogers, Research Associate
Urban Institute

"Alternative Futures—Alternative Schools Implications for a Developmental Counselor's Role in Affective Education—Strategies and Techniques"
Carol I. Marshall, Developmental Counselor
Duluth Public Schools

"Lifelong Learning and the Future of the School: A Critical Analysis"
Frank Spikes, Dean
St. Mary's University

"Creating a Person Centered Growth Oriented Future in Education"
James J. VanPatten, Professor
University of Arkansas

"Toward a University-Based Flexibility in Lifelong Learning"
Arthur W. Eve and Dmitri Gat, Institute for Governmental Services
University of Massachusetts

"Toward the Education of Gifted Children in 2025"
Suzanne McFarland, James R. Johnson and Robert N. Wendt
University of Toledo

"Philosophy for Children: A Model for Education in the Future"
Joshua Weinstein, Professor of Education
University of Houston

"Health Logic and Values in Education for Prevention"
Larry Laufman, Baylor College of Medicine

"Logic and Moral Development in Education"
Dov Liberman, Assistant Professor
University of Houston

"Combating Prejudice Through Logical Reasoning"
Deborah Salvo, Student
University of Houston

"Some Characteristics of a Futures Oriented Elementary Classroom"
Shirley A. McFaul, Instructor
University of Houston at Clear Lake City

"Policy Mechanisms the State Can Use to Encourage Restructuring
of Education for the Future"
Weston H. Agor, Professor
University of Miami

"Can the Local School Board Survive? Local-State-Federal Relations
are Changing"
C. Taylor Whittier, Associate Professor
University of Texas at San Antonio

"Libraries and Educational Futures"
Dan Barron and Charles Curran, Assistant Professors
University of South Carolina

"Ten Scenarios for the Future of the Public Library in America"
Bruce A. Shuman, Associate Professor
University of Oklahoma

"Information Technology and Distributed Education"
Robert W. Swanson, Manager, Instructional Services
Trevor Swanson, Assistant Professor
San Diego State University

"Futurity and Health Care Careers"
Robert L. Patrick, Director of Health Technologies
Alvin Community College

"The Future of Medical Education"
Harold G. Levine, Director,
University of Texas Medical Branch

"A Futuristic Approach to Continuing Vocational Education for Clinicians"
John L. Gedye, Professor of Neurology
Wayne State University

"The Future Style of Science"
Robert J. Doyle, Professor of Biology
University of Windsor

"Influence of Science Fiction Upon Scientific and Technological Innovations"
Charles Waugh, Assistant Professor of Psychology
University of Maine

"A New Model for Primary, Secondary and University Level Education in Venezuela"
Felix Adam, President, Universidad Rodriguez
Juan Socias, Director, Futures Studies Program
Universidad Simon Rodriguez

"The Missing Component: Evaluation in Futures Education"
Geoffrey H. Fletcher and Gary D. Wooddell, Doctoral Candidates
University of Cincinnati

"Human Foresight and Moral Re-Education: The Work of the School"
Max R. Goodson, Professor Emeritus
University of Wisconsin

"The Individual—A Need for a Reconstructed View"
Thomas J. Venables, Assistant Professor
Rutgers University

"Educational Policies for an Ecological Society"
Rodger W. Bybee, Assistant Professor of Education
Carleton College

"Writing Futures Histories"
Les Humphreys, Dean
Goddard College

"Technology Driven Future Histories for Education"
Earl C. Joseph, Staff Scientist-Futurist
Sperry Univac

"Art Input/Art Output Versus Art Kaputt: Forecasting Educational Futures. . . ."
Virginia M. Brouch, Department Chairperson
Judith A. Kula, Assistant Professor
Florida State University

"Artists and Designers: Educating for the Future"
Roman J. Verostko, Professor
Minneapolis College of Art and Design

"The Endless Enigma: A Slide/Tape Retrospective and Prospective on the State of the Art of Schooling"
David G. Gueulette, Associate Professor
Northern Illinois University

"Take a Giant Step into the Future: A Visual Art Approach to Future Studies in the Middle School"
Darlyne Atkinson Killian, Art Resource Teacher
Atlanta Public Schools

"Social Ecology: A Reconstructive Approach to Renewal of Liberal Education"
James R. Nolfi, Dean, Goddard College

"Futurism as Educational Theory"
John Pulliam, Professor of Education
University of Oklahoma

"Two Models of Futuristic Thinking"
George B. Pepper, Professor of Philosophy
Iona College

"Alternative Futures and the Dominant Social Paradigm"
William S. Harrison
Lowell Technological Institute

"Federal, State, Local Roles in Educational Management: Appropriate Future Technologies"
Nancy L. Knapp, Assistant Professor
Northern Illinois University

"Young Global Futurists: A Proposal for an Organization for Young People Concerned with the Future"
Sherry L. Schiller, Teacher, Waterford Public Schools
University of Michigan

"Mid-South Futures—1990"
May Maury Harding, Director
Southwestern at Memphis
Walter M. Mathews
Associate Professor
University of Mississippi

"University-Integovernmental Agency Relations: Reflections on the Days of Futures Passed"
Arthur W. Eve and Peter Leousis, Institute for Governmental Services
University of Massachusetts

"Citizenship Education Through Participation in Shaping the Future"
Clem Bezold, Director, Institute for Alternative Futures
Antioch College

"Education at the Turn of the Century"
Stanley L. Freeman, Professor of Education
University of Maine

"The University President as a Midwife to Creative Change"
D. J. Guzzetta, President of the University of Akron
Abdul Al-Rubaiy, Acting Director of the Institute for Futures

"Desegregation, Integration and Quality Education: A Future Perspective"
Walter C. Farrell, Jr. Chairperson and Associate Professor
Alex Molnar, Associate Professor of Education, Univ. of Wisconsin
Bert Ollie, Administrator, Milwaukee Public Schools

"Mathematics: The Key to Science Literacy For the Future"
Lucy W. Sells, Consultant

"Self Actualizing Education"
Harold R. McAlindon, Vice President
Center for Health Studies

"Claiming the Gift of Evolution: Visions of Education That Allow Full Development of Human Potential"
Harold L. Hayes, Assistant Professor
Walter State Community College

"Some Friendly Criticisms of Futurism"
Lloyd P. Williams, Professor of Education
University of Oklahoma

"Roles for Educators in Human Services Futures"
Charles W. Case, Dean
University of Wisconsin

"Socrates Revisited? Values-Education and the Emergence of a 'New Pedagogy' in the Humanities and Social Sciences"
Harry G. Wagschal, Dawson College

"Model Construction: A Method for Participation in the Future"
James P. Marshall, Assistant Professor of Sociology
University of Northern Colorado

"Affective Issues to Be Considered in Helping Students Confront the Future"
J. Leonard Steinberg, Chairman
California State University

"The Future of I.S.D.—Instructional Systems Development and I.S.D. in the Future"
D.C. Wigglesworth, Management Development, Kaiser Permanente

"Futures Oriented Strategies for Policy Making"
Joseph T. Matava, Superintendent of Schools
Maine School Union 76

"Metaperspectives in Post-Secondary Education"
Howard I. Thorsheim, Associate Professor
Peder Bolstad, Student
St. Olaf College

Organization for Education
Albert Wener, Faculty Lecturer
McGill University

"A Mechanism for Refocusing an Institution"
James W. Kunetha, Director of Planning
Southwest Educational Development Laboratory

"From Cure to Prevention: Prisons, Parents, Teens—Teachers"
Joanne Moses, Consultant
Centennial School District

"Redesigning the Future—A Systems Approach to Education"
Robert W. Fitzmaurice, Assistant Professor
University of Houston at Clear Lake City

"Time, Type and The Future"
Norman P. Smith, Assistant Professor
University of Texas at San Antonio

"Seven Sides of Symmetry: A Paradigm for the Future"
Leonore W. Dickmann, Chairperson
University of Wisconsin

"Planning for the Future of Occupational Education—A Consortium Approach"
Charles F. Adams, Director, Onondago-Madison BOCES
Thomas Mecca, Assistant to President, Tompkins-Cortland Community College

"The Future of Higher Education—Public Versus Private"
Donald L. Pyke, Coordinator of Academic Planning
University of Southern California

"The Future as History"
Bruce E. Bigelow, Associate Professor
Denison University

"Educational Futures in the New International Order: An Argentine Scenario"
Alejandro Piscitelli, Ph. Philosophy
Ministerio De Planeaminento, Buenos Aires

"Rediscovering the Newspaper: A Media Anthropological Approach"
Susan Allen, Co-owner
Anuenue Press and Publication Services

"Future Images: Cross Age and Cross Cultural Comparisons"
Roy Weaver, Assistant Professor
Richard Porter and Janet Fisher, Los Angeles Unified School District
Terri Cooper, Gerontology Center

"The Study of the Future in Taiwan, Republic of China"
Lai Jin-nan, Professor
Tamkang College

"Two Futures for Education-Work Relations: Technocratic vs. Socio-Technical Design"
Arthur G. Wirth, Professor of Education
Washington University

"Schools for a Space Colony"
Sister Alene Faul, Administrative Assistant
Saint Louis University

"A Society of Elders: Education Only for the Old?"
Carol E. Kasworm, Lecturer
University of Texas

"Images of the Future: A Slide Presentation on How We Imagine the Future"
Dennis Livingston, Visiting Professor of Political Science
Marlboro College

"Can Social Systems Learn? How? Some Models. Impact for Educators and Futurists."
Jock McClellan, Doctoral Candidate
University of Massachusetts

"The Future Is Where We Are Going to Live. Why Are We Preparing for the Past?"
Eldon M. Meyer, Doctoral Candidate
U.S. International University

WORKSHOPS

"Futurist Teaching in Upper Elementary Science"
Norma Harrington Morrison, Roan Mountain, TN

"The Future Preschool"
Evan G. Nelson, Director, U.S. Office of Education
Robert B. Lewis, Director, Environmental Research Group

"Introducing Golden Rule Education: A Model for Intercultural Education"
Gwen Neser, Associate Professor
Monmouth College

"The Cell of the Self: A Dynamic Conceptual Educational System of Mind Mechanisms for Continuous Self-Evolution"
R. Duncan Wallace, Psychiatrist

"Discovering Your Cultural Roots: Guide Posts to Your Future"
Warren T. Kingsbury, President, American Training Lab., Inc.,
Morrison F. Warren, Director, I. D. Paine Laboratories,
Arizona State University

"Computer Automated Educational Simulations for Training and Decision Analysis"
Gerald Smith, Assistant Professor, University of Utah
Jerry Debenham, Adjunct Professor, University of Utah

"Classroom Teaching and Futurizing"
Don Glines, Director
Educational Futures Projects

"Watershed: New Approaches to Integrating the Arts and Humanities"
Ronald Dean Konetchy, Director
Schola Moderna, Inc.

"Energy Education: The Future Is Now"
John Steinbrink and Bobby Jones, Associate Professors of Education
University of Houston at Clear Lake City

"The Words and Ways of Tomorrow—Shown to Us Today"
Josetta Walsh, Instructor, Marylhurst Education Center
Nancy Martin, Teacher
Don Neraas, Architect

"Societal Metamorphosis"
Laurence J. Victor, Instructor
Pima Community College

"Lifespace Planning: A Counseling Process for Career-Life Planning"
Gary G. John, Richland College
Margaret L. John
Newbury-John and Associates

"Learning to Live in a Global Village"
Gerald L. Kincaid, Communication Specialist
Minnesota State Department of Education

"Educational Horizons: Learning in the Future"
Betty Barclay Franks, Teacher, Maple Heights High School
Mary Kay Howard, Teacher
John Carroll University

"Model for Future Studies in the Secondary Classroom"
Maurice Champagne, Howard Feddema, Teachers
High School District 214

"Futurizing the Curriculum Through Process"
Dennis VanAvery, Director
Westminster College

"Houston Area Model United Nations"
Andrea Flynn, Youth Committee Chairman
Peggy Chausse, Educational Consultant, United Nations Association
Dan Stoecker, St. Thomas University
Chuck Mays, Ronnie Joe and Michael Phillips, Rice University
Ronnie Gonzales and Alan Bethscheider, University of Houston
Jo Lynn Jones and Mike Pitman, University of Houston

"Educational Futuristics Experientially: A Sampler of Monday
Morning Activities"
Diane N. Battung, Educational Options Center Coordinator
University of Southern California

"The School and You in 2002"
Jim Isom, Lloyd Longnion and Zelda Rick
College of the Mainland

"Man-Machine Systems for Delivering Educational Services"
Austin D. Swanson, Professor/Chairman, State University of New
York
Edward J. Willett, Professor, Houghton College
Eugene Nelson, Graduate Student, University of New York

"Science Fiction and Science Fact in the Educational Environment"
Richard K. Preston, Vienna, Virginia

"The Three Rs Plus Two Rs: Basics Plus Reasoning and Relating"
Clara Orsini-Romano, Principal, Bryan Hills School District
Isabel D. Pascale, Associate Professor, Long Island University

"Teaching for Future Living: Ideas, Skills and Instructional Strategies"
Elliott Seif, Professor of Education, Temple University
Ed Betof, Management Development Instructor
Sperry-Univac Corp.

"Education: The Futures' Healing Modality"
Eleanor Vogt, Associate Professor and James R. Kuperberg, Assistant Professor
University of Wisconsin

"Futuristics: Theory and Application"
John Welckle, Project Director and Penny A. Damlo, Project Instructor, Futuristics, Burnsville Senior High School

"Some Suggestions on Futurizing Almost Anything you Teach"
Patricia M. Proctor, Social Studies
Westbury Senior High School

"Study of Role Changes and Techniques of Deliberate Enactment of New Professional Roles in Hospital Settings as a Method of Studying the Future of Medical Education"
Joe W. Hart, Professor, University of Arkansas

"Integrating Future Thought Into Current Reading Programs"
Michael Cooper, Reading Consultant
Perceptions

"Help Wanted: Architects for Transforming the Context of Education
An Equal Opportunity Employer"
Jeana Wirtenberg, Social Science Analyst
Rose Ann Alspektor, Equal Opportunity Specialists and Georgia Strasburg, Social Science Analyst
U.S. Commission on Civil Rights

THEME SESSIONS

"Teaching to Cope with the Future—Challenges and Possibilities in the Education and Training of the Greater Houston Area Public Schools"
Billy Reagan, Superintendent, HISD
Duke Brannen, Professor of Secondary Education, Stephen F. Austin State University
Dianne Hopper, English Teacher, Cypress-Fairbanks ISD, and Don Thornton, Assistant Superintendent, Cypress-Fairbanks ISD

"Common Characteristics of Utopian and Futuristic Models of Society"
Hans Joachim Harloff, Professor, Dr., Technische Universitat Berlin, Federal Republic of Germany

"A Dialogue on *The Far Side of the Future*"
Jim Bowman, Fred Kierstead, John Pulliam, Chris Dede, Robert Theobald and Charles Weingartner

"Women, Education, and the Future"
Anita Miller, President of the National Association of Commissions
for Women and Institute for Studies of Equality

"No More Pencils, No More Books, No More Teachers' Dirty Looks"
Charles Weingartner, Professor of Education
University of South Florida

"A New International Learning Order"
James Botkin, Co-Author, The Club of Rome Learning Report

PANEL SESSION

"Legislative Concerns for the Future of Texas"
William P. Hobby, Lt. Governor, State of Texas

"The Role of the State Executive in the 21st Century"
Stephen C. Oaks, Secretary of State, State of Texas

"The Fiscal Future of Texas"
Thomas M. Keel, Legislative Budget Director, State of Texas

SMALL GROUP INTERACTIONS STRUCTURED BY
PROFESSIONAL INTEREST

Preschool/Elementary Teaching
Secondary Teaching
Community College and University Teaching
Pre-College Administration
Post-Secondary Administration
Counseling
Non-Formal Education
Special Education
Educational Technology
Theoretical Research

Business Meeting, Education Section

Small Group Interactions and Organization of Communications Networks